Touchy Subject

The History and Philosophy of Education Series

EDITED BY RANDALL CURREN AND JONATHAN ZIMMERMAN

Integrations: The Struggle for Racial Equality and Civic Renewal in Public Education
by Lawrence Blum and Zoë Burkholder

Spare the Rod: Punishment and the Moral Community of Schools
by Campbell F. Scribner and Bryan R. Warnick

Homeschooling: The History and Philosophy of a Controversial Practice
by James G. Dwyer and Shawn F. Peters

Making Up Our Mind: What School Choice Is Really About
by Sigal Ben-Porath and Michael Johanek

Patriotic Education in a Global Age
by Randall Curren and Charles Dorn

The Color of Mind: Why the Origins of the Achievement Gap Matter for Justice
by Derrick Darby and John L. Rury

The Case for Contention: Teaching Controversial Issues in American Schools
by Jonathan Zimmerman and Emily Robertson

Have a Little Faith: Religion, Democracy, and the American Public School
by Benjamin Justice and Colin Macleod

Teaching Evolution in a Creation Nation
by Adam Laats and Harvey Siegel

Touchy Subject

THE HISTORY AND PHILOSOPHY OF SEX EDUCATION

Lauren Bialystok
and Lisa M. F. Andersen

The University of Chicago Press CHICAGO & LONDON

The University of Chicago Press, Chicago 60637
The University of Chicago Press, Ltd., London

Published 2022
Printed in the United States of America

31 30 29 28 27 26 25 24 23 22 1 2 3 4 5

ISBN-13: 978-0-226-82216-7 (cloth)
ISBN-13: 978-0-226-82218-1 (paper)
ISBN-13: 978-0-226-82217-4 (e-book)
DOI: https://doi.org/10.7208/chicago/9780226822174.001.0001

Library of Congress Cataloging-in-Publication Data

Names: Bialystok, Lauren, author. | Andersen, Lisa M. F., author.
Title: Touchy subject : the history and philosophy of sex education / Lauren Bialystok and Lisa M. F. Andersen.
Other titles: History and philosophy of education.
Description: Chicago : University of Chicago Press, 2022. | Series: History and philosophy of education series | Includes bibliographical references and index.
Identifiers: LCCN 2022010467 | ISBN 9780226822167 (cloth) | ISBN 9780226822181 (paperback) | ISBN 9780226822174 (ebook)
Subjects: LCSH: Sex instruction—United States—History. | Sex instruction—Curricula—United States. | Sex instruction—Philosophy.
Classification: LCC HQ57.5.A3 B53 2022 | DDC 613.9071073—dc23/eng/20220304
LC record available at https://lccn.loc.gov/2022010467

♾ This paper meets the requirements of ANSI/NISO Z39.48-1992 (Permanence of Paper).

For Rebecca and Naomi, obviously—LB

For Abigail Karlin-Resnick, whose grandma would be proud—LA

CONTENTS

Introduction

In 2015 the public schools in Omaha, Nebraska, updated their Human Growth and Development curriculum to include gender identity and emergency contraception, among other topics. A town hall to discuss the changes devolved into a verbal and physical altercation between more than a thousand parents, teachers, and students. "I have five daughters! Five daughters! Who's going to keep them pure?" shouted one woman. Other critics alleged that the curriculum "rapes children of their innocence" and that it came "straight from the pits of hell."[1]

The United States has a reputation for a particularly hostile brand of disputation over sex education. So great is this reputation that many districts fold when a whiff of controversy threatens, even before the allusions to hellfire. In Omaha, a partial rollback of the new curriculum struck administrators as the best way to keep the peace. District Supervisor of Human Growth and Development Karen Spencer-May explained: "What we tried to do was neutralize it a bit, because sometimes a curriculum is more extreme than we would do in Omaha, Nebraska, or say or think."[2] But are the needs of Omaha's students really so different from those in countless other places? And are values about sex education really so local? The United States might have the most extreme reputation, but American-style dramas over sex education play out in many places. At the same time as the town hall took place in Omaha, for example, a group of parents in Hamburg, Germany, protested a new sex education curriculum, raising many of the same concerns. Counter-protesters appeared, throwing snowballs and eggs. The police got involved.

Sex education evidently stirs up strong feelings. Despite contextual factors that vary across time and place, deciding what schools should teach children about sexuality is never easy. What values and reasoning should guide policy makers as they attempt to make principled choices about sex education in a diverse society? How do some topics secure a permanent place in the curriculum, and how securely are others excluded? Is there progress in sex education? What, if anything, is fundamentally controversial about sex education, and how might we be distorting it through our political discourse?

Most people think they know something about sex education, or at least about the controversy over it, but what we know is mostly based on spectacle. And the relentless emphasis on conflict may encourage our tendency to pick a side and then just check out, stopping short of reaping the rewards that only ongoing, reasonable deliberation is likely to yield. We rarely pause to reflect on *why* we hold the opinions we do, or to confirm whether our beliefs even correspond to reality. There are blind spots and hypocrisies in most people's thinking about sex education, no matter how sincere their beliefs.

We assume that if sex education is so controversial, there must be nearly equal numbers of people who support and oppose including it in school curriculum. But the vocal protesters who get quoted in news media are in the minority. In survey after survey, school-based sex education is more popular than Morgan Freeman, Tom Hanks, or Yoda.[3] Even in Omaha, a 2014 phone survey of district parents and caregivers had found that 93% of respondents wanted sex education curriculum and wanted that curriculum to include information about not only abstinence but also pregnancy and STI prevention.[4] And Americans want it taught not only at school, but also in the home and in places of worship, civic organizations, and medical clinics.

We think of sex education as a momentous battle between liberals and conservatives. And there are some flare-ups. But there is also substantial agreement between these groups, both of which generally contend that the aim of sex education should be to limit teen pregnancy, the transmission of sexually transmitted infections (STIs), and sexual violence. An emphasis on the liberal-conservative divide is distorting, moreover, because it obscures other contests shaping the sex education landscape. For example, social scientists with expertise in young people's sexuality have historically expected deference from the public and are shocked when they don't get it; the gap between experts and laypeople is revisited every time a curriculum adjustment is proposed.

We think of sex education debates as important because what kids learn at school is important. And it can be. But sex education also accounts for a meager average of 5.4 hours of instructional time per year in middle school, and

6.2 hours of instructional time per year in high school.[5] In the meantime, kids spend countless hours on screens, and most live with their families for eighteen years. Arguably there are few moments of the day when a young person is *not* learning about sex, gender, and sexuality. So how has *curriculum* become the locus of so many people's anxieties about youth sexuality?

We wouldn't be writing a book about school-based sex education if we thought it didn't matter. But young people's sexual well-being is most influenced by factors other than curriculum, and the aspects of curriculum that we consider highly controversial are often less relevant than aspects we aren't even discussing. School is an important site of sex education, but it's essential that it's not the only one.

In this book, we argue that divisions about sex education are not as large as they initially appear and aren't necessarily in the places we expect. They never have been. In fact, American educational stakeholders have already secured some precious common ground. This is significant because mistaken beliefs about where the debate is situated, and an assumption that no substantial consensus has already been reached, have gradually, over the course of a century, been creating the world that they purport to describe. Misunderstanding stymies productive deliberation, dwelling on tired debates rather than tackling important new questions. It is crucial to recognize that progress has already been made—and that we still have a long way to go.

Improving sex education requires a willingness to question what we think we know about schools, young people, politics, and each other. History and philosophy provide the tools we need to get a clearer grip on the rightful place of sex education in a diverse, modern society. Such a claim runs counter to conventional thinking; history is often critiqued for being backward-looking, and philosophy for being untethered from reality. Yet these disciplines enable us to explore and evaluate the strident positions expressed at angry board of education meetings, intuitions about abstract values, and historically grounded ideas about social norms. We suggest that history provides, if not prescription, at least an accounting of what is unlikely to work. Moreover, history illuminates the constructedness of our contemporary conceits—and hence makes the best case that our world has the capacity for change. Philosophy, for its part, helps us to assess our current practices and delineate the boundaries within which new ones should develop.

The interplay between these two disciplines, seasoned with academic detachment, allows us to circumvent some of the aggression in present-day stand-offs between parties affiliated with Comprehensive Sex Education (CSE), and Abstinence-Only-Until-Marriage Education (AOUME). Scholarly approaches resist a worldview wherein possibilities for thinking about sex education have been reduced to a bipolarity, with the usual suspects in each camp. If we instead take an objective look, one that illuminates the twisting history of sex education, we will be prompted to think beyond this gridlock. At various points in our history, the loudest advocates for sex education have espoused values that would be considered conservative by present criteria, such as gender double standards and classist views of purity; meanwhile, some of the most traditional and religiously motivated sex educators have dwelled on topics like happiness and pleasure, which are only starting to make an appearance in "comprehensive" curricula. By getting clearer about the nature of these value conflicts, we can recognize more common ground in our present-day battles and help professional sex educators, parents, students, and policy makers to better identify what's underneath familiar taglines and rallying cries.

History and philosophy also allow us to see what is truly "new," and thus to evaluate how changes in medicine, culture, and technology ought to inform our attitudes toward sex education. This perspective can help break through some of what most flusters educational decision makers, such as one member of the Omaha Board of Education, who confessed her bewilderment that "our world has changed so much in the 15 years since I graduated high school. . . . We didn't have sexting, we didn't have the Internet, like we do now."[6] The content of sex education is inescapably contextual: what we need to tell children and at what age depends on what they already know, what they are doing, and what other influences are working on them. Consequently, there is no static slate of facts, skills, or discussion topics that can define appropriate school-based sex education in every time and place. Importantly, some views that have held more currency in the past are less tenable now simply due to advances in medicine and technology, as well as cultural changes in the world young people inhabit. The protection of premarital chastity may have been more defensible in an era before access to reliable contraception and when women had fewer economically and socially viable pathways outside of marriage. The aim of sheltering youths from graphic sexual images was more realistic before the advent of ubiquitous digital pornography. The unapologetic heteronormativity of earlier educational paradigms was less remarkable before the legalization of same-sex marriage. Things change, and so must education.

Still, the more things change, as the saying goes, the more they stay the same. This is in part because the march of time does not, on its own, diffuse profound differences in beliefs about such topics as sexual morality, the nature of parent-child relationships, and the purpose of education. There was diversity in American opinion on these topics at the turn of the twentieth century, and there is diversity on them now. In fact, on most of these issues, we should not expect to reach consensus. The challenge for peaceful modern societies is not only how to cultivate agreement but how to manage disagreement. We need sensible ways of dealing with the topics that cause otherwise nice people to shout insults and throw snowballs at each other.

In this book, we make the case for sex education, explaining why it's worth fighting for and which kind most deserves our fight, despite all the inconveniences and compromises along the way. In chapter 6 and the conclusion, we'll outline the significance of our analysis by suggesting how to narrow down the options, protect sensible debate, and design defensible sex education curriculum. Our vision of Democratic Humanistic Sexuality Education (DHSE) offers a framework that can be applied even in a tumultuous political environment, making the most of existing democratic institutions and norms.

What we call DHSE is at least as much a description of how educational stakeholders should set goals and conduct their curriculum development as it is a set of curricular requirements. In fact, we think that there is a strong case for leaving curricular content somewhat open-ended and customizable. While there are some universal basics, the information students need is always changing. To talk of a final product in sex education is as silly as, well, thinking that a seventeen-year-old will have no more questions about sex throughout the rest of their life course. Sex education's content will change because the world will always change, and it is hubris to think that the term "comprehensive" can be taken literally.

In that spirit, while this book is a defense of Comprehensive Sex Education, our goal is not to enumerate once and for all what that ideal requires. We argue for a historically and philosophically informed approach to sex education that aligns with democratic and humanistic aims and responds to the salient features of young people's worlds, including the inequities that put some students at much higher risk of sexual harm than others. In practice, DHSE will facilitate curriculum decisions that include what are currently considered highly comprehensive standards, incorporate ethics and civics education, and substantially modify some aspects of teacher training and school design. It will also assign different responsibilities to different actors inside and outside schools. We are quite far from realizing such an approach in most of the world, including the United States, though it is less unthinkable now than it would have been fifty, or even ten, years ago. Throughout our inquiry, we will see how sex education has progressed and how the very concept of "progress" remains contestable.

We mentioned that parents in Germany have expressed many of the same objections to comprehensive school-based sex education as parents in the

United States. Still, gender identity and sexual diversity were still on Hamburg's primary school curriculum in 2018, and attendance was compulsory. Germany has one of the lowest teen birth rates in the world, at about 5 births per 1,000 girls aged 15–19.[7] Meanwhile, when Omaha's district prepared to roll out its modestly revised sex education curriculum in 2016, the state's teen birth rate was 22 per 1,000 girls aged 15–19, and the county's chlamydia rate had reached an all-time high.[8]

These contrasts are a good reminder that there is a range of approaches to teen sexuality in similarly positioned nations, and that different outcomes are possible. In this book, we focus on the American context, occasionally commenting on other districts' experiences and what we can—or can't—learn from them. While certain countries in northern Europe are often touted as leaders in sex education, in this domain as in so many things, the United States also serves as a case study that the world references. Globally, sex education vocabulary has been framed in part by the distinctly American tensions between liberal rights and conservative values. Moreover, the United States wields enormous influence over policy in other developing countries that depend on the American government for international aid, which has been conditioned on abstinence-only programs and the withholding of condoms and abortion services.[9] American philanthropies, such as the Ford Foundation, have then created programs that can subvert American government's policies by providing reproductive education and health services that the latter refuses to provide. Understanding the history of American sex education helps explain how much of the world has ended up where it has.

This book's chapters are organized into two parts, highlighting how historical experiences have opened philosophical questions that persist to this day, and how philosophical questions can only be answered in historical context. Chapters 1–3, written by historian Lisa Andersen, combine scholarly synthesis and original research to delineate the history of school-based sex education in the United States. Some of this story will already be familiar to historians. Against the backdrop of America's expanding public school system and dynamic sexual norms, these chapters explore how educational institutions accommodated students' sexuality, the political vulnerabilities of deliberative democracy, the contours of educational expertise, the interplay between popular culture and curriculum design, the construction and disruption of heteronormative and racialized discourse within sex education curriculum, and the strategies employed by reformers and activists. To this end, each chapter describes a key question shaping a period's sex education, and thus how the building blocks of contemporary sex education were assembled. Chapter 1 features the late nineteenth- and early twentieth-century thinkers who grappled with the question of whether one should first learn about sex, or have sex and then learn about it. Chapter 2 investigates how midcentury sex educators pondered whether the purpose of sex education should be family-oriented or health-oriented. Chapter 3 explores the late twentieth-century debates about who should be in charge of educating youths about sex. This catalog of questions and resolutions should once and for all put down the specious assumption that sex education is just a way to tally the relative power of social conservatives vs. liberal activists. At the same time, these chapters suggest how the pervasiveness of this misconception has threatened to become a self-fulfilling prophesy.

Chapters 4–6, written by philosopher Lauren Bialystok, disentangle what should and should not be controversial about sex education, which values underpin different positions, and how to make justifiable educational choices about sex in the contemporary context. Philosophical arguments about sex education have usually proceeded from classical liberal aims, such as educating for autonomy, ensuring state neutrality, and protecting reasonable pluralism. The philosophical content of this book endorses the basic structure of liberalism, showing that the majority of conflict and missteps in sex education can be mitigated by referring to the overriding values of freedom and equality. At the same time, it exposes the limits of a narrowly liberal mindset, which has tended to miss the problems with institutionalism, the permeation of the private and public spheres, and the inequalities that sex education can exacerbate. Building on an assortment of qualitative evidence and critical perspectives, these chapters argue that liberalism is still the best way of framing ethical disputes over sex education, yet the answers are sometimes more complex than what liberal philosophers have suggested. Each chapter in this section of the book also takes up a key question. Chapter 4 asks how much room there is for disagreement and posits that debates about sex education must be bounded by available evidence and the norms of liberal pluralism. Chapter 5 explores the question of educational authority and argues for a model of distributed responsibility over sex education. Finally, chapter 6 asks what schools are for and challenges the appropriateness of schools as the *de facto* site of sex education, arguing that schools are obligated to educate students to navigate the evolving sexual landscape that far exceeds curriculum.

In other words, this book explains what led to the stable premises and obvious contradictions of our present moment, and how to build upon the former while getting past the latter. Collecting the conclusions to each of our historical and philosophical questions, we show that sex education based on democratic and humanistic aims would maximize the strengths of our existing structures and implement lessons from the past while keeping pace with the changing realities of youth sexuality and education in the twenty-first century.

This book's aspiration therefore parallels that of sex education itself. Sex education has generally been premised on the idea that knowing about sex and sexuality should help young people make sense of their world, and that this sense-making is comforting, especially when nothing else goes as planned. Sex education helps people to avoid both isolation and unhealthy relationships, navigate risk, and better understand sensitive issues. Likewise, knowing about the history and philosophy behind sex education should help today's sex educators—and everyone else—make sense of which educational principles are worth defending. In this book, we show that there is a long tradition of adjusting our ideas about youth sexuality and about formal education to be more compatible. There is comfort in knowing this, and hopefully some inspiration.

And we hope that this book will show exactly what is wrong with sex education, too. Even when sex education delivers crucial information, sexuality eludes the institutional structures and rational deliberation presumed by most formal education, as well as public health promotion. Indeed, it is the passionate and potentially reckless nature of so much adolescent sexuality that seems to incite panic among adults. Our futile efforts to bottle it up only underscore that the appeal of sex lies in its very unwieldiness. If sex were all rational and predictable, it wouldn't be *fun*. Cramming sex into the school curriculum, or summing it up with a handy A-B-C acronym,[10] thus imposes a highly mechanistic paradigm on the most unruly of subjects. Where does this leave the mystery, the excitement, or perhaps the sacredness of sexuality?

We won't downplay the irony that sex education—and books about sex education—probably can't, and shouldn't, be remotely sexy. But school-based education can and should at least give young people the information and tools they need to make their lives sexy and healthy. This can only happen in the context of reasonable public discourse and informed policy-making about sex education. Our aim in this book is to help bring about such a context.

CHAPTER 1

Prudish or Prudent: The Origins of Classroom-Based Sex Education, 1880–1922

Historians have standards: avoid assumptions, read widely, and aspire to verify everything. Historians of *sexuality* must work especially hard to meet these standards because, inconveniently enough, people in the past generally sought to hide or keep private any information about their sexual lives. This information rarely appears in public records (unless it violates a law), and so historians of sexuality broaden their search. They consult medical records, diaries, and correspondence. In the pages of these domestic and personal sources, there are occasional insights into people's habits, desires, or partner choices. The scarcity of these occurrences makes them all the more precious.[1]

Consider then the amazement of historian Carl Degler when he came across the research notes of Dr. Clelia Duel Mosher, a Stanford faculty member who left in her records a set of unpublished interviews with forty-five married women, most of whom had been born before 1870.[2] They had come of age during a time when dresses were long, divorce was difficult to obtain, and contraception was illegal. Theodore Dreiser's *Sister Carrie* (1900) was censored for depicting an unrepentant woman who has premarital sex. Yet not only did Mosher's survey takers—I think of them as "the Mosher wives"—bluntly answer Dr. Mosher's questions about their sexual histories and ideals, but their answers overturned scholars' preexisting assumption that this generation of middle-class women had been sexually repressed. It turns out that many women understood sex as not only the basis for reproduction but as a source of pleasure.

That revelation about sexual pleasure strikes most historians as the most important finding. But for me, in the midst of writing a history of sex education, it was another pattern that stood out: many of the Mosher wives confessed to very limited knowledge about sex before their weddings. The Mosher survey therefore provoked a question that most modern Americans would never think to ask, because to us the answer seems intuitive: Should women know about sex before having it? Or, more tastefully, what is the appropriate relationship between knowledge and experience?

For adult women to remain ignorant of sex, there are a lot of other things that would have to be true. Books, for one, would need to be restricted in some way. To investigate, I followed up on the comments from one Cornell graduate who described her premarital education as "very slight and indefinite" despite having read "parts of *Tokology*," a manual delivering information about childbirth and child-raising. Now having myself read Dr. Alice B. Stockham's *Tokology*, an enormously popular volume first published in 1886 and then continually until its author's 1912 death, I can affirm that it's possible to read the entire book and not emerge any the wiser about human sexuality. Consider this, the only explicit description of heterosexual copulation in the 400-page book:

> Conception or impregnation takes place by the union of the male sperm and female germ.[3]

Another description from a marriage and sexuality manual appears below, simply because I want to convey how much this genre of writing was (to moderns like us) hilariously uninformative. One tactic was to use technical language that obscured as much as it enlightened, and then to compound the problem with circular references in which unexplained terms were defined via other unexplained terms. Consider this passage, penned by John Harvey Kellogg (better known as the sage of Battle Creek Sanitarium, and the brother of Kellogg's cereals' founder):

> The act of union, or sexual congress, is called *coitus* or *copulation*. It is accompanied by a peculiar nervous spasm due to excitement of special nerves principally located in the *penis* in the male, and in an extremely sensitive organ, the *clitoris*, in the female. The nervous action referred to is more exhausting to the system than any other to which it is subject.[4]

The passage was, it should be noted, unillustrated as well as unilluminating. It is exemplary of a trend that Dr. Margaret A. Cleaves described in 1906 as one wherein "the simplest physiological facts are imparted in such a manner that the child is left to puzzle over the meaning of words and to associate a term with the thought that it is something which they are not intended to understand."[5]

Alternatively, there was the option of complete silence. *What a Young Woman Ought to Know* (1898) said exactly nothing about copulation, although the author, Dr. Mary Wood-Allen, did provide an ideal schedule for bowel movements, a lecture on avoiding restrictive clothing, and a summary of best etiquette for the engaged. Anyone who might then look toward *What a Young Wife Ought to Know*'s chapter entitled "Marital Relations" for enlightenment would, I assure you, also remain completely ignorant of what "marital relations" actually entailed.

The spate of new sex and reproduction manuals whose popularity rose in the mid- to late nineteenth century did not, it seems, enlighten everyone. It was possible for a woman who held a bachelor's degree from Syracuse University to describe her premarital knowledge as "none to speak of. Nothing at all definite in my mind," despite having read "Miss Shepard's *Talks with Girls*." She was "so innocent of the matter that until I was eighteen I did not know the origin of babies," and her knowledge did not substantially increase until marriage. Likewise, a Pacific University alumna had known "not the least in the world."[6] Carl Degler would point out in his summary of the survey results that almost half of the surveyed women claimed to have no premarital knowledge at all, with many others describing their knowledge as minimal. What would eventually disrupt such ignorance is the story of sex education.

THE CONSPIRACY OF SILENCE

Could such ignorance be credible, or was it just performative? The first sex education advocates would describe themselves as working against a conspiracy of silence wherein parents, doctors, and even married friends collaborated to keep knowledge of sex from young women. Reformers often compared this collusion to how family members withheld from children the truth about Santa Claus because it was ultimately for the young woman's own good. If a woman didn't know about sexual intimacy, then she would not independently develop unchaste thoughts and would never act upon a lustful impulse. She would remain virtuous.

Any gender or social historian would be quick to note that this pattern of ignorance was a social norm limited to middle-class women—the literate daughters and wives of merchants or attorneys, who lived in multi-story urban homes employing a few domestic servants—and marked their sharp distinction from and superior status over working-class women. Parents in middle-class families kept their daughters from complete knowledge about sexuality as a means to guard their value as prospective wives. To put it crudely, a wife's chastity was one of the currencies with which middle-class husbands established their prestige. For middle-class African American families, women's respectable chastity was further politicized as a strategy to uplift the profile of the entire community; conformity to this middle-class norm would bolster the fight for civil rights.[7] Many people were deeply invested in young women's chastity and took on extraordinary inconveniences to make sure that no stray word would lead the young women of their family and community off course.

The special status that middle-class families accorded to women's premarital virginity was meaningful precisely because most men could not shelter women family members from seeing sex, hearing about sex, or being sexually exploited. Women who worked in factories, lived on farms, or were employed as domestic servants had greater exposure to sex as a by-product of their smaller family residences, the necessity of breeding animals, and mingling with male workers on the shop floor. Employment could thwart Mexican American families' preferred strategy of protecting adolescent daughters through the judicious use of chaperones, for example.[8] And some women learned about sex via their harassment by men, many of whom (unfairly) categorized poor and non-white women as sexually available, even inherently promiscuous. These women became, as Harriet Jacobs described in her memoir of slavery, "prematurely knowing." In an age in which "knowing" was widely understood as the kindling for desire, a woman's condition of "knowing" was used by men as evidence of desiring, even if they themselves had been the ones to "pollute" a young woman with "foul images."[9]

Some scholars nonetheless suspect that the Mosher wives professed ignorance that they did not have, and did so for the sake of appearances. This is plausible.[10] One Mosher wife, for example, claimed that she was told about sex by a friend at age fourteen but simply "didn't believe it." This was a convenient disbelief given that her mother had already instructed her that "such things were not only not talked about but also not thought of."[11]

A similar *willful* ignorance might be attributed to American author Edith Wharton, who claimed that her mother refused to explain to her "what being married was like" before her 1885 wedding.[12] Literary critics have questioned how much of Wharton's narrative is authentic, and how much of it is simply an artist performing a version of her life so as to titillate an audience and control the production of her legend.[13] Wharton even quoted her own mother as asserting, "You can't be as stupid as you pretend!" Yet the elements of Wharton's narrative—childhood requests for information, a series of rebuttals concluding with "It's not nice to ask about such things," a "sense of contamination" upon learning that babies did not come from flowers, and the disapproving glare of her mother during their last interview—capture a narrative in formation. This was not the "coming of age" story but rather the "infantilized femininity" saga.

This cultural script would gain traction in the 1910s alongside the popularization in America of Freud's theory that sexual suppression led to neurosis. Wharton would claim that her own ignorance of sex stunted her sexual life with her husband to the detriment of their relationship; her marriage remained unconsummated for ten weeks after the wedding and, according to Wharton, never really took. It also seems worth noting that Wharton's own description of what she didn't know was written with the vague manner she had critiqued in others. Rather than explicitly stating that she had not known about *sex*, Wharton confessed obliviousness about "processes of generation."[14] Presumably she didn't mean gardening.

So, it is possible that some women maintained a facade of ignorance because admitting otherwise would seem immodest and make them feel ashamed. On the other hand, the Mosher wives agreed to participate in an interview about their sex lives and provided frank descriptions about the frequency of their sexual relations during pregnancy, their preferred means of contraception, the regularity of their orgasms, how many sanitary napkins they used per period, and their "ideal habit." I'm therefore inclined to take the Mosher wives' words for it: they hadn't known much about sex.

For me, the fact that the women in the Mosher survey who *did* claim knowledge of sex previous to marriage often noted, like one Radcliffe alumna, that she had "never *talked* with anybody on the subject except my husband" supports, rather than undermines, others' claims of ignorance; this particular respondent had benefited from access to her physician father's comprehensive home library. One of the other knowledgeable women, also a physician's daughter, described how "during one of the vacations [from school] I read some of my father's medical books. With that and what was taught in the school [in physiology class] I had a fair knowledge of sexual physiology of the female." But even she conceded that "of the male I knew but very little if anything."[15] Another respondent, whose *mother* was a physician, further illuminated the extent to which having a knowledgeable parent was not necessarily helpful. The college graduate recalled:

> My mother was a physician but refused to instruct me when I asked questions. . . . I remember well the first time I asked a question which showed that I already had the idea there was something shameful about child bearing. Yet she told me I would read books about it when I was older, and I never asked again.[16]

And really, if a mother physician withheld information about sex from her daughter, doesn't it seem likely that other less-prepared authorities might have routinely fallen short?

Consider also a second area in which silence on an intimate body issue was demanded of and by physicians, people who presumably had an obligation to helpfully inform their patients. From the late nineteenth to early twentieth centuries, physicians widely agreed that they should not tell married women if these women had a sexually transmitted infection, on the grounds that doing so would violate the confidence of their husbands, who had presumably been unchaste and then passed the infection on to their wives. To put it more bluntly, doctors conspired with husbands to hide evidence that suggested these husbands' adultery. This practice was justified on two grounds: it eliminated a potential inspiration for the widely condemned practice of divorce, and husbands paid the doctors' bills.[17] How many women were treated for syphilis and gonorrhea without knowing the name or type of their illness? We're not quite sure, given that such ailments were routinely—even systematically—underreported.[18] But to think that treatment without communicated diagnosis was standard practice, justified and recommended in documents circulated among physicians, is pretty horrifying. It created a precedent for future violations of patient rights, including the forced sterilization of African American, immigrant, and poor women, practices sanctified by the Supreme Court with *Buck v. Bell* in 1927.

But back to the unmarried women. If they were not taught about sex in school, if their parents were reluctant to have frank conversations, and if they had somehow missed out on having a helpful friend or cousin enlighten them, or on coming across a credible book, then how did these women actually learn about sex? One educational model was suggested by the unfortunately named advice writer Orrin Giddings Cocks, who envisioned a husband having a conversation with his bride. Cocks urged would-be husbands to educate themselves for this challenge, counseling: "Let me emphasize the necessity of going to someone who states things clearly and simply and from the scientific standpoint, to have the whole reproductive apparatus explained" because

> if you are to marry the ordinary type of American girl, you will find that a great many of these questions will be asked you by her. It is wise that you should know, and that you should learn from persons who will tell you in the right way.[19]

In other words, Cocks reinforced a belief that a wife would never need to know about sex in general, but only about what sex with her particular husband would include. Writing for an African American middle-class audience, the authors of *Golden Thoughts on Chastity and Procreation* would likewise advise newly engaged men that "ignorance on the part of the bride" was to be expected, but that "delicate attention" could prevent a disastrous first intercourse. In a separate chapter for women readers, they advised a young woman to consult "freely with her companion on these relations" before entering "into the physical relations of marriage." That was the best way for a woman to learn about the content of "these relations," whatever the heck they were.[20]

How did husbands prepare to teach their wives? Like women, young men might read works marketed directly to their demographic. Men's respectable literature was a bit more explicit than women's, and there were more titles dedicated to a male audience. While Stall's Sex and Self series featured parallel titles, for example, Cocks's work was published as part of the Association Press's sex education series, the subtitle of each volume being *Talks with Young Men*. Even the texts with gender-neutral titles were probably more available to men, if my own catalog of copies purchased off eBay can be temporarily substituted for a more systematic research method—in my collection, most of the texts with a previous owner's name printed inside the cover feature a man's name. And perhaps parents also felt more obligated to help their sons, as opposed to their daughters, understand and manage sex. Still, these factors and possibilities are not necessarily enough to explain the knowledge gap between the sexes.

Fundamentally, the assumption that husbands could educate their wives rested upon an uncomfortable premise: from boyhood onward, they received access to information about sex, including the fact that sex could be pleasurable, because they were encouraged to "sow wild oats." Why "oats" was the chosen euphemism eludes me, but their wildness is well documented. In his *Traps for the Young* (1883), social purity reformer Anthony Comstock warned that preparation for oat-gathering began before puberty. The cheap periodical stories sold to boys, Comstock claimed, provided lots of salacious details followed by brief boilerplate warnings to remain moral. What historian Anthony Rotundo has called "boy culture" provided access to these materials; boys were expected to be outside and unsupervised all day, starting at around age six. As they aged, they joined rowdy social clubs, wherein they swapped tales of how they pursued "chippies" while courting girls from "good families."[21]

As for grown men, they frequented saloons—male sanctuaries—in which both pornography and prostitutes were available. To understand this era, it helps to think of a world where the following song is hilarious and delivered with a wink-wink. I give you "You'll Miss Lots of Fun When You're Married" (1890), with lyrics by Edward M. Taber and music by John Philip Sousa, and which you should imagine at march tempo:

Now what could be sweeter and better in life
Than avoiding its weary turmoil,
And be welcomed at home by your own little wife,
When you've finished your diurnal toil.

Of course you must give up your bachelor ways.
And the style that you always have carried,
And think with remorse on your old reckless ways.
[Spoken:] Nevertheless
You'll miss lots of fun when you're married.

This was the notorious double standard. It was a pair of claims—namely, a young woman should be ignorant about sexuality and a man would likely acquire premarital sexual experience—that made advice such as the following make sense.[22] When posing the question of "What things should be told [to his fiancée] about the earlier life of the man?" Cocks responded to his own inquiry by conceding that "many times it is better to say little and to speak in general terms, because of her innocence and her probable failure to grasp the idea properly" because "if the girl is innocent, and unsophisticated, and is confronted for the first time with one of the great fundamental issues of life" (that is, information about sex), "she may totally misunderstand when a man talks frankly about his past, about some of the relationships in which he was involved when he was younger."[23] Grounded in this reasoning, Cocks urged that it should be the young woman's brothers and father who inquired about the would-be husband's sexual history, rather than his future wife.

Sexual knowledge was something that men held in common, and from which middle-class women were shielded. As late as 1906, reformers at the semi-annual American Society of Sanitary and Moral Prophylaxis convention expressed significant doubt about the necessity of providing classroom-based coursework explaining sex. One speaker outright concluded that "sexual physiology and hygiene need not be formally taught [to] girls."[24] What follows is the history of how the once unthinkable became common sense.

THE NEW WOMAN

The idea of having sex education as part of the public school curriculum gained traction only when social reformers came to see the alternative—that is, protecting unmarried, middle-class women from sexual knowledge—as less and less manageable. Perhaps most important in convincing reformers of universal sex education's necessity was the New Woman phenomenon, which combined demographic generational distinctiveness and myths about the youngest generation of middle-class women. Most historians describe the New Woman as an early twentieth-century phenomenon.

The New Woman was typically, but not exclusively, white, and she borrowed from working-class trends, just as working-class women borrowed style from her. She had an independent source of income, often working as an office clerk or as sales staff in an upscale shop. The New Woman probably hadn't visited a male beauty contest or Harlem drag ball, but she might know someone who had, and had likely read about these fashions in the newspapers.[25] She might attend a middle-class cabaret, or dance at an afternoon tango tea and be spun about by one of the professional male dancers. Maybe she engaged in one of the sensuous dips that were being banned at hotels and clubs, exhibiting what one historian has called "the power of pleasure whereby women might feel liberated to imagine and reinvent themselves."[26] The New Woman didn't "date" per se, but likely had admiring companions to accompany her out and about.[27] Hugh Cabot, a reformer and writer, would reflect in 1913 that "this half century has seen the achievement of the economic independence of women and has been marked by a general relaxation of conventional restraints." It followed that "the dangers arising from the mismanagement of the sex instinct are increasing."[28] Historian Jeffery Moran summarizes that "in the reformers' view, the poor had perhaps always behaved badly, but when white, middle-class young people began to visit dance halls and prostitutes, that was cause for alarm."[29] The New Woman was not a flapper—that was still two decades in the future—but she was less domestic and more cosmopolitan than her mother had been.

Young, middle-class women insisted upon education, and they found a commercial world ready to meet their demands. There were increasing numbers of public lecturers and clinicians who provided information about eugenics (the racist pseudoscience of human breeding) and anatomy, two topics closely related to sex. Some of these speakers were radical, advocating free love and divorce, often with a side of socialism. For example, Luisa Capetillo, a Puerto Rican labor leader and feminist, offered New Yorkers lectures on free love, as well as lectures about service to the poor and women's suffrage.[30] Other cutting-edge speakers referred their audiences to the writings of Europeans like Sigmund Freud, Havelock Ellis, and Richard von Krafft-Ebing; this era's research included some of the earliest attempts to present sexual pleasure medically, and to define what we would now call homosexuality or transgender identity.[31] The twentieth-century student of sexuality had new reading options that avoided the pitfalls of being either useless or pornographic. Print historian Jennifer Pierce has identified 1913 as a key point in the history of sex education manuals, noting that in this year the field was large enough to have its sales tracked independently by publishers.[32] Overall, there was what some scholars have called a "new presence of the erotic in the public realm, not as an illicit underground but as an accepted feature of daily life."[33]

In an age without radio or TV, the most significant entertainment rival to lectures and books was the theater. And in New York, the 1913 production of Eugène Brieux's *Damaged Goods* set a precedent for respectably explicit productions with the story of a middle-class man who visited a prostitute, only to later infect his wife with venereal disease. Financed by the journal *Medical Review of Reviews*, actors performed *Damaged Goods* for a select group of social workers, physicians, clergy, politicians, and society women.[34] Given the blessing of this prestigious audience, there were not any significant censorship campaigns against either the play or the film version that was later developed, and republished editions of the play circulated widely.[35] Indeed, the play's 1913 novelization reprinted a letter of praise from Rev. Richard Bennett, the pastor of Henry Ward Beecher's former congregation at Plymouth Church, in Brooklyn. This complimented an editorial review from the Washington Hebrew Congregation's Rabbi Abram Simon, who would later become a member of the Washington, DC, board of education. Rabbi Simon proclaimed his wish that he "could preach a sermon one tenth as powerful, as convincing, as far-reaching, as helpful as this performance of *Damaged Goods*."[36]

Given the new pervasiveness of tenuously respectable sexual entertainment, reformers hoped to prompt a type of sex education that would uphold and reinforce rather than destroy social order.[37] Such instruction must start with the family, they decided. Reformers therefore wrote books and tracts to coach parent-educators, and for parents to share with and give to their children. Prominent examples included Rose Wood-Allen Chapman's *How Shall I Tell My Child?*, Nellie M. Smith's *The Mother's Reply*, and Helen W. Brown's *Child Questions and Their Answers*.

Underwriting this domestic strategy was the not-quite-extinguished fear that talk about sex was inherently arousing. It is telling that in the mid-nineteenth century, lecture audiences wherein women addressed both men and women listeners had been, no matter the topic, referred to as "promiscuous audiences."[38] Cocks exemplified the continuation of this concern when questioning "whether it is wise to give such facts before a large group of children, either boys or girls, or both," only grudgingly acknowledging that "it may be that this whole subject will have to be dealt with in the schools."[39]

Reformers were loath to resign themselves to the fact that parents had abandoned neither the conspiracy of silence that made young women vulnerable to rakish advances, nor the double standard that encouraged young men's promiscuity. Reluctantly, reformers turned to the untried strategy that was left: sex education in schools.

A BRIEF HISTORY OF SOCIAL HYGIENE

The reformers who advocated school-based sex education were not a homogenous group, but rather a set of allies who had been attacking the consequences of unmarried and illicit sexuality—ethical, religious, economic, health—in diverse and often incompatible ways since the 1870s. They did not fit squarely into the modern categories of "liberal" or "conservative," and should instead be understood as well-organized experts who elevated themselves above lay opinion. Medical experts were the first to identify themselves as having an interest in social hygiene, that is, an area of study that emphasized sex's central role in human experience and that focused on the diagnosis and reporting of sexually transmitted infections, genital and bodily cleanliness, eugenics, and masturbation.

Social hygiene physicians met at national professional conventions and would unite as the American Society of Sanitary and Moral Prophylaxis—*prophylaxis* describes interventions that prevent disease—which later became the American Federation for Sex Hygiene, and then the American Social Hygiene Association. These physicians' most notable foray into public policy was a very early twentieth-century campaign to regulate prostitution, and to thereby prevent venereal disease and so-called eugenic decline. To repeat: Physicians who sought to eliminate venereal disease prioritized the safety of male clients over the well-being of poor women for whom prostitution was the best means to support themselves and their families. The resulting regulation of women prostitutes might—as it did in France, Great Britain, San Francisco, New Orleans, St. Louis, Cincinnati, El Paso, or San Antonio—include medical inspection, the licensing of brothels, or detainment and forced sterilization, as well as attempts to bring such women into rescue homes.[40] In an era in which American government was expanding at both the municipal and federal levels, an endeavor such as the careful control of an illicit trade seemed more promising than it ever had before, though physicians' respect and care for women had not discernibly increased.

What physicians did, inadvertently but effectively, was ignite a countermovement. Social purity advocates, also known as anti-vice reformers, argued that prostitution's regulation would amplify ethical problems.[41] First through municipal civic organizations, such as the American Purity Alliance, and then as the American Vigilance Association, social purity reformers drew upon experiences created in the course of living in settlement houses, conducting social work, ministering to congregations, and managing philanthropies. Social purity work was consistent with Social Gospel, a late nineteenth- and early twentieth-century strain of Protestantism that emphasized works of justice and charity, and elevated these forms of worship at least as much as adherence to doctrinal creeds or the pursuit of personal salvation.

Men and women of the social purity movement saw themselves—and were widely seen—as progressive because they wanted to extend the most obvious blessings of middle-class life to everyone. This they advocated despite the fact that many of the women reformers chose not to marry, a middle-class woman's customary achievement, and instead chose long partnerships with other women or else life in communal settlement houses; they spoke with the aged authority of motherhood without having becoming mothers themselves. Whether working within organizations explicitly focused on social purity or something broader, reformers like the Woman's Christian Temperance Union's Frances Willard opposed not only prostitution, but also polygamy, prizefighting, and gambling, and mostly favored women's suffrage, dress reform, and Sabbatarian laws.

For social purity reformers, it was age-of-consent legislation, not the regulation of prostitution, which best illustrated government's capacity to uplift American social life. Age-of-consent legislation was predicated upon the assumption that young women did not know—should not know—about sex, and therefore did not know to guard against potential sexual predators.

The problem was that social purity reformers, so quick to defend everyone's right to chastity, often forgot to ask poor, working-class, and non-white women if they *wanted* to live within middle-class women's confines; reformers advocated chastity, not agency. These reformers were ill-equipped to understand that some working-class women had a standard of sexual decency that included selective premarital sexuality without indiscriminate prostitution. One example is the custom of treating, wherein a young man paid for a woman's evening amusements in exchange for her company, and possibly for dancing, kissing, or sex. Working-class women and men of the urban North frolicked in dance halls, jostled together at amusement parks, escaped on boating excursions, and kissed in darkened nickelodeon theaters.[42] Public signs of sexuality among unmarried women were hard for some reformers to understand, in part because many in the reformers' ranks still insisted that women had few sexual desires. Cocks epitomized such assumptions when he described how women, as a gender, "oftentimes *endure* rather than seek or desire physical relationships."[43] Biologist Thomas W. Galloway would contend that even prostitutes "naturally desire home, constancy, and children" more than they wanted sexual satisfaction; so much greater would these domestic desires be among the non-prostituted, whose licentiousness had not been artificially cultivated.[44]

What finally united social hygienists and social purity reformers was that they both found Comstock Laws—federal statutes prohibiting the circulation of sexual information through the mail—very inconvenient. Physicians were frustrated that they could not mail anatomy volumes to other doctors. And social purity reformers' campaigns against forced prostitution (so-called white slavery) and venereal disease were hampered when they could not mail pamphlets describing these problems. They assembled a plan to avoid dependence upon the mail altogether.

Social hygienists and social purity reformers sought to capitalize upon the spread of mandatory schooling in most states as a means to diffuse sexual knowledge and thereby redirect the New Woman's interests along respectable lines. And schools could reach even more people than pamphlets; in 1900 over half of school-age Americans were enrolled in school for at least part of the year, and most states would have compulsory attendance policies by the end of World War I. Reformers wanted their message to reach young people, and young people were increasingly centralized in schools—and so it was to schools that they went.[45] Their expertise was propped up by a cosmopolitan community; the social hygiene/social purity proposal exemplified an international elite's approach to schools, one that emphasized their role as institutions for preserving public health, understood not only in terms of protecting young citizens' bodies, but in terms of the nation's eugenic future. In the United States and Canada, and even in largely Catholic Mexico, concerns about poverty, race, and congenital disease gained traction and informed school reformers' understanding of why students needed to know about reproduction.[46] If sex education had once been restrained to protect middle-class young women from sexual knowledge, the fact that such young women now had at least piecemeal knowledge meant that there was less innocence lost in the process of getting accurate information to those young people most needing it.

Of course, schools were more than a place where children were located. Educators added to reformers' justifications for school-based sex education a set of arguments related to schools' distinctive mission. The New Education movement had recently prompted extraordinary changes; schools' curricula celebrated modern life with more coursework in physical education, civics, vocational training, and health and physiology, preparing students for an adulthood of social collaboration. Appreciating the appeal of an alliance with this movement, Benjamin C. Gruenberg proclaimed that sex education was fundamentally about spreading "the newly acquired knowledge and wisdom and skill of a rapidly changing scientific age . . . to the people at large."[47] Likewise, Maurice Bigelow would describe the purpose of sex education as being to "develop an open-minded, serious, scientific, and respectful attitude toward all problems of human life which relate to sex and reproduction." Sex educators would teach not only personal chastity, but also family and eugenic responsibilities.[48]

One hurdle, however, threatened to upset the otherwise promising relationship between sex education advocates and the New Education. The latter cohort tended to favor a pedagogy of "learning by doing," whereas sex education advocates had spent the last two decades arguing that young people should absolutely learn about sex *before* doing it. So how could sex education advocates create a plausible pedagogy drawing from object teaching, student-directed learning, and skill-based curriculum—hallmarks of New Education pedagogy—without resorting to an obscene solution wherein students engaged in sex with classmates? Here we find an explanation for the otherwise bizarre insistence on referring to sex education as the "birds and bees."

Watching flower pollination or the chicken who lays an egg made visible the processes of mating and conception that were otherwise both difficult to view and obscene to witness. The "learning by doing" in this context came through witnessing, identifying, and caregiving. From here, sex education advocates assured their readers and listeners, children would not only learn basic properties of sexual acts, but also arrive at a suitable interpretation of sexuality's meaning. Sex, these reformers came to argue, was part of the natural world, special because of its commonness and necessity. A disaster narrowly averted, sex education advocates were ready to attach their newly devised approach to the New Education and take on the world.

Sex education's advocates remained blissfully oblivious to the liabilities of harnessing their program to trendy New Education. Tending to view themselves as creators of a common civic faith, progressives like John Dewey had what some historians have described as a "blind spot when it came to other people's strongly held conservative religious views," especially those of newly ascendent Fundamentalists.[49] Catholics were also not uniformly fans of progressivism. They had observed that Protestants often took the lead in other progressive reforms like prohibition and, in schools, English-only instruction, which demanded conformity as the price of Americanism. This reluctance regarding progressivism was not entirely defensive, either, given Catholic and Fundamentalist concerns that, at its most basic level, the natural sciences framework for sex education devalued sexuality's spiritual blessings, thereby degrading the human species that was alone capable of recognizing this dimension within reproduction.[50] Thus, while there was common ground upon which progressive reformers and religious critics might have united—civic actors overwhelmingly acknowledged that a public conversation about sexuality and sexual values was overdue—deep-rooted suspicions persisted. An ensuing tension would haunt sex education in the coming decades and was in no way deescalated by the decision to place sex education within biology courses.

HOW SEX EDUCATION BECAME PART OF BIOLOGY

Buried in a 1922 report on American high schools is a gem of a line, an expression conveying the first of reformers' many disappointments regarding sex education's implementation. The author dryly observed that early high school would become the typical age at which information regarding intercourse and reproduction was conveyed, noting that this was not "because of a conscious plan to give such instruction when it is most needed, in early adolescence," but rather because "the subjects including it [biology, health, physical education] happen to be taught then."[51] It was because one could easily wedge information about sex into the biology curriculum, and because biology was most commonly a first-year class in high school, that sex education became a first-year class, too. To me, this seems a strange choice given that, at the time, only 1.1% of public high school students registered for biology. Perhaps more took a variation of the course, such as life science, nature study, or general science?[52] Overall, this decision, sex educators claimed, was not necessarily the most pedagogically or medically sound option. It was the *easiest* option, because it did not demand a reframing or elimination of other parts of the curriculum but could instead be incorporated into existing institutions.

To understand the ensuing disappointment of the American Social Hygiene Association (ASHA) reformers requires some understanding of the optimistic way that they had batted about the question of "What specific knowledge of sex should be imparted to pupils at a given age?" throughout the previous decade.[53] Physicians had exerted great influence upon social purity advocates, impressing upon them the information that too many youths had "a practical knowledge" of sexual diseases "while yet in their early teens"; in other words, they contracted syphilis or gonorrhea. As early as 1913, Marrow had urged that many children should be instructed at age ten or eleven, especially if there was a need of "anticipating evil outside influences," because children as young as this age sometimes grew "accustomed to debauch." The goal should be to "teach in time to preserve."[54] Sex education would have to intervene in advance of sexual activity if the goal was to eliminate the spread of sexual infection.

In any case, the movement for sex education appeared to be gaining momentum: reformers had mostly resolved to support sex education in schools, they had united in a single reform association, the ASHA, and they had defused tension within their ranks. Most important, the federal government provided the movement with significant funding after it discovered high rates of venereal disease among WWI military recruits.[55] The Chamberlain-Kahn Act (1918) created the Division of Venereal Diseases in the US Public Health Service and ordered the US Interdepartmental Social Hygiene Board to coordinate a coherent program. The federal government would fund hygiene departments at over forty normal schools, colleges, and universities in the years immediately after the war.[56] With the federal government firmly supportive of sex education, and prepared to fund a previously cash-strapped movement, there were suddenly new pamphlets, displays, and posters. This was the beginning of a massive public health movement.

THE COURSE NO ONE WANTS TO TEACH

One nagging question remained: Where were the school-based programs? Looking for positive signs, the Public Health Service and the Bureau of Education conducted an extensive survey to chart the emergence of sex education in schools.[57] *The Status of Sex Education in High Schools*, published in 1922, suggested that about 40% of high schools offered sex education in some form. However, the sex education was not thorough; it skewed heavily toward patchwork measures such as meetings with individual children, the distribution of pamphlets, or presentations by visiting lecturers. The tentative nature of this approach is further suggested by the fact that most new programs lasted only a year or two.[58] As summarized by one parenting manual, "The question of sex knowledge has been debated in education circles, the necessity for it has been admitted, yet no move has been made."[59] Resolutions are not the same thing as action.

Some reformers concluded that teachers were the obstacle. Indeed, the personal reservations individual teachers might have about teaching sex education were undoubtedly amplified by the public's variable responses to the first sex education courses enacted in the 1910s. Historians and journalists preserved some information about sex education offered in St. Louis; Cincinnati; small-town schools around Oregon; Winnetka, Illinois; San Francisco; the Bronx; Buffalo, New York; and Montclair and Glouster, in New Jersey.[60]

One experiment in particular seemed to provide teachers with a lesson, its imprint being larger than others. In Chicago, Superintendent Ella Flagg Young arranged for three lectures scheduled at each of Chicago's high schools. A less-detailed version of this talk was also given to middle-school girls and boys; this was particularly important because it meant that the information was more likely to reach children from immigrant and low-income families. Young was initially successful in gaining public and board support for sex education lecturers because she defined sex education as an element of health education, a field that already had a toehold in the curriculum.[61] She also leveraged her respectability and authority. Young had been a John Dewey student, a Chicago teacher and principal, and a National Education Association president, and therefore could not be dismissed as a radical outsider.

According to one Chicago teacher, the lectures were well received by students such as a freshman young woman, who seemingly channeled the Mosher wives: "I knew nothing before the lectures: Mother thought me too young. My instincts and imagination told me some things and then I overheard a conversation between mother and a lady visitor, so guessed at part of it, but did not have any definite information until the lectures." Recording her opinion anonymously, a more knowledgeable senior described how the lectures supplemented her mother's instruction about menstrual periods and also served to dispel the "dark view of things" that had been prompted after an uncomfortable conversation with friends at age ten.[62] However, neither churches nor settlement houses offered parallel educational programs, which might have provided the public and board of education with a reassuring precedent for providing information about sex.

The specter of sex education in public schools accelerated an intra-denominational debate among Catholics regarding whether parochial schools should be understood as an "unfortunate necessity" or a "moral alternative" to public education, and thus whether the goal should be to make public schools less hostile to Catholics, or instead to lobby for state funding of parochial schools. For some Catholics, sex education was another sign that public schools were inherently dangerous because they featured Protestant teachings masquerading as "progressive." Seemingly in-school readings from the King James Bible—common at most American public schools during this time—were not the limit of Protestant proselytization.[63] The fact that the president of the board of education and several other board members were Catholic did little to assuage these Catholics' concerns, and they flooded the board with letters of complaint.[64] When the lecture materials were declared obscene under the Comstock Law, the board of education insisted that the program be discontinued.[65] The board of education then pressured Young to resign her position.

In all likelihood, Chicago's board of education despised Young more for her support of teacher unionization than for the sex education program she introduced. As summarized by historian Marjorie Murphy, "Critics pictured Young as virtually giving away the store to public school teachers out of her feminist sentimentality, her Catholic sympathies, and her alleged near-senility."[66] Out of all the things that Young accomplished—increased teacher pay, after-school programs, speech pathology specialists, vocational electives—a small series of sex education lectures should probably be understood as one aspect of an overall approach, the general arc of which was offensive to a pro-business board of education.[67] Yet the claim that Young lost her job over sex education appears to have had traction, regardless of its veracity.[68]

For some teachers, this meant that they would continue to provide no instruction. I would argue that the situation of women religious (Catholic nuns), whose inexpensive labor made possible the extraordinary early twentieth-century expansion of American parochial schools, represents an exaggerated version of what was the case for teachers everywhere; sisters were the least compensated and most over-managed within an occupation where this was generally the case. State requirements increasingly delineated the standards and required time for core subjects, and the sisters were simultaneously asked to prioritize religious instruction and endure diocesan oversight. I've found no document suggesting that these teachers were excited to teach sex education, and it would surprise me if they were.

Teachers who were without the constraints of religious messaging or personal celibacy, and who decided that teaching sex education was essential, still came to view their responsibilities conservatively. Consider the example of New York's Morris High School biology teacher James E. Peabody. Peabody, a rare teacher asked to address ASHA, began his 1921 talk by briefly outlining what he, as a father, shared with his children about sexuality. This is useful to know because it suggests what Peabody believed was best practice. When his children were quite small, Peabody's son and daughter bathed and dressed in the same room, thus presenting to them the differences in female and male bodies. Before they were five, Peabody told his children that babies came from inside the mother's body; he told his son about "the father-function" at age ten, drawing the analogy between the boy's own parents and a set of mating birds that they had witnessed. Peabody assured his son that the birds were not fighting, but instead "transplanting to the mother the sperm cells to fertilize the egg cells." In the same year, Peabody explained to his son the meaning of seminal emissions, even before his son had started to experience them.

However, in his role as a teacher, Peabody taught his classes quite differently. At Morris High School, first-year biology students received information about plant and bird reproduction, seniors' coursework included information about mammalian reproduction, but to boys alone was the following offer announced: "If you care to remain after school, say on Friday, we will talk things over, and I will try to answer any questions you may wish to ask." Peabody described himself as fielding questions about masturbation, prostitution and sexual necessity, and nocturnal emissions. Still, during the after-school session, Peabody refused to answer questions about sexual practices. He summarized his response to the students as follows: "I told the boys frankly these were topics that did not in any way concern them at their time of life. I urged them, however, to feel perfectly free to come to me as soon as they were engaged to be married, and I would gladly tell them, so far as I could, all they wished to know." Peabody also refused to teach female students about sex and reproduction. At Morris High School, "none of our women teachers thinks herself prepared to these talks," so Nellie M. Smith, author of *Mother's Reply*, was annually called upon to provide two talks. The young women were first required to bring a note from their mothers.[69]

To me, the significant differences between how Peabody educated his own children and how he taught his high school students suggest the large gap between what he thought best and what he thought feasible. His talk registered four compromises that would make sex education appropriate for teachers to teach: directing it toward older students, refusing to provide information on sexual practice, gender-segregated instruction provided by a same-gender teacher, and requiring parental consent from young women.

Peabody's caution also prompts us to explore why many teachers taught a very limited sex education curriculum or else avoided teaching sex education altogether, even if they were not celibate nuns and did not teach in religious schools. First, teachers in most states did not have tenure, that is, protection against arbitrary dismissal. The first state tenure law was enacted in New Jersey in 1909, and Illinois enacted a similar law in 1917; Rhode Island did not enact tenure until 1946 and excluded married women from protection. In an era during which labor conflict was frequent (and sometimes violent), labor unions had uncertain legal standing, and a series of politically motivated mass firings had plagued the profession throughout World War I, teachers were not looking to give administrators an excuse to fire them.

Second, there was the issue of optics in local communities. American schools were subject to local control and financed through local taxation. Most teachers lived in the same community in which they worked. These factors created circumstances that dis-incentivized teaching that might challenge community traditions and norms. When comparing local pressures to conform against national pressures to innovate, the former was a stronger force. Moreover, reformers, superintendents, and principals had done little to gain teachers' trust, and much to undermine it. This collection of educational authorities had most recently promoted centralization policies that over-managed teachers' lesson plans, blunted teachers' ability to impose classroom discipline, and transferred teachers between schools without consideration of how it might disrupt housing arrangements and family life.

Finally, there was the gender dimension of this labor problem. Peabody was something of an exception in that 80% of teachers were women, at least in cities with 25,000 or more residents after 1900.[70] This assured that teachers—as women—were vulnerable to the charge of being too interested in or too inexperienced with sex, charges tantamount to casting a woman as a whore or spinster. The stakes of being so cast were quite high for both African American and white women teachers, even if one did manage to remain in teaching: being shunned at community events, difficulty finding housing (especially in rural areas, where teachers often boarded with local families), and losing otherwise promising opportunities to gain social mobility through marriage. African American men represented a small percentage of the teaching force, but for these men the specter of lynching constantly loomed; so ready were white mobs to believe any account of Black men's sexual impropriety that such an accusation could result in death.

Reformers were thus demanding something unreasonable from the mostly middle-class women whom they had strived to keep innocent only a few decades before: be on the front lines of teaching sex education. Speaking from a position of historical amnesia, reformer Maurice Bigelow would dismiss as "absurd" the claim that unmarried women be exempted from teaching sex education. "Personal experience is not always necessary for teaching in any line," argued Bigelow. In many fields, Bigelow reminded fellow reformers, "these teachers have learned, not from personal experience, but from the great accumulations of scientific knowledge of medicine, hygiene, and education." In other words, knowledge both could and should precede experience, even for middle-class women.[71]

However, from the woman teacher's point of view, if her own sexual respectability was challenged, she could not—as women physicians might feasibly do—defend herself by asserting that actions deviant for other women were, for her, merely expressions of disinterested professionalism. The prevalence of women in teaching had long made teachers' work a semi-profession, one in which women were ostensibly getting paid for doing womanly things (i.e., caring for children), rather than for executing a task requiring particular training or skills.[72] The scale of the problem whereby teachers' gender discredited their labor as "work" is further supported by the fact that men teachers, who were a significant portion of the high school teaching force, deliberately formed separate professional associations to minimize the contaminating influence of femininity.

The women teachers at Morris High School demonstrated the interactions of gender and occupational stigmas in their response to teaching sex education. By design or spontaneously, the women teachers leveraged the second stigma (that women teachers were not professional) to protect them from the full force of the first (that women discussing sexuality were necessarily promiscuous). They pointed to their lack of normal school training in social hygiene as an excuse not to teach the subject. In citing their incompetence, they briefly joined forces with the school reformers they typically resented: those who blamed teachers for all of schools' failings, attempted to "teacher-proof" the school with standardized curriculum, and subjected teachers to administrative bureaucracy. Not only that, but the self-portrait of incompetence surely undermined the (mostly men-led) unions' attempt to promote teachers' image as experts who stood equal to administrators and teacher educators, and whose possession of specialized knowledge merited respect and deference.[73] The distorted idea that women teachers lacked an understanding of sex had the benefit of being just barely reasonable enough to work—after all, almost three-quarters of the Mosher wives had attended normal school, half going on to teach before their marriages, and were thus teaching before they knew much about sex. It was nonetheless disingenuous, given that increasing numbers of women teachers were married and mothers. Teachers' refusal to teach sex education traded on the ridiculous idea that sexuality was a technical topic comprehensible only to the finest scientific minds.

As teachers dragged their feet—not at every school, never exactly the same way—sex education reformers affirmed the possibility that teachers and principals were a bit incompetent, not having thought through the best way to provide a social hygiene education to their students, even as they also signaled some awareness of the possibility that teachers were refusing to teach out of self-interest. Consider, for example, how *The Status of Sex Education in High Schools* (1922) explained that only 5% of home economics courses had any information about sex instruction. The report noted that "apparently a large majority of the teachers of these subjects fail to realize that their subjects can include this instruction, or they consciously exclude or avoid it."[74] The report's author seems to have assumed that home economics was an appropriate locus for sex education both because sex belonged to married people in their homes, and because the course was generally sex segregated; an all-girl class would assure propriety and decorum.

Reformers came to accept that which appeared inevitable. They were generally persuaded that the best time to educate children would be before high school—developmentally, from a public health standpoint, and in terms of reaching the most people—but also knew that this just wasn't going to happen. They compromised, proposing that an explanation of sexual copulation and reproduction might be reserved until high school and elaborated upon in college, when puberty was well underway and marriage on the near horizon. This compromise position had been foreshadowed by Thomas Balliet as early as 1913, when he conceded that "so far as high schools are concerned . . . pupils at this age have already acquired extensive information in regard to sex, much of which has been obtained from impure sources and has connected with it in their minds impure associations. The chances of doing harm by giving such instruction prematurely, which some people fear in case of elementary pupils, are therefore reduced to a minimum in the high school."[75] Perhaps early high school could be the sweet spot wherein reformers reached students—and yes, their focus still prioritized white, middle-class students—after first knowledge but before first experience.

The 1922 report *The Status of Sex Education in High Schools* had proven to be a crucial document if not a turning point, one that accommodated the different interests of reformers and teachers. Reformers began to concede the question of when—fine, grumbled reformers, it would be early high school—and to instead emphasize the importance of a multidisciplinary approach, both pedagogically and tactically. They sought fully integrated curriculum taught by trained classroom teachers. Pedagogically, if information about human sexuality peppered the curriculum over a span of years, and was also divided among the various disciplinary courses, it might effectively convey the topic's importance. This reasoning was the same as that offered by civics advocates favoring the discussion of citizenship in multiple courses.[76] I would argue that this strategy had the same pitfalls as that used by parents who bring a toddler to a party; everyone is supposed to watch the kid, and therefore no one watches the kid, and the next thing you know all the pots are out of the kitchen cabinets, there's a spill in the front room, and no one can find the dog.

Tactically, I find the argument for spreading sex education throughout the curriculum more persuasive. Balliet embraced the benefits of never titling a single course "Sex Education," noting that "some of its connotations are vulgar; to others it seems to be of questionable wisdom for schools to give, imagining as they do that it means simply giving children information about the physical aspects of sex."[77] A distributed curriculum would not necessitate approval from a school board, could thereby avoid attracting public notice, and thus offered teachers a way to deflect some criticism.

So effectively did school-based sex education make itself discrete and discreet that almost no one noticed when its decline continued. In the late 1920s and 1930s, the idea of sex education still circulated in ASHA, but its presence in school classrooms was virtually extinct.[78] The problem here, as would be the case in ensuing debates, was not that sex educators failed to advance, but rather that their retreats were completely non-strategic. They neither vigorously circled the wagons around their most important ideas, nor preserved precious resources and institutions for future battles. They simply scattered in a haphazard fashion. This all but assured that the next generation of sex education crusaders would start from scratch, arguably robbed of their intellectual birthright.

SHOULD WOMEN LEARN ABOUT SEX BEFORE HAVING IT?

In an age when young, middle-class women became more difficult to supervise and were courted by new amusements, the possibility of keeping from them information about sex was impractical, much as it had always been impractical to keep this information from poor and working-class women. Classroom-based sex education emerged as reformers' second choice, a bargaining point, and a compromise. Understanding that sex education's origins came at a cost—the admission of failure—helps us to better understand why it is that, even now, almost everyone wants young people to receive sex education, but almost no one agrees about what and when students should be taught.

Today's debates are also grounded in past miscommunications. People invested in sex education, then and now, tend to assume that parental questions about sex education are an opening gambit aimed at pruning the curriculum, that religious people are anti-science and underestimate the pervasiveness of sexual activity among young people, and that teachers who hesitate to instruct in sex education are fundamentally ignorant about sexuality itself, or else need to grow a backbone. Resolving these miscommunications would leave room for better debates about what the content of sex education should be, when it should be taught, and by whom. Much depends upon the question of what we generally want from schools, and whether we think that information about sex is similar to or different from information about other subjects.

While thoughtful citizens now have some breathing room to reason about sex education, teachers in the early twentieth century had no such luxury. These teachers often discovered that when it came to sex, the path of least resistance was to teach late, infrequently, and superficially. Teachers were accountable to local communities in ways that national reform associations were not. Institutional impediments, including a lack of teacher training and an absence of tenure, meant that the risks of teaching sex education as reformers recommended were incompatible with teachers' interest in keeping a job and avoiding social pariah status. Only reformers truly blind to the realities of classrooms and schools would think that middle-class women, the group most often forbidden sexual knowledge in the late nineteenth century, were now going to lead sex education curricula. For African American teachers, respectability remained hard-won and precarious, and the risks and consequences of being branded sexually promiscuous were arguably the greatest. New supports emerged, such as a course called "Sex Education" taught by physician Sara Brown, which was the most-enrolled course at Howard University's 1929 summer session. But these endeavors to make teachers qualified did not directly address the underlying problem: teachers' fear of community backlash.[79]

Sex education—to the extent that teachers could bring themselves to teach it—first took root in biology classrooms, or sometimes in physical education or home economics. In the course of observing the natural world and mastering anatomy, students could learn about sex and reproduction without a sense of shame. The goal was to make sex seem boring. It would only be in the 1940s that a new generation of teachers and reformers would place greater emphasis upon sexual pleasure. Placing sexuality in a social, rather than natural, context, midcentury advocates would ascribe to sex education a new purpose that ASHA physicians and social purity reformers never would have imagined: strengthening families.

CHAPTER 2

Happiness or Public Health: Sex Education's Shifting Purposes, 1920–1970

When I first set out to read midcentury sex education textbooks, I expected to find a bevy of ridiculous statements: euphemisms and threats, melodrama and naïveté. What warnings would textbook authors marshal to discourage bobby-soxers and greasers from sexual dalliance? What horror scenarios would they present as inevitably visited upon the sexually reckless, those teens who necked in parked cars while listening to rock music, or perhaps snuck away to their parents' fall-out shelters?

But as I began perusing old, musty midcentury textbooks, I was struck by a surprising pattern. It was a pattern of absence. Among those textbooks promising Family Life Education (FLE), there was consensus that premarital sex was inappropriate, and yet the bugaboos of both early twentieth-century and modern twenty-first-century sex education—venereal disease and young pregnancy—made relatively brief appearances. After spending several afternoons gazing at almost two dozen textbooks, some for college students but most written for high schoolers, I noticed that authors typically provided as little as one paragraph and at most five pages about these two problems, combined.

This absence must have been deliberate. I found evidence that the scholars who produced midcentury curriculum guides, interviews, and journal articles overwhelmingly agreed that venereal disease and young pregnancy prevention should be near the bottom of educators' priorities.[1] As early as 1939, Benjamin Gruenberg urged that it would be "extreme" to use sex education to "make boys and girls 'good' by frightening them with the horrors of the venereal diseases and the stigma of unwanted pregnancies." In 1943 Frances Bruce Strain sounded a death knell when she dismissed social hygiene as mere "venereal disease control," insufficiently sophisticated for a modern age. Listing the qualities of a satisfactory high school textbook, two scholars in 1946 argued that "a sex education which begins and ends . . . with a discussion of the kinds of venereal disease" offered only "a myopic and distorted variety of education."[2]

Midcentury textbooks thus provoked a historical and philosophical question that might otherwise go unasked: What *is* the purpose of sex education? I had always assumed that its required characteristic was protecting public health. But midcentury Family Life educators saw things differently. They argued that the purpose of sex education was not to keep young people away from dangers, but to help them manage family transitions and achieve happy marriages. FLE advocates promised that their students would not "miss the pleasures and satisfactions of warm, fulfilling relationships with parents and grandparents, wives or husbands, simply because they have never fully understood what makes the sexes and the generations tick."[3] And sexuality, they contended, was the tick-starter. By preparing for responsible and routine sexual pleasure, students would gain access to sexuality's extraordinary social benefits: companionship, children, and community standing.

THE SEXUAL LANDSCAPE

To some extent, the midcentury's declining rates of sexually transmitted infections (STIs) explain the conspicuous absence of harangues. Cures, including penicillin, could be quickly provided and hence limit transmission, assuming one had access to a medical provider. Likewise, an absence of tirades against unmarried pregnancy could be explained by its stabilization, plateauing at around 5% of total births throughout the 1940s, 1950s, and 1960s. Contraception and abortion (legal and illegal) were available, literature about them was not banned from the mail, and contraception gained in respectability after endorsement by the Federal Council of Churches and then the National Council of Churches. Moreover, Americans were marrying at a younger age and remained likely to marry in the case of an unplanned pregnancy.[4]

The benefits of declining rates of STIs and young pregnancy, however, were not enjoyed equally by all Americans. For example, rates of premarital pregnancy and STIs for African Americans had not dropped as steeply as those of their white counterparts; the National Medical Association (the Black alternative to the segregated American Medical Association) noted that African Americans were more likely to live in poverty, a condition that limited access to medical treatment.[5] Rather than accepting this logical explanation about resources, some medical and governmental authorities instead interpreted

African Americans' higher rates of young pregnancy and STIs as evidence of their cultural and genetic inferiority. In the American South, some white people advocated extensive sex education to limit African American families, even while refusing programs in white segregated schools. Why? Employers hoped that sex education might assure Black women's uninterrupted availability as domestic laborers.[6] When the Federal Health Service's National Negro Health Movement lost funding in 1951, opportunities to document the impacts of racism and poverty on health evaporated.[7] Nowhere was the medical establishment's menacing attitude toward Black bodies, pain, and families more evident than during the Tuskegee Syphilis Study (1932–72), wherein researchers withheld treatment from individuals whose syphilis might have been easily cured, just to see what would happen.

And yet it would be too much to mistake a declining problem—or a problem that was systematically discounted because it disproportionally hurt poor and marginalized people—with no problem at all. In 1950, 141,600 babies were born to unmarried mothers and approximately 100,000 newborns had congenital syphilis.[8] So our question might be refined: Why was a problem that was still substantial (if recently improved) minimized in sex education coursework and textbooks?[9] To answer this question, we have to consider not only what the facts were about STIs and young pregnancy, but what the communication of information about these problems really meant. And for that, we need to start with Freud.

IN PURSUIT OF ADJUSTMENT

As summarized by historian Jeffery Moran, "Sigmund Freud and all he represented exploded in popularity in the 1920s because Americans were more than ready." Freud's writings "offered a new vocabulary—personality, repression, adjustment, and other psychological terms—that Americans could use to refine and give voice to their new impulses for self-indulgence."[10] Flappers were dancing close at speakeasies, daydreaming about Paris, enjoying automobile rides with their beaux, and listening to Duke Ellington phonograph records. Old restraints had fallen away under the pressures of consumer culture, with even the most sheltered and chaperoned young women having some knowledge of sex. Now that sexuality was part of public life, the discussion could only be what to do about it.

From the vantage point of Freud's American adapters, emphasizing STIs or pregnancy was counterproductive; it would traumatize a young person to the point that he or she might vow perpetual celibacy, and then become sickly or dangerous, even developing a neurosis such as chronic illness, schizophrenia, hysteria, or criminality. A shamed girl "whose just-emerging interest in boys at thirteen is denied by strong refusals of toleration by her parents, may at sixteen show no interests at all or become one of those shy misfits one sees in every gathering."[11] Educators and scholars warned that "irrational attitudes, deep-seated fears, and easily aroused feelings" might substitute a new problem—precocious anxiety and pervasive suspicion—for the old problem of sexual promiscuity.[12] America's maladjusted were party poopers with hang-ups, as the kids liked to say.

What Americans chose as their focus was not the only way one could have defined maladjustment in a national context. For example, Freud's Egyptian adapters were concerned about maladjustment's political manifestations; young people's demonstrations in 1935 and 1936 spurred a strain of psychology contending that the sublimation of sexual anxieties and inferiority complexes provoked actions that disconnected individuals from society and social mores. Egyptian social scientists, like those in the United States, began to argue for sex education that would prevent "deviance" both sexually and politically, especially in newly coeducational universities.[13] And Freud was not appealing everywhere, at every moment. One scholar of Freud's influence upon Chinese literature and literary theory has noted that Freud didn't really catch on in the 1930s because, even though Chinese scholars had translated Freud's work, "the general population was chiefly concerned with problems of economic survival and was not in a position to study and appreciate Freud's theory." Economic concerns were a desperate distraction, Freud's emphasis on sexuality would require a near reversal of cultural norms, and social scientists lacked the prestige of experts in the physical sciences.[14] Appreciation for Freud's theory required an element of right time/right place, and China was not especially fertile ground.

In 1920s and 1930s America, however, psychoanalysts' selective reading of Freud's theory—one that emphasized sexuality anchoring selfhood, the importance of developing personality, and the personal costs of maladjustment—was rapidly communicated among social scientists. The National Council on Family Relations (founded in 1938) facilitated scholarly exchanges, as did journals such as *Marriage and Family Living* (founded in 1939) and the *Family Coordinator* (founded in 1952). Some of the most cutting-edge research was completed by sociologists, anthropologists, and psychologists who interviewed married people, used a Freudian lens to analyze their results, and then developed prescriptions for people contemplating marriage. I have been struck by how much the ensuing recommendations—the substance of Family

Life Education curriculum—disrupt our modern dichotomies of liberal or conservative, comprehensive or abstinence-only, and coercive or anything goes. This is perhaps best demonstrated by a few examples.

Consider first the case of premarital sexuality. The recommendation made by social scientists advocated for virginity much like the Progressive Era sages, but made this argument in different terms. Rather than suggesting that virginity would safeguard health and preserve purity, midcentury Family Life educators argued that women should remain virgins until marriage simply because, as Ralph G. Eckert taught in Stockton Junior College's Psychology of Marriage course, "most men want to marry virgins."[15] From the perspective of a Family Life educator working within an adjustment framework, the goal should be to help women students remove impediments to their ability to become wives and mothers, and hence achieve social acceptability.

In defining "adjustment" as a practical goal, social scientists used the term to describe not the opposite of "freedom" but the opposite of "frustration." For example, educators who valued conflict-free marriages advised students to conform to gendered divisions of labor, because so doing would delineate each partner's responsibilities without extraordinary negotiations. Given that so many authors of Family Life Education curricula were members of mainline Protestant churches, the people authoring this advice were likely influenced by theological understandings of biblically mandated gender roles.[16] But their recommendations were explained not in moral or religious terms, but rather framed as the result of psychological research. As explained by one Purdue University home economics professor, maturity meant "adjusting oneself to the inevitable limitations and restrictions of community life without waste of energy or loss of satisfactions."[17]

Along the same lines, Family Life educators reported social scientists' finding that couples where both spouses came from similar backgrounds had better communication, and therefore recommended avoiding "mixed" marriages. What did "mixed" mean? Unions between people of different generations, races, classes, or religions were discouraged by FLE not because of ethical, religious, or eugenic concerns, but on the grounds that such marriages had historically higher rates of divorce.[18] Moreover, if a mixed couple did remain married, then they would still be unhappy because of the likelihood that they would be alienated by their community, members of which might have ethical, religious, or eugenic reasons for shunning them.[19] While Family Life Education might draw upon interfaith support for a common "Judeo-Christian family," historian Kristy Slominski notes that this praise "did not lead to support for marrying outside of one's religious tradition."[20]

As for marriage between two men or between two women, such commitments were likely doomed because they would deny to both partners the joy of children, and would subject them to the highest level of social alienation. For FLE advocates, the rationale behind any decision to shun (or, rather, lack of rationale) was less important than the point of fact that such shunning would occur. It was thus practical for would-be gay or lesbian young people to adjust their behavior so as not to offend mainline Protestants' conviction that "although God made us to love all people, His design in nature and scripture is clearly for heterosexuality and against homosexuality," a position that one midcentury scholar summarized as "judgmental" if "tempered by concern."[21] In a rare punt to medical authorities, FLE advocates noted that "doctors are working to find ways to help homosexual people. They want to help them learn how to give love to and accept love from people of the other sex."[22] Left out of this narrative was how medical "help" had often been cruel, coercive, and stigmatizing. For example, the California Sex Deviates Research Act of 1950 had investigated homosexuality's origin through an experiment that castrated male sex offenders.

Overall, the American model for sex education was distinctive for how it combined the aspiration of a divorce-free society, the leadership of social scientists, and its location in schools. As a point of comparison, Chinese political leaders shared with American social scientists a vision of family as a lynchpin for governance, yet held a very different understanding of divorce. China's 1950 Marriage Act upheld marital monogamy by making it *easier* for unhappy married people to divorce, which government planners considered a superior option to finding an extramarital partner. The Chinese government then provided contraception as part of an overall plan to *lower* the nation's future birth rate, even as the United States entered peak baby boom; some Chinese middle schools introduced courses on birth control in the late 1950s.[23] As another international point of reference, Cuba shared the United States' aspiration to preserve marriage by minimizing divorce, but relied upon different authorities and different forms of education. Cuban legislators wrote new prenuptial laws to prevent some marriages, and physicians took the lead in marriage preservation, using popular magazine columns to teach husbands to increase wives' sexual pleasure.[24] Social scientists had a comparatively meager role.

One of historians' biggest responsibilities is to point out contingency, that is, the way that innumerable choices and constraints contribute to a given timeline. And historians glancing at international examples will notice that there were paths not taken when American social scientists rushed forward to popularize their plan for a nation of happily married people. These same historians will wryly observe that midcentury social scientists did some mediocre historical thinking. Namely, midcentury social scientists sold educators and policy makers on the idea that the past is *prescriptive*—it is a set of lessons describing a failure (divorce and then social alienation) that can be avoided by obeying a natural law (such as "like belongs with like"). They were thus blind to how their interpretation of the past was not neutral, but in fact created the conditions that made change so difficult. Such influence is exactly why most contemporary historians aspire to avoid prognostication.

FAMILY LIFE EDUCATION

In the classroom, teachers were confronted with rows of awkward and pimply children, making the ideal of "adjustment" seem impossibly far off. But teachers really did try to apply the Freud-informed curricula they had learned in teacher-training programs. New courses appeared, most with titles such as Marriage and Family Living, Family Relationships, Sex Education and Family Living, Preparation for Marriage, and Human Relationships. And as Freudian abstractions and social science theory were applied on the ground, a clear pattern emerged in which FLE came to exemplify a curricular trend: functional education.

Functional education was a midcentury fixation about making education useful in tangible, measurable ways that would help individuals maximize their personal success after graduation. History was rebranded as "social studies" and mathematics as "business math," and some new classes were added. And while Family Life Education advocates sometimes argued that being "thrown into the same pigeon-hole with 'driver education,' 'alcohol education,' 'consumer education' and the like" trivialized the importance of their work, there were common features that justified this connection.[25] Consider, for example, the matter of classroom design. Just as the wood shop resembled an industrial space, so did Family Life Education classrooms increasingly feature living-room-like spaces with carpet and draperies. And while students could not be asked to demonstrate proficiency at sex—that would be illegal and untenable in countless ways—teachers could ask students to demonstrate skills related to personality improvement and social adjustment. These achievements would provide the foundation for a good married life.

Skill 1

Instructors presented the process of becoming gendered and adult as inevitable, and thus urged students to accept changes in their bodies because "you cannot help being tall or short or stocky or thin."[26] Educators sought to soothe and comfort young people undergoing bewildering changes, such as the first nocturnal emission, breast development (or lack of breast development), growth spurts, and hairiness, all of which were equally likely triggers for "fears and anxieties relative to individual sexual development and adjustments."[27] Students, educators proclaimed, should start their adjustment by conducting a reasonable inventory of their changing attributes. Then they should recategorize these attributes as resources rather than traumas. In general, this was good advice for girls becoming women and boys becoming men, a meaningful counterweight to stereotyping messages on TV and in magazines.

In illustrations and words, textbooks also offered the lifeline reminder that young people with changing bodies retained control over their cleanliness and hygiene, the importance of which "can scarcely be overemphasized."[28] Family Life educators offered chapters upon chapters about grooming, which makes more sense if one considers the pivotal role that education about menstruation played in most sex education curriculum design, at least for girls. Teachers often relied upon sex education materials that were developed and published by the companies producing supplies for menstrual blood collection: Coets, Tampax, Kotex.[29] These companies clearly had an investment in targeting a female-only market for a complicated blood-management process, including sanitary belts. Clothes should be protected, and pamphlets and films emphasized the need for disguising one's menstruating status from others, especially boys and men. Cleanliness, to elevate its importance, was being sold as a proxy for something else: "the task of assuming sex roles."[30] To be discreetly clean was to be mature, and to be mature was to be gendered. The TAMA Division of Professional Productions, who made training aids for teachers, named its first lesson "What It Means to Be a Boy or to Be a Girl."[31]

Left out of this discussion was the fact that people did not in fact need to accept the body that they possessed. They could modify it quite a bit. Cosmetics offered an immediate solution to the problem of pimples. Reconstructive surgery could change injured veterans' faces, and shapewear could revise a silhouette. And in 1952, gender-confirmation surgery first entered public knowledge in the wake of Christine Jorgensen's media appearances. Such surgery remained unavailable in the United States until the mid-1960s but signaled possibilities. Furthermore, the advice to accept and care for one's body could be applied irregularly and cruelly, especially when it was directed at people who were intersex. A baby who was born intersex at midcentury often underwent infant surgery; parents did not want the baby to become someone who accepted an intersex body, but wanted the baby to grow into a child whose puberty had established developmental milestones, and for the child to accept the body that they were assigned after their infant surgery rather than the one preceding it.[32]

Skill 2

Having established that "men and women are essentially different," teachers now needed to provide students with lessons in how to "grow socially in order that they may be able to get along comfortably and satisfactorily with their peers of both sexes" and form "healthy heterosexual relationships."[33] There were rules to memorize and perform: "It is usually considered poor manners for a girl to call a boy and ask him for a date" and "When eating out, the girl orders first."[34] More lecherously: "In courtship men assume the role of the pursuer while women assume the role of pursued. Women respond favorably to pursuit by men; men respond unfavorably to pursuit by women."[35] As for women's responsibilities, Bennett College's Art of Living course explained to freshmen women that being "popular with the opposite sex" required adherence to two rules: young women must "look their best at all times" and prepare to "have something to talk about, especially something that interests boys such as Sports."[36] While a midcentury woman was expected to be passionate in ways that her grandmother had not been, it still remained her (unfair) responsibility to anticipate and redirect the sexual passions of her partner away from copulation before marriage. So knowing about sports could be an asset.

Teachers coached students to practice social interactions with classmates, building social skills over time. By the 1950s, classes with both young men and young women had become the norm for sex education because, as noted by one college instructor, "to separate pupils defeats one of the purposes of this type of education. If they are to live together, they should learn together."[37] Teachers directed students to complete exercises such as "plan a sociodrama where the boys and girls act out 'being at the party.' " Importantly, one should "provide the kinds of entertainment that boys as well as girls enjoy"—the examples being making popcorn, treasure hunts, and square dancing.[38] Sociodramas, in turn, might build toward another opportunity to showcase heterosexual sociability: a school dance. Here, young people might have some opportunities to challenge adult standards; the Lindy Hop, mambo, and the Twist were part of what one historian has called a "sonic cultural exchange" across ethnic and racial boundaries, and also represented a transition in social dance wherein coupling no longer required constant contact but simply orientation toward one's partner.[39] Despite the promiscuous possibilities therein expressed, "the date" remained a prerequisite for inclusion in schoolwide social life, and often tickets for school events were sold only in pairs. Thus, "in most high schools many of the most important social activities require the participation of dating couples; and one must date to rate."[40]

Family Life Education tended to emphasize dating's diverse benefits. As summarized by an ASHA-affiliated teachers' group: "Not only is dating fun, but it can contribute greatly to personality development."[41] In the 1950s, ASHA suggested that it was the norm to "begin dating at about the junior high school level and begin going steady in college."[42] Instructors advised that "the prudent young person will give himself every chance to date as many friends as possible. All of us need a basis for comparison," adding that "out of such experiences they will also expand their own personalities."[43] The stakes here were very high, namely that "those college students who seldom or never date or who started dating late in high school and who have never had more than one 'steady' are predominantly socially retiring and show a predisposition to be emotionally maladjusted."[44] The eventual goal of all of this dating was to become a person with a "marriageable personality," to select a suitable mate, and to form a loving marriage.

Skill 3

The transformation of children into young dating adults tended to create family tensions that Family Life Education textbooks promised to help students diffuse.[45] Use of the family car for dates was a notorious sticking point. In a moment of humor, one textbook described a teenager who told his parents, " 'Don't worry about reckless driving and an accident—we won't drive much of the time—we'll park.' " As the textbook authors explained, ". . . that hardly relieved his parents' minds. Most parents know something about the hazards of parked cars; many of them would prefer the risk of motor accidents."[46]

Some evidence suggests that the standards for dating recommended by Family Life educators would be peculiarly difficult for Black middle-class women to follow or for their parents to endorse. For these women, safeguarding their respectability was one of the few available strategies for deflecting sexual stigmatization and exploitation, especially, though not exclusively, by white men. And because individual respectability was the cornerstone of community respectability, the greater community had a big stake in the matter of whether, not just how, Black women might present themselves as potential dates.

The professional papers of Gladys Groves (by all appearances a well-intentioned and respected white professor of Family Life who taught at several of North Carolina's HBCUs) suggest how some middle-class African American women balanced the tension between embracing sexuality and guarding respectability. These students appreciated psychological approaches to child-rearing and marriage that were "implicitly sex-positive," according to historian Christine Simmons. And their written work included resolutions that sexuality "must be respected but not allowed to become master."[47] But in terms of dating, both Groves and her students were concerned that having many dates, and going to many social outings, could lead to dangers that were greater than the benefits of dating. The best solutions relied upon support and protection from an older generation, because the parents of dating-age women could arrange church outings and events in private homes, wherein the potential for abuse could be mitigated.

Skill 4

Family Life educators did not believe that all family styles were equally appropriate but instead encouraged students to adopt a "democratic" form. The term could be misleading as used in this context, so let me clarify. A democratic family was *not* one where all issues were up for a vote—"parents are the leaders in the democratic home"—but rather one in which parents tutored each family member to undermine communism; it was the family, not the individual, that was the unit of democratic strength because "when we have strong homes, we have a strong nation."[48] In part through an ongoing insistence that students should imagine how they would someday educate their own children about sex, Family Life Education prepared future parents to ward off the "ethnocentrism, political-economic conservatism, and anti-democratic trends" that would otherwise leave the individual ripe for authoritarian recruitment. Schools vowed to amplify and perfect the family's democracy-instilling work.[49]

If strong families were what upheld democracy, then FLE advocates had also, perhaps unwittingly, offered racists a corollary: people who had sex outside of marriage should be refused democratic participation. Studying 1960s Louisiana, scholar Melinda Chateauvert has traced instances where sexual "bad character"—defined by having children out of marriage—was used "as a proxy for race" and grounds for disenfranchisement. She chillingly quotes the testimony of African American Joe Kirk before the US Commission on Civil Rights, who described being called "a damned liar" by the registrar after she asked if he had any "illegitimate children," and he answered negatively. His voter registration would be denied. Thus, when civil rights advocates countered racism along these lines by foregrounding "the Black Family" and the respectability of Black women, they did so because it conveyed "the emotional appeal to motherhood and the call to solidarity among black kinfolk" as well as communicating political legitimacy.[50] Laying the groundwork for this important civil rights strategy, Tuskegee initiated a new Family Life Education program in 1961, and Bennett College created a new position for a director of Family Life in 1962.[51]

All this is to say that in the context of family, "democracy" was about identifying insiders and outsiders rather than about egalitarian deliberation and shared decision-making power.

In light of the active role churches would play in developing abstinence-only education in the late twentieth century, it's worth exploring another related question: What kind of church-based sex education was offered during midcentury? Was it Family Life Education? Or did it fill any of the gaps for young people who did not attend high school, or for those whose middle and high schools did not offer Family Life Education? On the one hand, the Federal Council of Churches had worked with ASHA since the 1930s to develop sex education guidance for parents and ministers who wished to counsel young people, and had explored the goals and values such sex education should promote. However, the National Council of Churches did not create student-friendly audiovisual kits until the 1950s, and most mainline Protestant denominations did not make significant investments in sex education curriculum for Sunday schools until the mid-1960s.[52] The earliest guidebook I've found for young people in the Church of Latter-day Saints was published in 1970, its authors explaining that "this book was written because in our youth we found no place to read about sex as it relates to courtship and marriage, especially something written by anyone with an understanding of the gospel."[53] Had they been so inclined and in agreement among themselves, people with religiously informed understandings of sexuality might have developed more congregational or denominational programs and shared them widely; their churches and religious education programs were spaces that people of faith already controlled, unlike public schools, in which they were one constituency among many.

When Protestants developed Sunday school curricula in significant numbers, they did so with an eye on what public schools were offering. For some mainline Protestant denominations, it was a matter of some relief that "schools are better equipped than churches to deal with the physiology and biology of sex" because it liberated Christian churches to explore sexuality's biblical meaning, and how sexuality might interrupt or support one's relationship with God. In the pages of the *Chicago Defender*, a prestigious African American newspaper with a national readership, a consensus emerged that churches should "be a part of the sex education now being taught in schools" and also compensate for the education that adults had been denied in their own childhoods. With perhaps too much confidence, one scholar who collected church-based curricula noted that there was "no opposition to sex education in the public schools by any denomination."[54]

THE USUAL PROBLEMS: ASSESSMENT AND CONTROVERSY

Scholars, for their part, weren't quite sure if FLE programs were creating better marriages, even as they continued to advocate for more sex education in schools. John F. Cuber, a sociologist, created a helpful list of the problems inhibiting FLE program assessment: the difficulty of isolating the variable of Family Life coursework from the whole set of experiences leading to marriage, the lack of a clear way to measure marital "happiness" other than simply avoiding divorce, the lack of longitudinal studies with multiple check-in points, and the difficulty of determining the role of individual mental health in marital outcome.[55] Even if avoiding divorce was taken as a proxy for successful marriages—and, goodness, that is a rather modest standard of "success"—it would be at least a decade before educational researchers could hope to determine whether or not any given Family Life program accomplished its goal.

In the meantime, educators and researchers used student assessments to make tentative program assessments. Student assessments included such standardized methods as matching or multiple-choice quizzes for knowledge. Students also took personality quizzes wherein they self-evaluated their character and sociability, and then compared their self-image to the perception of family or teachers. Teachers using these assessment tools sometimes acknowledged that they might, fundamentally, be grading students on the basis of how well they mimicked teachers' values, or whether or not the teacher found them likable. But then again, being a good listener and having an appealing personality were course learning objectives.

At the college level, instructors supplemented exams and personality inventories with journals and mandatory one-on-one interviews with the faculty member; recording the journey to self-actualization provided instructors with evidence that students understood key course vocabulary while at the same time generating evidence that their programs shaped students' personalities and decisions. For example, Lester Kirkendall described one college-credit course he taught to GIs as conducted without a textbook, but with requirements for one-on-one counseling and a "thoughtfully prepared paper on How

My Life in the Army Has Affected My Attitudes and Experiences Toward Marriage, Sex, and the Family."[56] Instructors Gladys Groves, Alfred Kinsey, Joseph Kirk Folsom, and Henry Bowman—pathbreakers in marriage coursework—all included interviews as part of their courses.[57] The possibility that forcing students to share their personal lives with people who had the power to grade them might be a massive and unwarranted invasion of students' privacy did not seem to have been a deal-breaker for midcentury teacher-researchers. Yet, at the same time, it seems likely that some students were desperate to share personal decision-making and trauma with a compassionate listener. I can only conclude that such interviews and self-reflection papers met a real need, as well as being invasive and a mediocre means of student assessment.

School and administrative leaders, however, were mostly worried that Family Life Education would violate community norms, or that angry parents would *think* that these programs had violated community norms. They resolved to intervene early, and did so in ways that meant few Family Life Education courses were conducted as designed, making program assessment still more difficult. For example, a committee of citizens charged by the school board with setting Family Life curriculum expectations gave the following list of "don'ts" to a Renton, Washington, high school teacher:

> The following topics shall not be a part of the course:
> a. Information on details pertaining to coitus
> b. Approval of masturbation
> c. Approval or discussion of homosexual relations
> d. Discussion of religious interpretations pertaining to any phase of the course
> e. Discussion of any type which would have a tendency to approve or advocate divorce
> f. Birth control and contraceptives
> g. Approval of pre-marital or extra-marital sexual relations

Teacher Patricia A. Smith noted, rather dryly, that "many students have inquired" about "why pages are missing from the text books." Responding to this question could be tricky because she, like many teachers, was caught in a difficult position: she suspected her students needed something more but hesitated to risk her job by providing "details pertaining to coitus." An article about her experience, however, had a passive-aggressive flair.[58]

Smith was hardly alone in offering a compromised version of Family Life curriculum and could count on fellow teachers to sympathize when she blamed school administrators for course deficiencies.[59] Recalling the previous semester's sex education module within a Family Life course, teacher Anna Laitala commented, "Unfortunately this unit was dropped before its completion. I was told very emphatically and bitterly that I was not meeting the needs of my students and I was harassed into starting my cooking unit at once!" She continued, "I knew that some administrators react in this way to this subject over which 'controversy' might develop, but I did not expect it in an area in which the need for a school-centered program is so vital," concluding that "in spite of this experience, I will again repeat these sessions and I plan to continue after these kids have assimilated, talked about and evaluated what was presented."[60] Likewise refusing to let controversy deter them, a department of (women) home economics faculty openly mocked the (men) physical education teachers who shied away from providing sex education: "Somehow, one is surprised to discover that Home Economics is alone in presenting a highly idealized but, nevertheless, relatively complete program of sex and family life education, and that where these ladylike crusaders lead, the masculine physical education teachers do not dare follow."[61]

Other teachers relied upon authoritative filmstrip narrators to mediate between faculty and their fearful school boards and administrators. The most popular film was *Human Growth*, first distributed in 1947 by the Oregon Social Health Association. Over the next decade and a half, two million children would view the twenty-minute film, as would thousands of parents at Parent-Teacher Association meetings.[62] As described by Laitala, "It was not enough to show the film once. It had to be shown over and over and over at their [students'] request," a comment meant to convey both her students' low starting level of comprehension and the compelling nature of the material.[63] The staff of the trust underwriting *Human Growth*'s distribution praised the film for securing the central place of "a new discipline, that of psychology" in sex education. The E. C. Brown Trust would further describe the film as marking "the gradual extension of ideas which were, ten years ago, only hints," such as "the understanding of the fact that for teen-age boys and girls, a knowledge of the physiology of sex and of human reproduction does not pass for sex education," with the most relevant information instead being "social relations within the family and of family members with the world outside."[64]

CHALLENGE FROM THE LEFT

Family Life educators might have expected gratitude from students but got something altogether different. Historian Susan K. Freeman argues that educators had inadvertently given young people "tools with which to challenge adult hypocrisy and silences as well as the limitations of the domestic ideal."[65] Against the backdrop of feminism and civil rights, and with a nod to the emerging sexual revolution, young adults added up what adjustment to social norms cost, and explored the sometimes soul-destroying forces with which a well-adjusted person became complicit. What if social adjustment is neither normal nor good because it requires adjustment to a flawed society?

By the mid-1960s, it was clear that mass movements from the Left had made possible new choices, which set new standards for social permissibility. "Adjustment" was now a moving target. Responding to the legal and cultural precedents set by *Pérez v. Sharp* (1948) in California and *Loving v. Virginia* (1967) in the Supreme Court, rates of intermarriage between partners with different religions, ethnicities, and races were on the rise. New forms of contraception gave many married and unmarried women opportunities to enjoy sex without early pregnancy, and to thereby engage in personal experimentation or develop partnerships in advance of having children. More women sought paid employment and kept working after marriage and childbirth.

What would sex education have been like if it did not presume that women and men needed to get married, needed to marry each other, and needed their marriage to be their most important relationship? By the time that Adrienne Rich would pen "Compulsory Heterosexuality and Lesbian Existence" in 1980, gender theorists would have cataloged ways in which legislators, medical authorities, families, and commercial culture had historically directed women toward husbands, making options other than marriage elusive for all but a small number of "marriage resistors." When we look at what political thinkers from the second half of the century were saying, we can see the contours of what was lost when FLE had failures of imagination. African American civil rights and welfare rights activists emphasized how the courts, social workers, and legislators had pathologized single mothers' sexuality, discredited their kin and near-kin networks, compelled sterilization, and initiated nighttime surprise investigations by social workers.[66] Young people who had been alienated by their biological families founded cooperatives and communes, where their friends became their new families. Transgender people sidestepped unfriendly hospitals and unhelpful insurance policies when they shared information about medical centers offering specialized services, and they created houses grounded in ballroom culture.[67] If not financially dependent on husbands or stigmatized for being unmarried, Rich and others noted, women might acquire friendships, sexual partnerships, and cooperation with women, and ultimately advance all women's liberation.[68] Activists forced the issue until FLE advocates could see the possibilities.

Looking back over four decades of teaching and research, Lester Kirkendall would conclude in 1966—in a rather awed tone—that "educators are now dealing with a generation of youth which looks for evidence, asks for reasons, weighs and evaluates," a generation that rejected tradition unless it was accompanied by reason and justice.[69] The most adventurous educators began suggesting that teachers should explore how "family roles can so easily lead to the teaching of outmoded stereotypes," and concluded that it might be better to teach students that as families change over time, so do the roles and obligations of each individual within them.[70] Of course, not all sex educators demonstrated such open-mindedness. But this only meant that, as summarized by historian Jeffery Moran, "when a small minority of youths," soon to be a much larger number, "began to revolt openly against the older sexual standards, the grown-ups would no longer be united to quell the rebellion."[71]

In part to facilitate communication among the diverse groups of researchers on sexuality—not only social scientists and professors in schools of education, but also those in theology and medicine—and from these researchers to classroom educators, a new organization emerged in 1964 to fill an unoccupied niche in the Family Life landscape: the Sex Information and Education Council of the United States (SIECUS). Led by former Planned Parenthood medical director Mary Calderone, SIECUS dedicated most of its energies toward producing study guides, a newsletter, bibliographies, and reprints for distribution.[72] SIECUS was embraced by Family Life educators as a much-needed support for their work, categorized as professional and moderate, and was an important conversation space for sex educators of diverse religious, academic, and regional backgrounds. It was a whole new world, and Family Life educators (mostly) resolved to modernize.

CHALLENGE FROM THE RIGHT

Just as sex educators were incorporating feedback from the Left and carefully tending to alliances with religious liberals and moderates, recently organized social conservatives raised a different, and often incompatible, set of concerns. California's sun-soaked city of Anaheim would be the locus for a conservative political response, with its anti-sex-education movement becoming the model for others. Within a year of Anaheim's backlash-to-end-all-backlashes, the National Education Association would catalog that "communities in 13 states have canceled, postponed, or curtailed their sex education programs as a result of extremist attacks; 20 state legislatures are considering legislative proposals for investigation, restriction, or prohibition of sex education in public schools."[73] In fact, over forty states would experience some sort of controversy in 1968–69, with about half considering legislation that would neuter Family Life courses.[74] What had energized this backlash? Seemingly coast to coast, a new consensus emerged among social conservatives, coordinated through organizations such as the National Council of Christian Families Opposed to Sex Education in Public Schools, Parents Opposing Sex Education in Public Schools (POSE), and, tellingly, the John Birch Society. Family Life Education, these organizations argued, was a communist plot.[75]

This attack would strike Family Life educators as so preposterous that they had trouble taking it seriously. Modern sex educators will recognize in the Anaheim School District's implementation plan many elements now considered best practices. After finding that a mind-boggling 90% of Anaheim adults—the *real* majority, not some imagined Silent Majority—supported sex education, educators in the school district had begun a multiyear curriculum-development process.[76] The committee charged with creating the curriculum in "Family Life and Sex Education" had reviewed teaching materials with community members, included students in some parts of the planning process, and run teacher workshops to test curriculum. They had turned to SIECUS for help at the final stage, crafting a new curriculum guide so coherent that it would be published by a prominent commercial press, with the idea that other districts would likely adopt it.[77] Family Life Education professionals lavished praise on the program, with Lester Kirkendall proclaiming that the grades 7–12 program "would have been hailed enthusiastically by any family life teacher."[78] When teachers guided students' discussions about values, encouraged students to weigh the benefits and consequences of sexual roles and behaviors, and emphasized how each choice advanced or inhibited integrity, empathy, or exploitation, they engaged in what Family Life's researchers and educators widely considered the best pathway to successful marriages. Family Life educators promoted what we might now call *critical thinking*: values discernment, values identification, weighing evidence, defining a position, and learning how to make good choices.

And yet there were rumbles of discontent, which Family Life advocates ignored at their peril, given that these complaints came from a small number of people willing to make a very large ruckus. Starting in 1967, conservative parents began to read course materials and to investigate and organize against their district's Family Life Education curriculum. To parents visiting classrooms, the years spent mulling pedagogical options and the multiweek social context that Family Life Education provided for sex education were not immediately apparent. Arriving on a date when reproduction was being discussed in a Family Life classroom, all that sex education opponent Eleanor Howe could see was a list of sexual terms written on the blackboard.[79]

From conservatives' vantage point, much of what happened in the sex education classroom neglected students' moral development, or even inhibited it. Conservatives expected education to help students to master a body of knowledge; educators' job was to compress information so that students could build upon a strong foundation and avoid bad choices.[80] But when teachers claimed that sexuality could be understood through an exclusively secular, scientific lens, they taught an untruth. Even worse, teachers who guided students in values discernment exercises were permitting students to learn and proclaim untruths in service to relativism, a foolish and false doctrine that conservatives had learned to recognize. Within Christian denominations, conservatives engaged in a parallel battle against proponents of the "new morality"—a Protestant theological elaboration upon situation ethics, one eschewing moral absolutes and prioritizing the adaptation and application of Christianity to modern culture.[81] Ultimately, Christian conservatives concluded, relativism was as dangerous in FLE as it was in Christianity, not only because of the likelihood that students would learn incorrect content but because of the inherently flawed pedagogy through which untruths were taught: open-ended exercises encouraged students to contemplate disobedience to their parents' instructions.

For conservative Christians, the fact that a lot of other Christians were leading or embracing sex education did little to diffuse their concerns. I can't say this enough: Christians were not in agreement.

Other Anaheim parents who might not have identified as either Christian or conservative heard bad things about sex education from their children, or were horrified by incidents that most likely never took place. Community members reported an incident of sexual intercourse in the classroom. A second rumor, printed for distribution by flyer, asserted that an unnamed teacher stripped for her class.[82] Flyers circulated, and Christian TV and radio reported. Evangelical Christian Tim LaHaye, the pastor at a San Diego megachurch and a future founder of the Moral Majority, proclaimed his disgust that seventh graders were graphing the results of sexual frequency after interviewing their parents.[83] This was the stuff of urban legends and suburban nightmares, and just as fictional. But "fictional" is not the same as "ineffective."

Soon, Howe and others created a local organization called Mothers Organized for Moral Stability (MOMS) to host anti-sex-education workshops. Once organized, MOMS received support from national anti-communist moralists, including Gordon Drake and Billy James Hargis, as well as the Christian

Crusade. These national organizations provided MOMS with pamphlets, including the Drake-authored *Is the School House the Proper Place to Teach Raw Sex?* (The answer: No, schools are not a good place for raw sex. Go figure.)[84] The overall effect was to amplify the volume and potency of MOMS's complaints, providing political novices with a veneer of professionalism and expertise.

Anaheim parents' accusation that Family Life Education turned children against their parents became supercharged, reemerging as a conspiracy to use sex education to destroy families for the purpose of leaving the nation vulnerable to communist takeover. Opponents of sex education seized upon the "subversive affiliations" of some SIECUS board members who had been forced to testify before Joseph McCarthy's infamous House Un-American Activities Committee in the 1950s.[85] Through the logical fallacy of guilt by association, sex education's opponents channeled McCarthyist energy, describing their aspirations "to promote Christianity and to defeat Communism and to preserve Christian ethics in our country."[86] What had begun in Anaheim developed into a nationwide movement, with opponents such as those identified with the Highland Park Baptist Church in St. Paul, Minnesota, claiming that sex education "will 'bury us' morally, and perhaps physically. The Communists will not have to dig the hole; we will do it ourselves!"[87]

The extraordinary turning point in the Anaheim case was a school board meeting in October 1968, where local protesters read (decontextualized) passages from the published curriculum for three hours, including bits and pieces of rhetoric drafted by Gordon Drake. The 90% of district parents who had supported sex education seemingly evaporated. As understatedly summarized by historian Jeffery Moran, "While a large majority of parents who had been surveyed supported sex education in general, their endorsements were passive, and in many cases what they had in mind may have differed greatly from what the district was implementing. In contrast, MOMS members were highly motivated and ideologically united."[88] One sex educator ruefully noted that "it became evident in 1968 and 1969 that many parents, in addition to the organized opposition, were not reconciled to guilt reduction, regarding guilt as insurance against evil behavior and as deserved punishment for departures from traditional codes."[89] After a low-turnout municipal election in 1969—only 14% of eligible voters cast a ballot—anti-sex-education candidates won a majority of school board seats, gutted the Family Life program, and demoted the superintendent. The decades of work required to make a curriculum like Anaheim's Family Life Education possible had been diminished in a single academic year. The ex-superintendent would have a heart attack shortly thereafter.

Family Life Education soon became a curricular zombie. When they chose to publish their curriculum, Anaheim's Family Life educators had volunteered their community as a test case for how an exemplary program might operate, and though they might now wish that they had not done so, the scrutiny to which they had made themselves subject was now national in scope. Letter writers from not only all of California, but from around the country, wrote to the *Anaheim Bulletin* to share their opinions about what sex education should be and do.[90]

Principals became less and less willing to entertain the suggestions of Family Life educators, or physical education, biology, or home economics teachers, who wanted to include sex education in their courses. When principals received angry phone calls, they saw the specter of a mob. One California researcher, Doris Bloch, captured the anxious responses of principals to whom she had directed inquiries about district sex education offerings.

> I'm in trouble with an angry parent group right now; yesterday they descended on my office . . . and recently I had a petition.

> The opposition started in the fall. They had mass meetings. . . . We lost a tax election, and part of the issue was sex education.

> We are under completely irresponsible, vicious, obscene attack. We are surviving. Ordinarily I would be quite interested.

The fact that the researcher was a graduate student at prestigious UC Berkeley, which also had a national reputation for student activism, did not help: "I would have to spend hours explaining to the people in the community that we are not trying to pervert their kids. How about Berkeley? There are a lot of avant-garde ministers and social reformers there."[91]

Reporting on a quickly convened Inter-Agency Conference on Current Opposition to Family Life and Sex Education, a National Council on Family Relations staff member would note with some relief in 1969 that "the concentration lies in southern California," even while describing "evidence of organized opposition in 23 states."[92] However, a 1970 survey of sex education advocates around the country showed that the story was moving to a new stage: several out-of-state respondents would mention that "the action [against sex education] in their state was encouraged in some manner by the situation in California," even as "our California panelists documented at length the severity of the attack on sex education in their state."[93]

LESSONS LEARNED

Much as had been the case after Chicago's 1913 sex education fiasco, the story of Anaheim's Family Life troubles left sex education advocates temporarily shell-shocked. In the columns of the *Family Coordinator*, individuals who had acquired advanced degrees in Family Life, who had jobs in like-named departments, who had developed high school curricula, and who had defined best practices—in short, people who had dedicated their professional lives to strengthening marriages—complained that they were now accused of being petty pornographers. Responding to Gordon Drake's infamous *Is the School House the Proper Place to Teach Raw Sex?* pamphlet, one Family Life professor howled that his accusers were "playing upon people's fears and prejudices" and receiving "support from certain organizations with national dimensions," an allusion to the John Birch Society and the Christian Crusade.[94] Family Life educators lost this battle, despite having majority support. They had lost as much because principals and administrators *feared* that parents would revolt, as because of the actual parent revolts.

Post-Anaheim, the struggle was not over whether Family Life Education would be the method of instruction, but about whether schools would offer any sex education at all. Organizations such as the National Council for Family Life, which had only a few short years earlier admonished educators to avoid overemphasizing such matters, now foregrounded the public health benefits of sex education. It was the lack of opposition to this reasoning that made it key. It provided sex educators with a way to keep teaching and working without suffering public attack. No one was opposed to public health, and teaching about STIs—assuming the exclusion of information regarding prophylaxis—had for decades remained the least controversial topic for parents of high school students. Noted the researcher behind one such survey, in which parents widely agreed that discussing STIs and premarital pregnancy were the most important features of any sex education curriculum: "The majority of parents in the sample are likely to believe in the 'fear approach' in sex education programs as a deterrent to premarital intercourse. Such an approach assumes that one goal of sex education in the high school is to prevent premarital intercourse."[95] A single point of agreement—that sex education should inform students about painful diseases and the difficulties of early parenting—became the ultimate justification for the entire program of sexual education, replacing the earlier consensus that sex education should be about building happy marriages.

This transformation could perhaps best be measured by the creation of a new publishing category for high school and college textbooks: Health. Texts such as John LaPlace's *Health*, Benjamin Kogan's *Health: Man in a Changing Environment*, John Sinacore's *Health: A Quality of Life*, and Paul Brandwein and Daniel Collins's *Health: Decisions for Growth* entered the market in the late 1960s and early 1970s. Placing sex and reproduction back into a biology and anatomy curriculum, Health promised to accomplish many of the same goals as Family Life Education with less (appearance of) fluff or morals. Indeed, the Public Health Service's approach—which had improved testing for syphilis, provided training for physicians and outreach for citizens, and promoted a relatively frank educational program of counseling, pamphlets, and exhibits—had bided its time long enough to appear cutting-edge; this was, if not a reversion to the social hygiene approach, clearly a variation of that approach. Expanding its efforts from outreach to adults to outreach for school-aged teenagers, a task force at the Public Health Service (PHS) distributed a new pamphlet, *Strictly for Teenagers: Some Facts about Venereal Disease*, and began preparing text for *Teenage Pregnancy: Everyone's Problem.*[96]

There is some reason to think that the scandals of 1969 merely accelerated a pedagogical transition that was already underway. FLE did not have a documented history of assessment success to which its advocates could refer. Rates of divorce continued to climb and would reach an all-time high in the early 1980s; many Family Life alumni were among those divorcing. And while sexual restraint had never been Family Life's main goal, educators were left to wonder what to make of the finding that University of Missouri–Columbia students who had taken sex education (from diverse high schools, admittedly) had no lower rates of premarital "petting" or intercourse than their peers who had not.[97] The PHS's William J. Brown would paint a rather horrifying picture of the persistence of STIs, describing the incidence among teenagers of all races at around 200,000–300,000 diagnoses per year. If one expanded the age group from teens to young people up to twenty-four years old, the rate of infection was 1,500 per day.[98] In any case, it soon became obvious that the Public Health Service would neither be able to fill the gap left by Family Life Education's declining prestige and shift in priorities, nor solve FLE's research problem. Just as its public-health-based approach gained traction with professional educators, the PHS's funding was cut.[99]

Of course, there is reason to think that some social scientists would have loved to try to complete high-quality program assessment. But recall the problem mentioned by Doris Bloch, the young Berkeley researcher who had encountered the hostile principals. Teachers' and administrators' fearful retreat from controversy had cut short research on sex, education, and sex education at the very moment when findings would have been most useful for policy makers and parents. When concluding her article about the difficulty of acquiring research subjects, and the reasons provided by school administrators for their refusals, Bloch noted that "individuals on both sides of the question" regarding the value of sex education were "making statements that could not be supported by scientific facts, while they raised questions that needed to be answered by sound research." Bloch's own inquiry, for example, would have provided documentation regarding how much sexual information mothers shared with their daughters and how much the daughters retained.[100] This might clarify once and for all what content was essential for schools to provide.

Protestants, in the meantime, were at a crossroads with sex education: Should the next goal be to reform sex education in public schools—perhaps making it more about character and premarital abstinence—or to follow Catholics' lead and remove themselves from secular schooling? In 1962 parochial schools had been educating one in every eight American students, and many new Christian schools seemed anxious to follow this lead in the 1970s.[101] The question of Christians' investment in public schools was complicated by the fact that there were volatile disagreements both within and between Protestant denominations about what should be a "Christian" sexual standard, and hence whether the public schools could ever be sufficiently reformed. On the one hand, conservative Christians were beginning to harden their positions on what we now think of as cornerstone issues related to sexuality, including abortion. On the other hand, liberal Christians would show signs of switching from patronizing toleration to a warmer embrace of LGBTQ+ partnerships. They seemed content to develop denominational curricula, with the Unitarian Universalist Association's About Your Sexuality curriculum representing the most progressive edge. Across the board, Christians were clear that their faith mattered when discussing sex but were not in agreement about what that entailed.

And as for those activists from the political Left and the Right, the ones who had challenged Family Life Education and triggered the field's retreat back to public health justifications? They maintained their mutual dislike, clashing repeatedly over a series of issues that were never-ending: the Equal Rights Amendment, school bond issues, sexual harassment policies, evolution, school prayer, and affirmative action. On the educational front, they would initiate or renew advocacy for open classrooms, small schools, decentralized districts, centralized districts, and homeschooling. And that was just in the 1970s. Sex education, it seems, had merely been a stand-in for broader anxieties.

WHAT IS THE PURPOSE OF SEX EDUCATION?

Midcentury sex educators and reformers had imagined a curriculum in which sex education was not just about biology; it was also social. This curriculum included scrutiny of emotional and embodied sexuality, areas absent from most contemporary curricula—and which might be good to again include. Through textbooks and new Family Life courses, they had guided high school and college students to consider which sexual choices might advance their values and goals. They weighed when and how often to have sex, the selection of a sexual partner, and the pursuit of sexual pleasure. This curriculum was grounded in a significant body of social science research, especially the findings of sociologists and psychologists who interviewed married couples about the agreements, roles, and attitudes that had seemingly assured their marital success.

Miscommunication nonetheless continued to be the dominant theme in sex education debates. Some parents, boosted by anti-communist reactionaries, assumed that teachers' discussion of sexual pleasure was an endorsement of sexual experimentation, and that instruction in critical thinking would inevitably promote open rebellion. School administrators, in turn, tended to assume that an angry phone call was the harbinger for an angry mob, whether that initial phone call came from a district parent or someone in a whole other state. And when each side projected its fears as though those fears were already fact, it validated the impression that "culture wars" were everywhere, and entrenched people behind their battle lines. All of this conflict was facilitated by the parents who generally thought that sex education was a good idea until someone gave them a reason to think otherwise, but were disinclined to put much effort into its support during school board elections, curriculum meetings, or conferences. Likewise, churches could have offered an alternate venue for education in Christian values regarding sexuality, but because they didn't agree among themselves, they instead bickered about what should be taught in the public schools. Family Life Education's scholar-teachers, the people who cared the most about sex education as an independent issue, were left frustrated and flummoxed.

Sex education advocates were desperate to keep some toehold in the curriculum, especially as the American school system continued to expand and standardize. By identifying just two problems for which there were no proponents—teenage pregnancy and sexually transmitted infections—sex education advocates conveyed the significance of their curriculum while deflecting fears and ire. It was not a compromise position so much as it was a retreat.

This defensive maneuver was arguably shortsighted. It meant that there were few programs that sex education researchers could investigate, destroying a pipeline that might have created evidence of Family Life Education's positive outcomes—or else the evidence that there were compelling grounds for a different approach.

There is no way that reformers could have anticipated the unimaginable: the ascendency of a new and deadly sexually transmitted infection, one that would make public health more important than ever.

CHAPTER 3

Peers or Professionals: Authority, Activism, and Sex Education, 1970–2000

Want to find out all of the crazy ideas people had for innovative sex education programs? The place to look is in grant files because experiments cost money, and no public school is ever flush with cash. There's rich material in a grant file—correspondence, evaluations, publicity—but for me the most interesting document is the grant proposal. This is where applicants tend to say what they really think: complaints, ambitions, expectations. And when looking at grant files preserved at New York's Rockefeller Archive Center, I found one proposal that included all that and more: the "Peer Education and Referral Project" proposal, submitted by the Student Committee for Rational Sex Education (SCRSE) to the Ford Foundation in 1973.

This grant proposal first stood out to me because of its authors; teen voices are rarely found in archival records. As I read further, I could also see how a program like what SCRSE described would be an intriguing exception to what otherwise appears to be the doldrums in schools' sex education history, an era between the fall of Family Life Education and the rise of HIV/AIDS education. But most of all, this proposal and its ensuing program illuminate important questions that are now all but resolved and are therefore quite difficult to imagine as once unsettled: Who should lead sex education? What should authority look like? And are schools worthy—ethically and organizationally—of being a site where these authorities teach?

SCRSE's peer-education proposal illuminated the edge of what educational stakeholders could imagine. It aimed to create learning centers at fifteen New York City public high schools, with each "rap room" open for at least three periods per day. The grant writers envisioned trained peer educators providing one-on-one counseling, coordinating discussion groups, presenting information to health classes, offering pamphlets, and overseeing a small library. Peer educators would visit clinics and resource centers around the city, scouting for low-cost and friendly locations where parental consent was not required. The proposal was quick to note that the project "could serve as a model for sex education programs throughout the country."[1]

In tracing the original document scribed by Stuyvesant student Hariette Surovell and the ensuing proposal drafts, I developed a better understanding of SCRSE's radical vision, especially regarding why they felt that students should be taking on duties customarily assigned to administrators. This, they argued, would achieve consistency between the program's emphasis on student communication and autonomy, and its organizational structure. If students were to be trusted to make good decisions about their bodies, could they not also be trusted to make good decisions about the programs educating them about their bodies?

In 1973, when the Ford Foundation provided $280,232—the equivalent of $1.75 million in 2022 dollars—to a bunch of teenagers and encouraged them to talk about sex, it was a dramatic reversal of educational policy. Previous generations of educators had lived in fear of exactly what was now being funded: kids teaching other kids about sex. This was probably unprecedented, and definitely unusual, and I honestly have difficulty imagining that such a program could be funded at any other historical moment.

AN EXPERIMENT IN PEER-LED SEX EDUCATION

Outstanding through it was, the idea for SCRSE's program did not emerge from nowhere. Peer education was having its moment on the educational stage. Speculating a bit, employees at the board of education believed that there were at least twenty New York City schools already using peer education to attack drug abuse by 1972.[2] As noted by Maude Parker, the Bureau of Health and Physical Education program supervisor for Sex Education and Family Living, "The term 'peer' is 'education chic' and is widely used," even if there wasn't complete agreement about what it entailed.[3] Parker was here being a bit patronizing, suggesting through the use of "chic" that peer education was a superficial change of fashion. A less-dismissive contemporary scholar described how peer counseling had "emerged in the early 1970s as professionals gave increasing attention to the need of individuals, not just for information, but for opportunities to explore confusing issues in a setting of acceptance."[4]

A new peer-led sex education program might have normally attracted critical attention, but was easily overlooked in the context of New York City's dynamic educational environment. In Manhattan and Brooklyn, longtime movements toward integration were checked by Black nationalists who advocated community control of elementary and middle schools. These activists leveraged school boycotts to advocate for locally elected governance boards, exceptions from collective-bargaining agreements that would permit governance boards to hire more African American teachers and administrators, employment for parents and community members as assistant teachers, and control over budgets and building maintenance. Such changes, activists hoped, would improve students' lives by protecting them from inequitably applied disciplinary procedures and stereotyping faculty, and would create schools where students would have more dignity and opportunities for achievement.

But by the early 1970s, it was clear that a developing municipal budget crisis would limit the radical capacity of school decentralization. There wasn't money to experiment with new pedagogies, and many of the special programs that had previously distinguished one school from another—such as sex education courses—were trimmed from operating expenses because they were "on the bottom of the priority list."[5] What this meant was that while a citywide Family Life Education curriculum including sex education had existed since 1968, this curriculum was delivered in a rather haphazard fashion. Before ever penning the SCRSE proposal, Hariette Surovell contributed one of the most memorable descriptions of sex education, repeating for a crowd's benefit the advice of her hygiene teacher. When asked to recommend a form of contraception, the teacher had flippantly suggested "sleep with your grandmother."[6] And Surovell had been comparatively lucky; less than a third of New York City's nine hundred public schools offered any form of sex education at all.[7] In an early draft of their proposal, SCRSE students had expressed their frustration that in a typical school, "some written material was distributed one day during the year by those relatively few teachers who felt comfortable doing that."[8]

For the Ford Foundation, therefore, the SCRSE proposal was the right sort of project at the right time. It would test an educational trend and fill an educational gap.

NOTES FROM THE FIRST YEAR

How successful was the Peer Education and Referral Program's first year, in terms of compensating for New York City's sparse school-based sex education instruction? I think this is a story with two narratives. First, there is the story of plucky students and teachers overcoming significant obstacles. The training program began in September 1973 and was operating in around a dozen schools—which was fewer than the originally proposed twenty-five, and far fewer that the total number of New York City high schools, but was still pretty impressive. On-schedule rap rooms opened in February, with lagging programs mostly operational by April.

Madeline Oberle, a peer adviser at John Jay High School, explained how students found their way to the rap room: "A couple of guys came in with birth control questions the other day," she noted. "I told them to come back tomorrow with 15 kids and we'd have a workshop. We wound up with 30 or 40, including the whole football team."[9] At Adlai Stevenson High School, the room was open for two periods and averaged 15–30 student visitors per day.[10] Stevenson High School would have over two hundred student conferences by April of their first year.[11]

As peer educators developed their knowledge and communication skills, these young people injected a playfulness into the task that had been absent in previous eras of sex education. Sex, it turned out, need not be so serious. They gave their rap rooms tongue-in-cheek names such as "Living, Loving, Learning," "S.P.I.C.E.," "The Happy Room," and "Speakeasy."[12] Peer educators wore identifying T-shirts, handed out their pamphlets at student assemblies, and hung posters to inform fellow students about the new spaces. They showed films and demonstrated contraception devices.

To the surprise of no one who knows anything about schooling, structural problems interrupted momentum but could be and were creatively circumvented. For example, because many of the peer educators would train through elective offerings in health, the volunteers at most schools had to completely revise their schedules to accommodate the new course. Scheduling glitches also explained some problems with the rap room at Flushing High School in Queens; the school operated on end-to-end scheduling (wherein students have no free periods), and students were required to conspicuously obtain a special pass to leave the lunch room.[13] Then there was the scramble for space. At Martin Van Buren High School, the peer-education service would be relocated from an optimal space near the entrance after "the decorations were deemed inappropriate for evening meetings when the room is used for other purposes."[14] Other rap rooms were just glorified closets.

And yet, a closet is still a space, and overall the peer educators were successful at disseminating information. It was definitely a superior alternative to the silence on sexuality that had preceded it.

This success initially obscured a second, equally important trend: SCRSE was gradually forced out of the program. SCRSE's original proposal had emphasized that the organization would not only provide counseling, but also *manage and organize* the program district-wide, overseeing everything from room reservations to hiring. Understanding why students would desire such a logistically difficult and time-consuming responsibility, and feel that the program was inadequate without it, requires some consideration of SCRSE's interpretation of how schools worked.

Ultimately, this was about what we would now call *institutional sexism.*

SCRSE, and its earlier incarnation as the High School Women's Coalition, had routinely argued that schooling was a *problem* that amplified the oppression of young women. Take, for example, the way that schools routinely expelled young mothers (but not fathers). As reported in *Time* magazine, this procedure had been developed to protect "the good of the school" and was defended by New York City's board of education upon the assumption that permitting pregnant women to continue enrollment would "invite even more schoolgirl pregnancies."[15] High School Women's Coalition member Lynn Silver had complained that even when, by the 1970s, pregnant teens were "sent to special schools," it wasn't necessarily helpful: "All New York schools are in bad shape, and the schools for pregnant women are even worse—in terrible condition and overcrowded." As summarized by Silver, "What high school women face is the oppression of women combined with the oppression of minors."[16] Moreover, what might appear to be a neutral form of standardization—such as the creation of an academic calendar—could have profound consequences for new mothers. Unless a new mom gave birth in July, her maternity leave would make it impossible to acquire a complete semester's instruction.

SCRSE, persuaded that schools created obstacles for young women, saw what they had expected to see: the Bureau of Health and Physical Education tolerated peer education but did not necessarily perceive much value in letting students act as policy makers and program developers. For example, some faculty advisers were cherry-picking peer educators. Ford Foundation consultant Michael Carrera noted as early as February 1974 that "there seems to be an absence of any unified method by which students are selected," and that "to avoid the potentiality of an elitist, strictly homogeneous group," there needed to be a more open process. "At the very least all students must be made aware of [the program] and enfranchised to participate," declared Carrera, noting that this had been "the intent of the High School Coalition for Relevant Sex Education" since the program's origin.[17] By the end of the first school year, SCRSE had raised enough ruckuses that the Bureau of Health and Physical Education conceded that "students from other pilot schools or the Student Coalition for Relevant Sex Education could be involved" in recruitment.[18] For SCRSE activists, who at one point had proposed that it should be *students* who chose their *advisers*, this patronizing permission was further evidence that adults refused to help unless granted controlling authority.

It was especially frustrating for SCRSE when faculty-selected peer educators took for granted their own incompetence and the superiority of an adviser's knowledge. When peer adviser George Dunn remarked that "the most difficult part is when a pregnant girl comes in and wants to know whether to have the kid, have an abortion, or what. I'm not in a position to tell her," it was a forfeiture of his own authority as a counselor. This is not to say that Dunn should have told pregnant teens what to do, but neither should the faculty adviser to whom he referred such students.[19] It also begs the question of what he was doing as a "peer educator" if not educating. Were peer educators reinforcing the judgments of adults, merely puppets complicit in fooling other young people into thinking that they had agency and power they in fact did not possess? Advisers were likewise quick to take over tasks like budgeting, staffing, and goal-setting.

With a new year on the horizon and reports from schools still trickling in via training reports, SCRSE exploited a small opportunity to reopen the matter of which new schools might start new programs.[20] They got nowhere, and the board of education's previous promises seemed forgotten. The students turned sullen. At an Advisory Council meeting in which participating schools were evaluated for future funding, Ford Foundation staff member Adrienne Germain was initially frustrated that "the two students present did not say very much and they had no input to report." As someone who oversaw many of the Ford Foundation's international projects on population control, and who had ushered in a policy change that shifted the foundation's emphasis from medical interventions to women's economic development, Germain wanted young women to be at the forefront of sex education programming. Germain took the SCRSE representatives aside. At this point, she learned that "the Coalition feels isolated from the pilot schools because it is difficult, often impossible, for students to meet let alone visit the schools." It did not elude SCRSE that "if the Coalition had been involved in visiting the schools at the initiation of the project last fall, they could have been helpful in generating enthusiasm, giving advice from their perspective and so on."[21]

There was reason to suspect that the students were correct. Consider the case of Martin Van Buren High School, where the peer-education program had started poorly. The teacher-adviser had selected students who were "not well organized and not aware of the responsibilities involved in developing and operating a peer sex information service." Then the teacher-adviser became ill.

But the campus branch of SCRSE stepped into the void. With a new adviser "who had experience with students from the Student Coalition for Relevant Sex Education and who worked in peer centered programs," the situation improved; peer educators were running parent workshops, arranging for outside speakers, and moderating weekly discussion groups by May.[22]

Yet in his report submitted to the Ford Foundation, Irwin Tobin, director of the Bureau of Health and Physical Education, outlined a pretty superficial projection of SCRSE's future involvement. He offered a few meetings to discuss project progress and invited the coalition to visit pilot schools. Oh, and the bureau would provide trainers for SCRSE meetings, an offer that no documents suggest SCRSE had requested, and that anyone attentive to SCRSE's activists would realize was undesired.[23] The Ford Foundation vaguely considered even vaguer interventions: "We ought to reach out to the High School Coalition and try to involve them more intimately next year," noted Ford Foundation evaluator Michael Carrera. Otherwise, "I believe that the Bureau is willing to write them off."[24] Carrera would in coming decades emerge as a pioneering proponent of social services as part of pregnancy prevention curricula, receiving awards from Planned Parenthood, Advocates for Youth, and the American Association of Sex Educators, Counselors, and Therapists; he would take quite seriously what young people told him about what they needed to succeed. But in 1975 he was an early career professor who had been conditioned to expect that programs' efficiency depended upon only the transmission of sexual knowledge, rather than upon the matter of who directed the distribution of this knowledge. This assumption showed when he noted in his Ford Foundation report that "only a couple of students remain interested in its original work," a situation which was "disappointing but not surprising."[25]

Reflecting upon the struggle to be heard, Columbia social work student and SCRSE advocate Sharon Katz dryly described how the endeavor was "if not the most rewarding experience, a very educational one."[26] By the end of the second year, SCRSE was estranged from the peer-education project, with many student activists refusing to respond to summons by either the Ford Foundation or the Bureau of Health and Physical Education. From the SCRSE point of view, what remained of their program at the end of its first year was a stripped-down and soulless exercise that wasn't worth fighting to defend. From the bureau's point of view, however, the students were simply flighty. When Parker and her team published their findings in *Family Coordinator*, they would write SCRSE out of the narrative, refusing to even identify the students' organization by name, instead bogarting the credit for themselves.[27]

LACK OF FUNDS: ANOTHER WAY THAT SEX EDUCATION PROGRAMS DIE

In 1975 the Ford Foundation reconfirmed that it would not provide the ongoing Peer Education Program with any money beyond its second year. The previous years of funding had already accomplished Ford Foundation goals: creating a pilot program and assuring that information about this experiment was distributed to other districts around the country and world. But to assume that the board of education would independently fund this relatively successful program was a disingenuous hope, especially given the municipal budget's worsening condition. The board of education's employment ranks, for example, would be cut by almost 20% between 1975 and 1978.[28]

This was no doubt disappointing to Maude Parker, the supervisor of Family Living and Sex Education, who wanted to expand the program to twenty schools during the 1975–76 school year.[29] She regretfully noted in June: "I am not hopeful about refunding of the project by the Division of High Schools or the other sources that were contacted. It may be that we will have to think of our effort as another 'Camelot.'"[30] In a memo addressed to the Ford Foundation, Planned Parenthood noted the likely implications: "This action will, in effect, wipe out sex education in the school system, after years of struggle to get it going."[31] A few days later, a scribbled note from Parker found its way into the Ford Foundation grant files. It read, "Sex Ed. is dead; it seems I am being reassigned."[32]

As one scholar speculated in 1975, "Perhaps a historian looking back from his vantage point in the future may report that the greatest block to the proposals of the high school reformers of the mid-1970s was not the varied views of educators." Instead, it was "the total social setting of the time, racked by economic malaise, energy shortage, international tension, polluted environment, maldistribution of income, unemployment, stagflation." In such a context, of course schools would be "uncongenial to new education centers, organizations, and institutions on the scale envisaged; unreceptive to hosts of young people seeking meaningful jobs and social involvement."[33] There was no conspiracy to stomp sex education out. It just wasn't a priority.[34] Maybe that's why the adults had agreed to let students teach it in the first place.

THE ORIGINS OF ABSTINENCE-ONLY EDUCATION

Without peer education, New York City's story no longer stood out from the national narrative. In the 1970s, schools bowed to the pressure of budget cuts,

Cold War conservatism, parental protests, or all of the above. If parents and the community didn't really care about sex education, then a district's skeletal sex education was reduced to textbook-driven lectures on reproductive biology and "plumbing lessons" in physical education. This resulted in sex education that was insufficient. But in places where parents and the community were carefully watching what schools did about sex education, wary administrators implemented sex education that was didactic, provided selective data, and normalized the "traditional family." This was the sort of instruction favored by some well-organized evangelical and fundamentalist Protestants, recently joined by some Catholics and some Latter-day Saints. The question: Was this style of instruction really sex education, or was it misdirection calling itself "sex education"?

In response to criticisms such as the one I just made, conservative Christians explained that they were, in fact, sexual experts. Why would they make such a provocative claim? A market for marital manuals—what sociologist Janice Irvine has called an "alternative sexuality industry"—had recently exploded, filled with biblically inflected books marketed to newlyweds and couples in trouble.[35] Christian advice writer Marabel Morgan urged that a "Total Woman" is "not merely a submissive sex partner; she is a sizzling lover," but also that such sizzle must be reserved for a husband because "God planned for woman to be under her husband's rule."[36] Tim LaHaye and Beverly LaHaye's *The Act of Marriage: The Beauty of Sexual Love* (1976) exemplified how individuals active in protests against sex education in schools could also successfully position themselves as experts on sexuality; their book sold 2.5 million copies.

Social conservatives increasingly organized within national associations such as the Moral Majority and Focus on the Family to lend out-of-state support to local protests against sex education. And by 1980, they used their record of success to acquire leverage within the already-conservative Republican Party and proved integral to Ronald Reagan's election. From here, social conservatives continued lobbying for their new model of sexual communication in schools, now called Abstinence-Only-Until-Marriage Education (AOUME). In 1981 the Adolescent Family Life Act provided federal funding to programs that endorsed abstinence from sex as the only way to completely prevent young pregnancy, and that promoted adoption but not abortion. This new funding stream rewarded the conservative Christian groups developing programs customizable for public schools. All that was necessary was to reframe religious objectives (i.e., stay celibate to please God) in public health terms (stay celibate to stay safe).

A key premise in abstinence-only education was that if teachers vigorously and consistently provided a sex-avoidance message, students would not need more information about sex and contraception. Curricula such as the widely adopted Sex Respect, Facing Reality, Choosing the Best, and programs developed by Beverly LaHaye's Teen Aid, Inc., were silent about or condemned contraception and abortion, the development of sexual identity and desire, homosexuality, and the means to protect sexual privacy. Questions about condoms were cut short in abstinence-only curricula wherein the only reference to condoms was about their supposedly high failure rate, a distortion sometimes presented as fact. And these curricula were misleading in important ways: abstinence's failure rate is pretty darn high if we count all the people who depended on self-restraint and then changed their minds, and marriage is not necessarily a safeguard against STIs if one's partner has had other sexual partners.

SCHOOLS, POLICY, AND HIV/AIDS

When compared to the meager information provided through either a one-day hygiene class or AOUME, schools' administrative policies—dress codes, codes of conduct, employee contracts, school admission standards, and workplace safety guidelines—represented many schools' most robust communication with students about sex. Thus, when the HIV/AIDS crisis emerged in the mid-1980s, it was school policies, rather than sex education courses, which were the testing ground on which students, parents, and communities deliberated.

As each school revised one policy at a time, districts closely watched each other, modeling their strategies to mimic or avoid the decisions made in high-profile cases. The most scrutinized were episodes in Indiana and New York, with each district's policy-making process imagining a different course for how schools would relate to school-aged children living with HIV/AIDS. In Kokomo, Indiana, residents formed picket lines, pressed lawsuits, and used intimidation to keep sweet and photogenic preteen Ryan White from attending his neighborhood school in 1984. Arguing that schools had an obligation to protect other students' health, the superintendent and parents argued that White might have lesions, bite, or vomit while at school. So rapidly were scientific findings emerging that many parents were unaware of newer conclusions that such means of transmission were extremely unlikely, bordering on impossible. Yet the superintendent could not have referenced county guidelines even if he had so desired; the county health officer refused to develop a school admission policy in advance of the state.[37] The superintendent therefore ordered that White should study at home, receiving educational instruction over the phone.

White's mother initially achieved a small legal victory that returned White to school, where he was asked to use a separate bathroom and use disposable utensils. Even with these concessions, some district parents removed their children from the school and established a private school.[38] So deeply invested were they in the idea that Ryan White was dangerous—that their bullying of a child was thereby justified—that most Kokomo parents were unwilling to adjust their positions when the CDC's guidelines were finally released in 1985, and mountains of evidence suggested that HIV/AIDS could not be spread through water fountains, toilet seats, or cafeteria forks. As late as 1987, the Kokomo schools passive-aggressively failed to distribute the county's HIV/AIDS education materials among students.[39] Ryan White, in turn, would be comforted and eventually memorialized by figures of national and international importance, and his story would be the subject of sympathetic media reports and a TV movie. Kokomo's response would become the classic example of what not to do.

If Kokomo's story received the most media attention, it was New York City that would produce the nation's first significant legal case regarding school systems' responsibility toward children living with AIDS.[40] In Queens, two community school boards protested the board of education and chancellor's decision that children with AIDS could be assigned to neighborhood elementary schools, and that a single student would be so assigned in the fall of 1985. Confident that school administrators underestimated children's likelihood of transmitting AIDS, a multiracial coalition of parents in Districts 27 and 29 organized a school boycott. About eleven thousand students remained home on the first day of school.

Public policy scholar David Kirp recalls how one New York policy maker expressed his frustration: "New York City ought to be able to handle AIDS better than Oshkosh, for chrissakes!" Kirp suggests, and I concur with his interpretation, that this statement confused Kokomo with Oshkosh, "a completely understandable slip from a New Yorker's perspective," one that tends toward smugness. And yet here is the ultimate argument for education: it was the testimony of expert witnesses, presented day after day at a trial, that eventually persuaded Queens parents that children with AIDS should attend public schools.[41] Parents from Districts 27 and 29 sat in the gallery and shared the court's findings with neighbors at the end of each day.

For these parents, Dr. Polly Thomas's testimony proved peculiarly persuasive. Asked by the attorney for Districts 27 and 29 parents: "If your child was bitten by an AIDS patient and you knew that your child was bitten . . . would you want to have your child receive that blood test?" Thomas responded, "I would not," producing gasps from the gallery. Thomas, a pediatrician with the New York City Health Department, explained that the risk of transmission was so low that she would not feel like her child was endangered, and that she would risk her child's life upon the scientific findings thus far accrued. She had leveraged her authority as a mother to amplify her authority as a physician.

Education seems to have won not only the trial, but also the public's acceptance of the verdict: children with HIV/AIDS would attend local schools without wide-scale harassment. The mechanics that followed—assembling first-aid supplies, developing teacher training, creating protocols for protecting children's privacy—advanced this education still further. As noted by historian Jennifer Brier, in Queens "we see a portrait of a largely uninfected community trying to protect itself in a world in which information provided by the state changed on an almost daily basis," and that as a result of education, parents proved "capable of changing their minds."[42] The majority was, in this case, reasonable.

Starting with a small program during the 1985–86 academic year, New York City broke ground by hosting information nights for parents. A small pilot program featuring HIV/AIDS education followed. San Francisco began providing teacher in-service days on HIV/AIDS in the fall of 1986.[43] Given that school bureaucracies do not turn on a dime, this was progress, and it was only the tremendous spread of the HIV/AIDS epidemic that makes this transformation from policy development to curriculum development seem lethargic. Other school districts, even those who would disagree with New York City and San Francisco's policy decisions, would take the cue that it was time to formalize their practices regarding privacy, employment, and health resources.[44]

When Surgeon General C. Everett Koop—he of the amazing beard—ordered the distribution of an AIDS pamphlet in 1988, the national public finally received something long overdue: a coherent and authoritative explanation of what scientists and public health officials had thus far concluded about the virus's transmission. Perhaps most remarkably, *Understanding AIDS* put information about homosexuality and condom use into every household in the entire country. "Some of the issues involved in this brochure may not be things you are used to discussing openly," Koop explained in the cover letter. "I can easily understand that. But now you must discuss them. We all must know about AIDS." Furthermore, "your children need to know about AIDS. Discuss it with them."[45]

Despite serving in the conservative Reagan administration, Koop challenged social conservatives, who had long insisted that explicit information inflamed sexual passion where it did not belong. In the context of AIDS, Koop insisted, frank conversation was the best way to change people's behaviors.[46] No sex education campaign had ever before—or would ever again—have such reach. The document was small, and it was distributed just once, but everyone got it. And 82% of Americans actually *read* it.[47]

In creating and distributing this pamphlet, Koop drew upon his capital not only as the nation's physician but as a Reagan-appointed pro-life conservative, and gently pushed Americans to acknowledge that the new era required new practices. He had, in other words, done for sex education what no other stakeholders could do: he provided schools with cover.[48] The President's Commission on the HIV Epidemic, in turn, would recommend that state boards of education make HIV/AIDS education a requirement. Some districts began the long process of overcoming curriculum hurdles: teacher training, union contracts, classroom space, scheduling accommodations, textbook selection and purchase, and parent management.

However, in other districts, HIV/AIDS education lagged. Perhaps those curriculum hurdles were too high. Or, as expressed by one exasperated CDC program director, it could have been the case that "many educational administrators, having been burned in the past, are wary of installing educational programs that are apt to evoke a negative response from their communities."[49] As though discovering this fact for the first time, he fumed that it is very hard to make teachers and administrators do things that might get them fired.

PEER-LED SEX EDUCATION'S REVIVAL: ON-CAMPUS AND OFF-CAMPUS

Taking a cue from feminist cooperatives, and also acting in accord with a tradition set by SCRSE, young people explored peer-to-peer education as a practical adaptation when their schools' sex education offerings were insufficient. In the process, they discovered that peer education could do something no other pedagogy could accomplish: it made the difference between on-campus and off-campus education meaningless. For example, a teen trained to answer the phone with Teens Teaching AIDS Prevention in Kansas City, Missouri's Good Samaritan Clinic or at Boston's YO' Line could also answer friends' questions between classes, referring them to other resources as needed.[50] As explained by one teen, peer education was useful because grown-ups "can't ban students from school" the way they can ban adult activists from entry. "If young people are educated so that they can tell each other the facts, that cuts right through everything else."[51] This was true, if arguably putting an unfair burden on young people.

Perhaps the clearest and best-documented example of how young people became educational leaders was YELL (Youth Education Life Line), established in 1989.[52] YELL's founders were a small group of New York City teachers who were ACT UP members, ACT UP being a powerful direct action organization—eventually including almost 150 chapters—with the goal of pressuring politicians to fund the search for an HIV/AIDS cure.[53] It was thus with the purpose of pressuring board of education members, faculty, and staff into publicly stating their support for or opposition to expanded HIV/AIDS education that these teacher-activists unleashed direct actions.

It's important to note that YELL was not, in the grand scheme of everything that ACT UP did, the organization's largest or most impactful affinity group. But in the story of New York City schools and their response to the AIDS crisis, and hence a starting pistol for the national story, YELL was one of the most eloquent and organized advocates for sex education, and its history illuminates how activism can be a form of education during transitional periods. YELL members met weekly to plan "zaps"; they disrupted school board meetings, arguing that until a cure emerged, the schools were morally obligated to prevent every possible infection. Typical was New York City teacher and ACT UP activist Robert Rygor, who explained to the board that "when I die of AIDS it will be because of ignorance—we just didn't know. If these kids die of AIDS—you do know and it will be your fault!"[54]

The likelihood that people contracting HIV/AIDS would die, and the rate at which the virus was spreading through the teenage population, is the context explaining why the New York City Board of Education's response was inadequate. The 1988–89 AIDS Surveillance Update would confirm that while only 3% of America's teenagers lived in New York City, the city's population contained 20% of reported adolescent cases.[55] And HIV activists were quick to point out that the prevalence of HIV-positive people in their twenties suggested a teenage undercount. For women, non-white men, people in poverty or experiencing homelessness, and teenagers, the consequences of an HIV/AIDS diagnosis in the pre-HAART era[56] could be especially dire, given that clinical trials were one of the only ways that people who did not tolerate the standard antiretroviral treatment could receive treatment, and these groups were generally ineligible for clinical trials. To reduce variables that might otherwise result in outlying outcomes, scientists at the National Institutes of Health and elsewhere preferred to use subjects with identical sex and racial background, namely, adult white males.[57] Issues related to age but not exclusive to adolescence (i.e., transportation access) also played a key role in excluding young people from studies, as did scientists' concerns about compliance with medical protocols. This, of course, left as an open question how scientists might learn if any drug could work on women, children, and non-white men, a point that ACT UP affinity groups were pressing.

In the face of dire statistics, ACT UP pointed out, the city had underfunded HIV/AIDS education, instead requiring the board of education's AIDS Unit to operate with an unsatisfactory budget drawn from state and federal sources, which came to a mere eight cents per year per pupil.[58] Students sensed that adults' contempt for young people often amplified racism. Some of these students recommended peer education, heckled teachers during class, or else threatened to engage in unprotected sex if condoms were not made available.[59] Knowingly or not, such students extended the logic of earlier gay liberation politics, demanding recognition that did not cost them their sexual autonomy, and in fact using sexual expression to create political leverage.[60] YELL's goal was to (as activists) create sufficient pressure upon the board to assure that the board would, in turn, require teachers (often the same people as activists) to teach about HIV/AIDS prevention more thoroughly.[61] Given that schools still remained the location where large groups of teenagers could most easily be found, YELL urged schools to distribute condoms through school clinics.

What ACT UP did not necessarily anticipate was that "there were these kids, literally high school kids from New Jersey, [who] came in and started joining us in our zaps."[62] What had been envisioned as an affinity group advocating *for* students quickly became a collaboration *with* students. For example, YELL reports would note that "12 people, including 7 high school students, were arrested" after they had posed as a class field trip, and then taken over the Brooklyn borough president's office; unnoted in the report was the fact that the group had also stuffed Howard Golden's office files with condoms.[63] One of the arrested students, Kate Barnhart, would recall as an adult that YELL was at that point transitioning from "mostly adult teachers, who were concerned about the lack of AIDS education," to a group that dovetailed with students previously organized in opposition to the Gulf War. Evidently the students and teachers bonded while chained together in the precinct's waiting room. Barnhart noted, "That gave us a lot of time to talk and get to know each other." She was fifteen at the time and would soon find out that her mother was pretty angry that she had cut school.[64]

Adults can use youths in a variety of ways that are *not* empowering; youths can be mascots, or room-fillers, or even offered up for arrest to deflect from adults. And so one thing worth considering is how authentically YELL's young people were politicized and the extent of their autonomy. Here we have to rely upon admittedly scattershot evidence. Barnhart, now the director of a nonprofit supporting LGBTQ+ youths, recalls that "when I talked to these people from ACT UP, it was the first time I'd ever met adults who were not trying to manipulate me." She described her peer cohort as fiercely independent and political, and she herself had previously participated in antiwar protests and organized an HIV peer-education team at Stuyvesant High School. From her perspective, it was YELL students who "mobilized doctors who worked with adolescents, and teachers and young people and parents and all these people," rather than it being adults who organized student support.[65]

Barnhart and Sarah Kunstler—a fellow Little Red Schoolhouse alum, Stuyvesant High student, and leading YELL member—eluded even parental restraints. Barnhart recalls how at the 1991 action where they had taken over Golden's office, William Kunstler—Sarah Kunstler's father, a prominent attorney who had defended the Chicago Seven—was seen racing to the borough president's office from the Brooklyn Court House, where he had been representing a client. Noted Barnhart, "the cops just froze" when they saw the famous senior Kunstler running across Cadman Plaza with an early model cell phone in hand and hair flying behind him. "They were like, oh no, what have we done?"[66] And William Kunstler was as surprised as everyone else. Though such evidence of young people's independence is anecdotal, a description of YELL's antiauthoritarian organizational culture is consistent with that of ACT UP, whose own operating procedures required democratic and nearly leaderless organization.

Young people in YELL did everything they could to rally behind Chancellor Joseph Fernandez's new sex education proposal, which Golden had been slow to support. The proposal included K–12 classroom curriculum with revised lesson plans, professional development, educational brochures, AIDS education teams at each high school, condom distribution by trained staff, counseling, and resource libraries. YELL members got themselves to the meetings, created flyers, and used their allowances to finance printing. They pressured the board of education to drop all counseling and parental consent requirements for condoms.[67] A pilot program eventually emerged, with sixteen of the city's 120 high schools distributing condoms (accompanied by a sternly worded pamphlet urging abstinence) the following fall.[68] Condom distribution programs ensued in San Francisco, Los Angeles, and Seattle.[69]

National magazines and newspapers followed the spread of this strategy, which illuminated divisions within even the most politically unified communities. *Jet*, for example, pointed out that African Americans had honest differences of opinion regarding the programs in Chicago, Los Angeles, Philadelphia, and New York. The National Medical Association president thought that such programs might promote sexual activity; an employee with a Catholic diocese worried that condom distribution would feed the stereotype that minority students in urban public schools lacked self-control; the rector of a Chicago South Side church saw condom distribution as providing an important opportunity for educational intervention.[70]

Controversy about hypothetical consequences of condom distribution brought to the forefront a particularly difficult intellectual problem: Must curriculum decisions be resolved democratically?[71] Majority rule could facilitate resolutions excluding people who otherwise belong, whether these are sexually active youths, LGBTQ+ people, or any other subgroup. These outcomes might be counter to democracy's other requirements, including the principle that all people are heard. With sex education, the stakes are especially high because decisions are being made by adults who will not themselves be subjected to the rules they set.

YELL relied upon the democratic principle that all voices should be heard to press for sex education similar to what would now be called Comprehensive Sex Education (CSE). SIECUS—still the object of conservative fury but more conventional than ACT UP—began formalizing the criteria for a sex education program that might address the HIV/AIDS crisis, hoping to inspire NYC-like programs in other districts and among other community providers. In 1991 the National Guidelines Task Force articulated the first standards for CSE, a new term ascribed to what was basically Family Life Education plus descriptions of sexual response, sexual orientation, and abortion; the skills necessary to develop mutually pleasurable relationships (not necessarily marriage); and encouragement for the responsible use of contraception and other sexual health measures.[72]

The new guidelines influenced what information liberal religious communities decided to provide their young congregants. For example, the Unitarian Universalists and the United Church of Christ adapted their preexisting curricula to introduce Our Whole Lives, and did so in consultation with SIECUS president Debra Haffner, who was herself a Unitarian. For these communities, "comprehensive" did not necessarily mean "secular," and in fact Our Whole Lives contained more religious material than the curriculum it replaced. At the same time, designers did offer a customized version of Our Whole Lives to public schools and civic organizations, one with the faith materials removed. Discussions about what "comprehensive" education might require and entail were reinvigorating the field. But in terms of getting education into schools immediately, it would be the ad hoc and freewheeling work of groups like YELL that proved capable of the quickest response.

In celebration of its modest success, YELL's ranks seem to have filled with more and more teenagers every year—so far as one can measure such a thing in an organization without membership fees. More members meant more actions and hence more influence. Consider the ritual emerging when YELL showed up across the street from a NYC high school to distribute pamphlets and condoms in the minutes before classes started. While the information was not particularly controversial, and condoms could be purchased at any pharmacy, it was the method of having sex education be school-adjacent rather than in-school that was an innovation. YELL members had at first been surprised to find that there wasn't more resistance from administrators, given that sex education had so little traction in schools. An early zap, at Clara Barton High School in Brooklyn, handed out five hundred pamphlets and condoms, and was greeted by one teacher with the statement: "It's about time you folks got out here."[73] Activist Jeffrey Fennelly recalled a similar reaction by teachers at Washington Irving High School: "And the teachers were like, 'Keep it up, keep it up, keep it up.'"[74] School administrators would have had good reason to fear parent reprisal, and so perhaps they appreciated that YELL provided an alternative where students could get education without teachers having to stick their necks out. In any case, police were rarely called, and activists had the impression that the police were deliberately lax.[75] This was bewildering for ACT UP activists who, in the course of other zaps, had come to expect police harassment.

The work YELL was doing took on new importance after the board of education voted to restore counseling and parental consent requirements for condoms. A majority of the board came to agree with member Michael Petrides's concerns, because they shared his premise that parents were gatekeepers regarding their children's sexuality until those children became adults. Petrides declared that "when a child whose parent does not want that child to have a condom, and that child has a condom that fails—and some of them will fail—and that child dies eight years from now, somebody should sue the hell out of this Board."[76] At the behest of board member Irene Impellizzeri, the state of New York would soon disband the condom distribution plan on the technical grounds that it did not comply with state statutes.

Debates about sexuality and schools continued in 1992 when the board investigated a teacher guide for Children of the Rainbow, a multicultural project aimed at creating respect for diverse types of families, including those with one or two parents, gay or lesbian parents, adoptive parents, grandparents, or foster parents.[77] Community activists flooded board of education meetings, and many seemed to be holdovers still disgruntled by the 1990 initiatives in sex education and condom distribution. *Radical Teacher* noted that conservative organizers assembled a coalition of "their traditional white Protestant constituency with white Catholics in the outer boroughs and with Latino Pentecostals, Black Muslims, and immigrants to create a multiracial conservative coalition."[78] Some protesters seemed to think that being anti-gay was the best way to fend off HIV/AIDS, which they claimed God had inflicted upon the United States as a punishment for sinful sexual toleration.[79] Those protesters were especially loud. Literal fights broke out, and all of this was an uproar over a curriculum that was—wait for it—optional to use and would only be seen by teachers. Noted one school superintendent who supported the curriculum, teachers "put it on the shelf, and nothing happens. You have to understand how this works."[80] But for the minority of New Yorkers who got involved in debates, political acrimony was an end and not a means, and newly appointed replacements for board membership would assure that Chancellor Fernandez's contract was not renewed.

Perhaps no other example can better illuminate the fluid and unpredictable boundaries between constituencies debating sex education, and how these boundaries can create unanticipated outcomes. As a whole, the board of education for New York City—with its large gay population, economic and racial diversity, and cosmopolitanism—had arrived at a more conservative position than the evangelical Reagan-appointee Surgeon General Koop. Again unanticipated, Koop's position seems to have reanimated AOUME because it made so likely sex education's permanent place in schools; from a social conservative's perspective, the question would become how to manage that transition with the least damage possible.[81] Still, the largest tendency remained for schools to contract out sex education as much as possible, and parents to punt to the schools to provide it.

In New York, inaction would prove a turning point. When the board of education started treating HIV/AIDS as just another curriculum area—something to standardize and rationalize, needing committees to approve classroom materials, and requiring a perfect roll-out—rather than as an emergency intervention, it began a slowdown that meant irreversible damage in the form of missed opportunities to get grants, undereducated students, and possibly deaths.[82] Teacher training fell behind schedule; a compliance review would soon find that 35% of New York City's secondary-school educators and 28% of elementary-school educators who taught health remained untrained in HIV/AIDS instruction, with 30% of the elementary teachers who had received training nonetheless feeling undertrained.[83] HIV/AIDS community-based organizations such as the AIDS and Adolescents Network of New York (AANNY) feared that the old 1987–88 curriculum, which was supposed to be discontinued, was still used in many schools.[84]

By October 1993, the board of education's own HIV/AIDS Advisory Council was "pissed off about the process," frustrated that grants for in-school peer-led programs had not been renewed because of board foot-dragging, discouraged by the fact that "there's not enough teacher training happening," and annoyed that "schools are saying they don't know where to go to get AIDS education."[85] The Advisory Council even found fault with its own composition, noting that its 1994 membership initially included "no young people, no gay men, and no one with the HIV/AIDS virus." When three non-voting student representatives were added as a compromise gesture, their words were not recorded as part of the HIV/AIDS Advisory Council's minutes.[86] Seemingly, the people with the greatest risk of HIV/AIDS were the ones least able to influence board of education politics from within that institution.

YELL's ensuing direct actions not only expressed members' anger, but also created opportunities for people within municipal governance to express their support. On the board of education's HIV/AIDS Advisory Council, it was member Erica Zurer who campaigned to appoint Sarah Kunstler as a student representative. Perhaps it was when YELL had interrupted the Advisory Council's February 14 meeting to distribute valentines, temporarily stopping a discussion about abstinence-based education, that Kunstler made an impression.[87] As a second example, consider a feature in YELL's second 'zine, which depicted the aftermath of a disruptive board of education protest. An article featured a photo of "K" with her likewise grinning arresting officer. A scribbled annotation on the side explained that "K" and the officer bought the attending student activists pizza for dinner; many police officers were hostile to HIV/AIDS activists, especially those in ACT UP, but this particular officer became an ally.[88] Everyone had a part to play, assuring that protests dramatized the stakes of HIV/AIDS education, and that word of these events made the newspaper.

So the board of education proved a disappointment. YELL, however, knew that there were alternatives to teacher-directed on-campus education, and advocated for sex education through a peer-education structure, emphasizing the fit between this pedagogy and the lessons on sexual autonomy it espoused. Founding YELL member (and educator) Jeffrey Fennelly had, from the beginning, insisted that "in many ways a symbolic gesture, condom distribution is backed up by the demand that a student-directed program be instituted by the schools. Kids know what they are doing."[89] One might have as easily added that kids *had* to know what they were doing because parents, who hadn't received sex education for at least fifteen years, and were often in monogamous and heterosexual pairings, had such minimal knowledge about HIV/AIDS that they were not in a position to lead.

PROFESSIONAL PEERS

The processes and institutions underwriting young people's leadership in HIV/AIDS education—and undermining it—were dramatically showcased by a relatively new professional field: young adults as visiting speakers. These new speakers were quite unlike the physicians who had delivered lectures about venereal disease in the 1910s–1930s. Instead, individuals such as Leanza Cornett (Miss America 1993, at age twenty-two) and Kate Shindle (Miss America 1998, at age twenty-one) visited schools, showing off their crowns and, not incidentally, providing information about sex, sexuality, and STIs; both women had chosen HIV/AIDS as their outreach platform. Whether members of YELL or reigning pageant winners, young speakers were desirable visitors not because of their expertise, but because of their relatability. It was their job to convey that *no one* could assume safety from HIV/AIDS, and that *everyone* could possess the necessary knowledge to understand why.

Advocates for sex education and HIV/AIDS education couldn't help but notice that these young people also had a unique ability to access the scattered sex education deserts still existing. As late as 1992, at least one-third of American school districts did not require HIV/AIDS education and probably didn't offer it.[90] Regarding her post-inaugural tour, Cornett noted, "Being Miss America gave me entry to places an HIV/AIDS activist normally couldn't go." Shindle would agree that "the places that invited me . . . were the same places that AIDS activists couldn't get into."[91] In southeast Louisiana, for example, teachers told one scholar, "If a student asks what a condom is and the teacher answers, she/he can be fired. It's as simple as that!"[92]

HIV/AIDS education often required a dose of misdirection to placate cautious administrators. Shindle recalled that during visits to some districts, school administrators "would ask me to come and talk about AIDS, but then they would give me a list of words I couldn't say. I couldn't say 'condom' or 'gay.'" Yet young lecturers found that they could provide HIV/AIDS education in ways that cued student collaboration. "I quickly learned to say, 'oh, okay, but . . .' once we get to question and answer, for the sake of cred, if the kids ask questions I have to be able to answer them honestly." Shindle recalled that "if you say 'protection' enough times . . . then the first question is always going to be 'What do you mean when you say "protection"?'" The answer: condoms.[93]

The popularity of young speakers, independent-minded but nonetheless reliant upon corporate affiliations and professional speakers' bureaus to coordinate their appearances, also begs the question of how authentic this "peer" education was. After all, they were trained by adult professionals—school counselors, activists, or nonprofit organizations—and tended to emulate adult professionals in their style of delivery. Wasn't this a compromised authority because it was always contingent upon the authority of grown-ups?

In the case of *The Real World*'s Pedro Zamora (age twenty-two in 1994), arguably the most famous professional peer educator, media scholars have further considered how Zamora's message might have been diluted by producers and directors editing reality's raw materials. Producers never promised Zamora that the messages he wanted to convey would get airtime, nor that there would be no competing messages from other housemates. Yet performance studies scholar José Esteban Muñoz concluded, "Zamora was more than simply represented; he used MTV as an opportunity to continue his life's work of HIV/AIDS pedagogy, queer education, and human-rights activism. . . . He used MTV more than it used him."[94] Zamora could do this because he was not without media savvy. He had already been the subject of numerous newspaper articles and had been a featured guest on the *Oprah Winfrey Show*. He had worked as a peer educator for Body Positive in Miami and made presentations at schools and colleges.[95] And he seems to have used these experiences to highlight key ideas in HIV/AIDS education that young people—even open-minded young people—resisted.

Two *Real World* plot lines are exemplary. The first was an early episode in which the house's tenuous calm completely falls apart in a way that only a house full of twenty-year-olds could do. Puck, an abrasive bike messenger, blew his nose into his hand, and then used this same hand to scoop peanut butter from Zamora's pantry. To be clear, this would be gross no matter what. But Zamora explained to the house the distinctive stakes of concern to him, namely, that as someone with a compromised immune system, he faced greater threats from the housemates than the housemates faced from him. When Puck did not express remorse and would not commit to reforming his grossest habits, it didn't take long for the housemates to vote for his permanent exile.

A second example took place near the end of the series. Having courted over the course of the season, Zamora and his fiancé decided to make a lifelong commitment to each other. This storyline might have been filmed in a *Walk to Remember*-type tone, but it instead insisted that yes, people who have HIV/AIDS still want to date and have sex. Zamora's interest in finding a partner, and success at finding one, only made sense if there were ways to limit transmission risks or contain the likelihood of acquiring infections. In other words, it demonstrated that continued condom use or partnering with another HIV-positive person were options beyond celibacy for people who acquired HIV.

Yet the sympathy that housemates, and ultimately the viewing audience, felt for Zamora was not the ultimate aim of HIV/AIDS education and could potentially be counterproductive. The decision to frame education through autobiography risked what Roger Hallas calls the "privatization of the AIDS crisis." Such privatization is especially problematic when it diminishes what is otherwise an "imperative placed on the viewer to transform consciousness and to effect change."[96] In other words, a viewer might feel empathy for Pedro Zamora without necessarily feeling provoked to question the health care system that left him without insurance, problematic government procedures and bureaucracy that delayed medical research, and interference from some tax-exempt religious organizations with housing and hospital access. Without the counterpoint of ACT UP's high-profile actions, it might have escaped public consciousness that new treatments for HIV/AIDS were and would continue to be too expensive for many people with HIV/AIDS. It would be easy to miss that HIV/AIDS was a political problem requiring government investment in scientific research, subsidies for medical costs and the expansion of public benefits, public health campaigns that provided information about safer sex, and new policies to open drug trials.[97]

A description of one scene from episode thirteen might demonstrate what was lost when privatization ascended. Filmed while Zamora delivers an HIV/AIDS education lecture at an Arizona school, the tension in these scenes comes from the fact that a housemate's parents are teachers at that school; politically and religiously conservative, they have nonetheless welcomed Zamora into their place of work and into their home. How conditional is this welcome? In particular, the question is whether the price of this welcome will be Zamora's silence about his homosexuality. It would be very easy for a viewer to ignore all of the information Zamora provides to the students about HIV/AIDS, and simply worry about whether or not Pedro's feelings are about to get hurt. Left unasked might be questions about how institutions controlled by adults—schools, but also production companies—constrain the information young people receive about their own bodies.

If Zamora's educational successes were harder to assess than ACT UP's demands for financial and medical assistance, or YELL's pursuit of specific policy changes, this is largely because Zamora spoke, as Muñoz has noted, less to those who were already politicized, and "instead for a world of *potentially* politicized queers and Latinos; for a mass public that is structured by the cultural forces of homophobia and racism; for those who have no access to more subculturally based cultural production and grassroots activism. Thus, Zamora's activism preaches to the not yet converted."[98] From this vantage point, even a compromised version of Zamora's message could prove significant; about 58.8 million homes had cable TV in 1994, and pretty much every home with a teenager routinely tuned to MTV.[99]

Zamora's narrative ended with his death, coming in the days following *The Real World: San Francisco*'s season finale. Measuring the extent to which this death was a watershed event in public discourse, President Bill Clinton would introduce MTV's memorial film honoring Zamora. Activists might quite reasonably push back against the idea that haunting stories like Zamora's keep in circulation the unsound assertion that homosexuality meant death. Such an intellectual shortcut was neither helpful nor representative. But in a nation where their fellow citizens had denied gay people rights of marriage, military service, employment protection, and medical care, the direction of public sympathy toward a gay man who lived with and died of AIDS was an incremental step toward tolerance and inclusion. TV assured that the sexuality education deserts were getting smaller, and further apart, even as abstinence-only education was getting more federal funding and taking a stronger hold on schooling.

If Pedro Zamora—like the YELL kids, Leanza Cornett, and Kate Shindle—was almost too old to be a "peer," Zamora's *Real World* roommates and collaborators had the opportunity to amplify his message even as they completely aged out of being "peer educators." His roommates—especially Judd Winick—found themselves settling into the more conventional style of how adults educate young people; they became the establishment. Winick ultimately wrote an award-winning graphic novel, *Pedro and Me: Friendship, Loss, and What I Learned* (2000), which would in turn be recommended by the National Council of Teachers of English.[100] In other words, teachers could assign the story of a peer educator, told by a once-peer of that educator who was now an adult, who had been famous for being filmed by adults who wanted to talk to young people through other young people who were mediators. That delicate two-step of filming in schools so as to create a narrative that provided a form of sex education that was not contingent upon schools ultimately crafted an artifact fit for bringing sex education back into schools.

By the turn of the century, a map of HIV/AIDS would show the disease's aggressive spread in Sub-Saharan Africa and among North American gay men of color. This spread persisted even as HIV/AIDS would decline to the status of a chronic but manageable illness among the populations of people who had most benefited from national and global industrialization. With this demographic transition, largely due to the existence of new and improved medical interventions, but also due to prevention measures, American sex educators suspected that the third era of sex education was tapering off.

The federal government would nonetheless continue to tug local programs in divergent directions, using funding to pressure changes in how sex education was taught. Since 1996, the Personal Responsibility and Work Opportunity Reconciliation Act provided $50 million of federal funding per year for states' abstinence-only education programs. Among the criteria for receiving funds, the legislation specified that programs must emphasize the likelihood of harm from premarital sexual activity, without providing options other than abstinence for how to mitigate these harms. Not through force or protest, but rather through incentives, the federal government made its mark as the dominant authority among authorities. A final means to consolidate AOUME emerged in 2000, with funds set aside for programs that agreed to omit all safer-sex messaging and content about contraception. For social conservatives, funding that provided for the development of new curricula and teacher training constituted a massive government investment, making AOUME the status quo in some states. Even if the funding for AOUME programs should be eliminated in the future, the needed materials and instructors would already exist.

In 2007 a congressional study conducted by Mathematica Policy Research surveyed four major AOUME programs funded by the federal government and showed that the programs had no positive or negative impact on sexual behavior. A bit flummoxed about what to try next, state legislatures became occupied with assuring the medical accuracy of what is taught, a weak spot for many AOUME programs that often misrepresent the effectiveness of condoms or the likelihood of negative health outcomes from sex. While the major federal funding streams for AOUME (since widely rebranded as "Sexual Risk Avoidance" by its supporters) were eliminated in 2009, new congressional initiatives continue to fund both AOUME and CSE initiatives, with the latter receiving federal funds for the first time in 2010. Perhaps most puzzling for anyone who wants to figure out what young people do sexually, and why, there was a 67% decrease in teen birth rates from 1991 to 2016 that was, confusingly enough, accompanied by an increase in STIs.[101]

The mixed and mediocre quality of program assessment, sometimes the result of unresolved ethical conundrums, remains an impediment to good policy: support for programs that achieve what they set out to achieve and have valuable goals. When a lack of research is exploited for partisan gain, policy vacillates, as shown by a pruning of the Teen Pregnancy Prevention Program (TPPP), enacted in 2010 to pledge over $100 million annually for sexual health programs. In 2017 Trump administration appointees cut funding from ongoing programs during year three of their five-year grants.[102]

WHO SHOULD LEAD SEX EDUCATION? WHAT SHOULD THEIR AUTHORITY LOOK LIKE?

The 1970s were the doldrums in terms of formal, classroom-based sex education. To investigate the programs that did exist—such as the peer-education program introduced by SCRSE in New York—is to make visible the extraordinarily high bureaucratic hurdles that hold back sex education in even the most agreeable eras. Such hurdles, however, proved to not only discourage adult-led sex education but also to create an authority vacuum where student-initiated education was a viable alternative. Experiments that might have been deferred had room to grow.

HIV/AIDS was the crisis that changed everything. In what was perhaps the clearest measure of how seriously this crisis was taken, adults massively increased their support for sex education, and did so in ways that also increased their control over that curriculum. Yet administrators and teachers from both AOUME and CSE districts preserved relics from student-led endeavors, in particular embracing the premise that young people were more likely to accept information from other young people than they would be from adults. And this idea became common sense despite the fact that there was little program evaluation to support it. Schools, off-campus educators, and peer educators would thus prove to be neither rivals nor equals, but something else: a team.

I think that this history of recalibrating authority among people of different ages, and between on- and off-campus educators, is incredibly important because it explains the pedagogy and tone of sex education at this moment: maintaining at least the appearance of student-directed content and discussion is a critical part of most sex education curricula and not, for example, of most math curricula. This is a substantial common ground. But the story of AOUME vs. CSE is the higher-profile story in public imagination. And that story does highlight a truth: even as they attempted to stabilize their relations with young people, the adults were not in agreement among themselves. The miscommunications that had typified sex education debates throughout the century hardened into distortions, and as the debates became ever more heated, principals and teachers withdrew even more. It didn't matter whether bickering people were the majority or not; they were loud, and school administrators didn't have the time and energy to deal with them. And this story of AOUME vs. CSE conflict does feed back into the story I want to emphasize. When spreading sex education throughout the curriculum, or titling it something friendly like "Family Life Education," did not diffuse parental and community ire, schools began to shift the burden for teaching sex education to educators who visited but were not employed by schools. These off-campus educators became the most burdened team members.

A sense that sexuality was unlike other topics in education, but that it was hard to explain why this was the case, would point to a question for philosophers: How much room is there for honest, healthy, productive disagreement? Philosopher Lauren Bialystok takes up this question and more in the following chapters, suggesting which paths out of the quagmire are the most reasonable.

CHAPTER 4

How Much Room Is There for Disagreement?

As the previous three chapters illustrate, sex education has always been fraught with sensitive questions that can seem unresolvable in a diverse society. Some of these questions are inescapably philosophical in nature. Behind the strident positions of teachers, politicians, health care providers, and parents are intuitions about abstract values. What is the meaning or purpose of sexuality? What sexual ethics are required in a healthy society, and do the ethics vary with gender, social position, or other factors? What are the broader aims of schooling, and who is responsible for seeing them through?

On most of these issues, we should not expect to reach agreement. As noted in the introduction, the challenge for peaceful modern societies is not only how to cultivate agreement but *how to manage disagreement*. There has been progress in sex education when actors have been able to converge on critical aims in spite of their ideological differences—for instance, when the social hygienists and the social purity reformers joined hands in the early twentieth century to curb venereal disease. We believe that progress is still possible. In fact, progress depends on understanding where our values diverge and what relevance they have to public policy.

The next three chapters will interpret ongoing disagreement over sex education by distilling three recurring philosophical themes. This chapter focuses on the theme of legitimacy and pluralism. How can decision makers defend one course of action in the face of disagreement? How debatable is the evidence about sex education? The culture wars of the last half century have clouded our understanding of these issues. After dissecting some clashing opinions, I argue that sex education should be evidence-based and also be a type of ethics education, in which young people learn to reflect on and articulate their own values.

Chapter 5 considers the problem of educational authority and children's rights. When adults disagree about the best interests of children, who should prevail? There are powerful arguments for deferring to parents, but most parents also prefer for schools to take the lead. I argue that decisions about sex education should be the product of distributed authority, with parents, teachers, youths, and the state playing complementary roles, and with all of them prioritizing the interests of children.

Finally, chapter 6 considers attitudes toward the purpose of schooling and what they can tell us about the place of sex education in schools. Have we been wrong to dwell so much on what goes into formal curriculum? There are reasons to be skeptical about whether schools can live up to the job of Chief Sex Educator. I conclude that sex education must be provided in schools, but in a much more critical way than it currently is, and outside of schools as well.

This philosophical game plan will allow us to touch on almost all of the major arguments over sex education in contemporary North America and build up to more confident conclusions about how to teach and how to make public policy. Still, some might feel that this approach tries to shoehorn sex education into a rational paradigm that was intended for other topics. A recurring question throughout these chapters will be this: Is sex education *sui generis*, that is, a category of its own? Is it different from other educational subjects, or other moral controversies, in such a way that our usual thinking does not, or should not, apply?

Going forward I will grant that views about youth sexuality and education may not be neatly compressed into logical boxes and may not be entirely analogous to views about other topics on which there is considerable dispute. Indeed, sex education remains distinct from most other subjects on the curriculum, and properly so; nobody wants students to go home and practice sex the way they are encouraged to practice Spanish or the flute. Nonetheless, approaching sex education as a problem for rational deliberation and coordination—the way that philosophers tend to think about social problems—allows us to shed light on this issue that can mean so many things to so many people. The history of sex education shows us that social hysteria, chance events, outcry from a minority of the population, economic pressures, health crises, and general apathy can jerk us in different directions, leading to a mishmash of programs and muddled public discourse. Philosophy helps us to survey the disagreement and the evidence for pursuing some strategies over others, making more principled decisions that can withstand the changing cacophony. People may respectfully disagree about the place of sex education in schools—as well as the meaning of sexuality itself—but not all positions are equally defensible, and some are detrimental.

Even when we are talking about sex, then—that ultimate touchy subject—we are also talking about public reason. If our overarching goal is to cooperate enough to have a peaceful, healthy society, we have to agree on enough background assumptions that we don't have to go back to the drawing board—or battlefield—for every educational policy decision. I refer to the stated goals and procedures of free and open democracies (however imperfectly they are expressed) to ground arguments about how to reason through disagreement. Without them, social organization becomes a literal free-for-all where foundational rights, principles of fairness, and the meaning of "truth" itself are called into question any time we face a dispute.[1] This means that perspectives that flout these norms will by definition be less admissible in public discourse and reasoning about policy than others. But it also means that some perspectives with which I or others vehemently disagree might have to be given a place at the table.

At the end of these philosophical investigations, I articulate our vision of Democratic Humanistic Sexuality Education (DHSE). We support what is usually called Comprehensive Sex Education, but the historical and philosophical perspectives we offer here point to more specific, and in some cases more radical, ways of thinking about it. We've learned in the first three chapters how American sex education lurched over time toward some stable conclusions, such as the idea that women deserve to know about sex before getting married and that schools should be part of a public health response to viral threats. We can build on this progress by looking at the decades of evidence about the effects of different programs and taking seriously the objections and fears of people with different worldviews. The ideals of freedom and equality support providing young people with honest and complete information about their bodies and sexual health, which is inclusive of all races, genders, and orientations, while also respecting their diverse belief systems and the value of community. This education can neither be value-free nor confined to a designated cranny in the curriculum. When we take into consideration the contemporary information landscape, as well as cultural and technological developments, it is clear that an even more wide-ranging, critical, and holistic curriculum is necessary. Rather than writing out this curriculum in stone, DHSE provides a conceptual framework that is dynamic and context-specific, but rooted in democratic and humanistic aims. We argue that DHSE is both as practical as most alternatives, as well as the most philosophically defensible approach to sex education in a context that includes deep polarization and unequally distributed power.

At the end of the previous chapter, we saw how, by the late 1990s, American views on sex education had retreated into some of the most absolute and oppositional positions in its history. Not only had Family Life Education all but evaporated, but conservatives were consolidating federal funds and authority to prohibit any explanation of contraception in schools that may once have distributed condoms and supported peer-led "zaps." Meanwhile, progressive organizations like SIECUS and legions of liberals railed and rallied. How can we possibly get from such balkanized positions to an overlapping consensus on DHSE? To do so, we need to begin by understanding the anatomy of the disagreement.

MANUFACTURED POLARIZATION

Disagreement has been the defining characteristic of North America's experience with sex education. The titles of major scholarly books on the topic feature confrontational, even militaristic, metaphors, such as "battles," "debates," and "war."[2] Campaigns to change sex education—whether from more conservative to more liberal or vice versa—are described as "revolutions."[3] Politicians may rise and fall on their promises about how to deal with sex education.

You probably knew before picking up this book that the United States and other parts of the Western world have been engaged in relentless political warfare over sex education. But you may have believed that there are precisely two types of sex education, incompatible as day and night, from which we must choose. The historical emergence of sex education in the United States, as we have seen, puts the lie to this contemporary conceit. Sex education is constantly evolving. Once people agree that some sort of sex education should happen in schools, hundreds of details remain to be debated: What information? At what age? Delivered by whom? In what subjects? And what is the message? Plumbing and prevention?[4] Pleasure and liberation? The list goes on. Individuals across the political spectrum and other axes of difference may advocate or oppose many individual aims or types of sex education and not others; attitudes toward sex education are not (necessarily) a package deal. Yet the discourse about sex education, the policies associated with it, and, increasingly, the political parties to which each position corresponds have all fallen into bifurcated stances, at least in the United States. Putative liberals supposedly support Comprehensive Sex Education (CSE), while putative conservatives supposedly defend Abstinence-Only-Until-Marriage Education

(AOUME). Sex education is Exhibit A in a phenomenon of ideological polarization, whereby an individual's or group's position on one hot-button topic serves as a reliable bellwether for their views on myriad others.[5]

This polarization is unfortunate because it inflates the actual degree of disagreement over individual components of sex education, as well as the common aims undergirding them. Moreover, despite the public's overwhelming support for the many possible components of CSE, AOUME has become the default method for teaching sex education in wide swaths of the United States—even in those jurisdictions that technically allow for or require CSE.[6] This pattern distinguishes the United States from most other Western nations, also ostensibly democratic and rights-respecting, where a thorough version of comprehensive school-based sex education became normalized in the same time period. Far from protecting its image as a bastion of diversity and progress, the United States mirrored and joined hands with global conservative movements, traditional sexist cultures, and even theocracies.[7]

We saw in the previous chapter how the push for AOUME resulted from a confluence of factors and gelled when social conservatives got the upper hand in the culture wars. The Adolescent Family Life Act of 1981 delivered the first federal funds to AOUME. Against the backdrop of the AIDS epidemic, the rise of the Christian Right, and Reaganism, AOUME accelerated, along with nationwide surges in the anti-abortion lobby and opposition to gay rights.[8] The institutionalization of these attitudes had more than symbolic effects on the public's understanding of the politics of sex: it cemented an entire educational infrastructure and public vocabulary for measuring sex education against the norm of "the abstinent heterosexual."[9] Since the 1997 amendment to Title V, funding for AOUME has required adherence to the A–H (later A–F) guidelines.[10] Anything outside the guidelines was in practice dubbed "comprehensive." While some states have declined the funding in favor of their own, less restrictive curricula,[11] federal AOUME funding in the United States has been disbursed to the tune of over $2 billion and counting.[12]

Because the AOUME, or "Sexual Risk Avoidance," guidelines set the bar for "comprehensiveness" so incredibly low, the semantics of sex education have been deceptively skewed. In light of the false dichotomization created in the public's understanding of sex education, CSE can refer to anything as parsimonious as AOUME with a one-hour class on contraception, all the way to an integrative, yearlong course on the physical, social, political, and emotional dimensions of puberty, sexual identity, relationships, and gender (in theory, anyway). Advocates of CSE have thus been backed into the illogical position of trumpeting anything that surpasses the draconian Title V guidelines as an example of CSE, even when they know that effective sex education should go much, much further.[13]

Internationally, CSE has also been associated by default with "fact-based" sex education, as opposed to moral education, which has in turn been held up as the exclusive province of AOUME advocates. This is another false dichotomy. The lines on the battlefield derive from crusty beliefs about neutrality and education. Liberal democracies affirm that people can pursue diverse conceptions of the good life, whether based on religious or other worldviews, and the state isn't supposed to take sides as long as those worldviews accept the rights of others to do the same. Public schools are properly non-denominational. So, when the claim is made that sex education must involve God or specific moral injunctions, liberals may bristle and retreat to the position that sex education is "purely factual"—covering anatomy, disease prevention, and the mechanics of contraception.[14] The ethics of sexuality according to diverse worldviews may be described to students but not promoted. Critics charge that this attempt at "neutrality" is nothing more than "relativism"—a "you do you" attitude to high-stakes moral questions.

Liberal educators reply that parents can supplement the "facts" learned in school with whatever ethical overlay they want to add at home. This way, children will come to appreciate that sex has moral or spiritual dimensions according to whatever their families believe. But this attitude toward diversity, far from confirming the importance of parents' values, can have the effect of undermining them. Some claim that it invites the child to regard the home culture as an optional add-on or curiosity, which is in competition with other frameworks. For the devout religious parents who complain of the curriculum's treatment of sex, it is not satisfying for their values and worldview to survive their child's autonomous scrutiny. They feel affronted by having them subjected to scrutiny in the first place.

Nor do critiques of "fact-based" sex education hail only from the side of religious or moral conservatives who worry about the clandestine ideology of secularism. Even among educators and theorists who espouse liberal approaches, the "just the facts" attitude earns much-deserved criticism.[15] For one thing, empirical facts about, say, the symptoms of herpes do not provide students with the kind of sex education that really matters. If you don't want herpes, what matters is how to make choices, communicate with others, develop health-promoting behaviors, assess risks and desires, and other such soft skills. The abstract scientific approach to sex education that prevails in some forms of CSE conveniently sidesteps much of the discussion that would actually make the "facts" about herpes applicable to young people's lives.

Moreover, there *are* important values to be promoted and discussed here, such as self-care, truth-telling, and mutuality. Sexual choices can only be made in a normative context—that is, where some values are already in play. No one thinks that having all the facts about biology entitles people to have sex with whomever they wish, whenever they wish. Although traditionalists and progressives often disagree on the interpretation of values, the information provided in sex education can only matter if it helps to advance what philosophers refer to as a "conception of the good."

We should therefore reject the notion that successful sex education can be uncontroversially limited to "facts" and the corresponding misperception that conservatives have a monopoly on values education. Any type of sex education that can withstand pedagogical and political scrutiny must involve both facts and values. The values are unavoidable even if not made explicit, and without facts—well, what kind of education provides no confirmable information? Neutrality is the wrong target. The philosophical task is to determine *which* facts and values ought to be enshrined in education policy given the reality of irreducible diversity. In the remainder of this discussion, I continue to use the terms "CSE" and "AOUME" as they map onto current public discourse, while stressing that they are neither accurate nor exhaustive.

WHAT ARE WE ARGUING ABOUT? MEANS VS. ENDS

At least two kinds of disagreement about sex education should be distinguished: disagreement about means and disagreement about ends. Ends are value-laden goals that structure the pursuit of activities—for example, losing weight could be an end. Means are choices about how to achieve the ends—HIIT, intermittent fasting, keto diet, or any of the thousands of other strategies on offer. While it may seem as though various camps in the sex education debates have incommensurable values, there is more agreement at the level of ends than at the level of means. For example, it is usually taken for granted that we do not want adolescents to become pregnant[16] or contract sexually transmitted infections (STIs). Regardless of one's political views, these aims are nearly universal, and sex education, in all its guises, has been deployed to achieve them. In every era, people have been spurred to action by high rates of "bastard" babies and syphilitic adolescents. Today, everyone on the sex ed stage—from Planned Parenthood to the Heritage Foundation—prioritizes the unquestioned aims of preventing disease and unplanned pregnancy. They agree so much, you might say they are awkward bedfellows.

Progressives and conservatives even agree to a surprising extent that abstinence is the ideal for youths, or at least that sexual activity should be delayed, and promiscuity minimized as much as possible. There is some scientific rationale for this: all sexual activity carries some risks—and the more sexually active one is with more partners, the greater these accumulated risks. But on some level, adults, and especially parents, are probably apt to feel anxious by the thought of school-aged kids having a lot of sex, whatever their own political proclivities. Less sexual activity among young people is, rightly or wrongly, a baseline aim that enjoys broad support.

It's worth taking a brief look at the treatment of abstinence in various sex education curricula and guidelines to drive this point home. Opponents of CSE appear to have cornered the market on preaching youth abstinence, often portraying advocates of more extensive sex education as amoral libertines who encourage young people to experiment sexually early and often. This depiction is demonstrably off-base. Here's the Centers for Disease Control talking about why sexuality education is important:

> It can help young people . . . *[d]elay sexual initiation until they are ready*. Comprehensive sexual health education teaches abstinence as the only 100 percent effective method of preventing HIV, STIs, and unintended pregnancy.[17]

Note that the CDC's endorsement of abstinence as an aim complements its defense of CSE as a means.

Even Planned Parenthood—a favorite target of social conservatives—measures the effectiveness of sex education against the goal of delaying sexual activity, along with "reducing the frequency of sex" and "reducing the number of sexual partners." Its website has a whole page devoted to the benefits of abstinence.[18] It even measures the success of its own initiatives, such as the Get Real program, against the benchmark of delaying and reducing teen sexual activity.[19] So much for sexual libertinism.

The 2015 Ontario CSE curriculum that garnered considerable pushback was also accused of promoting "promiscuity"[20] despite identifying "delaying sexual activity" as the number-one learning objective.[21] In a contentious section about sexual decision-making, students were expected to

> explain the importance of having a shared understanding with a partner about the following: *delaying sexual activity* until they are older (e.g., choosing to *abstain* from any genital contact; choosing to *abstain* from having vaginal or

> anal intercourse; choosing to *abstain* from having oral-genital contact); [and] the *reasons for not engaging in sexual activity*.[22]

These are awfully indirect ways of encouraging promiscuity.

In short, AOUME teaches abstinence as an end very conspicuously, but anti-AOUME programs offer different means toward the same goal.

So, while there are some ends on which we see genuine disagreement—we will take up the juggernaut of sexual diversity presently—much of the disagreement among opponents on sex education has nothing to do with aims. This suggests that what opponents are often disagreeing about is *how* we ought to go about accomplishing widely endorsed goals. This might be akin to observing that different political parties all endorse the aim of having a strong economy but disagree about whether they should strive for it by reducing taxes or investing in infrastructure.

The means in question here are choices about educational policy and pedagogical practice. Indeed, we now have substantial evidence about the correlation between different educational means and the sexual health outcomes to which they are ostensibly oriented. Counterintuitive though it may seem, if the goal is to keep kids abstinent for longer, preaching abstinence as the exclusive form of "sex education" is a disastrous strategy. After years of aggressive AOUME in the United States, 77% of people had had sex by age twenty, 97% of sexually experienced Americans at age forty-four had had sex before marriage, and the teen pregnancy rate was among the highest in the developed world.[23] In Switzerland, the teen pregnancy rate is one-seventh of the American rate, and the teen birth rate is one-fifteenth.[24]

Since the United States claims it would like numbers closer to the Swiss ones, something has obviously gone wrong. The educational means—curriculum and policy choices in the United States—are not accurately calibrated to the educational aims—what we say we want to accomplish. Extensive research shows the ineffectiveness of AOUME at achieving its own stated goals.[25] International evidence and systematic reviews turn up the same disappointing findings around the world.[26] Moreover, CSE is as effective as, and sometimes more effective than, AOUME at the initial goal of delaying the onset of sexual activity and reducing the number of sexual partners; but it is much more effective at preventing the transmission of STIs, encouraging infected adolescents to seek treatment, and reducing unintended pregnancy.[27]

To the extent that both opponents and proponents of sex education agree about some of the ends, you might expect that they could agree on whatever means are most efficient at bringing them about. However, even after decades of exclusive AOUME funding in the United States has failed to produce the desired outcomes, a vocal contingent still holds that it is the correct means of delivering sexuality education. This phenomenon has pushed advocates of CSE into defending their approach by doubling down on the evidence. Unsurprisingly, those who object on principle are unlikely to be persuaded by having more evidence waved around. What is at stake is the very role of evidence itself. How much disagreement about *evidence-based education* is worth entertaining?

EVIDENCE IN EDUCATION

"Evidence-Based Policy" and Its Discontents

Since at least the 1990s, policy makers in Western countries have faced mounting pressure to design and justify policies based on research or scientific evidence. Strengthened collaborations between researchers and government agencies have been intended to facilitate this knowledge mobilization.

What if many of the problems in schools could be alleviated by paying more attention to educational research?[28] It might be tempting to believe that if research evidence offers the best guidance about how to make policy, we could just put researchers in the position of policy makers and the rest of us could go home.

Alas, it's not so simple. Put aside for a moment the obvious complications of political pressures, economic incentives, and the glacial pace of bureaucracy. Even among researchers, the notion that anyone could draw a straight line from evidence to law is dubious. The effectiveness of educational interventions depends a lot on the context, the interests and capacities of the stakeholders, and other policies and practices. Getting from educational research to better educational policy is no "mechanical . . . algorithmic process."[29]

Because of these types of concerns, we may prefer to speak of "research-informed policy" rather than "evidence-based policy."[30] Research is critically important to how we ought to make public decisions. But there are still gaps to be filled between the studies published in social science journals and the policies signed into law.[31] Besides, in many areas germane to social policy, the evidence is inconsistent.

There is no significant inconsistency to speak of when it comes to the evidence on sex education, however. Leading research agencies have released independent guidelines for sexual health education over the last decade that form a pattern of consensus, not disagreement. While they lack the clout of official policy, guidelines issued by, among others, the Centers for Disease Control and Prevention (CDC), a partnership of American nongovernmental adolescent health organizations called the Future of Sex Education (FoSE), the Sexual Information and Education Council of Canada (SIECCAN), the WHO Regional Office for Europe, and the United Nations Educational, Scientific and Cultural Organization (UNESCO) unanimously endorse multiple components of sex education—most of which would be explicitly excluded by Title V's A–H (or A–F) guidelines.[32]

Attitudes toward Evidence

If the evidence about sexuality education points inexorably to certain types of policies and away from others, then we should, in a fairly straightforward—even "mechanical"—way, follow the evidence; but we don't. Something is getting lost in translation. Is the problem that people don't trust science?

Popular wisdom holds that social conservatives are skeptical about science and liberals embrace it. When contentious policies are debated, Democrats point to evidence and Republicans go with their gut. Although there are disparities between Democrats' and Republicans' deference to science overall, the truth is more complicated.[33] Most people defer to scientific experts on topics where evidence is available. When we resist it, there's usually a reason. Our willingness to accept evidence depends on the degree of consistency or tension between our preexisting commitments and what the science tells us to believe. The more ideological the issue, the more we stick to our guns. People of all political persuasions do this.

These kinds of biases are well established in psychology. For example, "'motivated reasoning' occurs when people encounter information that is inconsistent with their existing attitudes or opinions on a subject, and then discount that information to mitigate cognitive dissonance."[34] In other words, people have an impressive capacity to ignore information that is inconvenient. It's part of our psychological software.[35]

This tendency is almost certainly exacerbated by the polarization of political views and the strong imperative to stick with one's political tribe. Many voters may be agnostic about certain controversial issues until they receive a signal from a trusted source within their own camp.[36] Once the signal is received, the impetus to seize the relevant evidence and discount opposing evidence is strengthened. The echo chamber effect of Google algorithms and our self-reinforcing news diets makes it additionally hard to encounter alternative views, or at least to encounter them in a nonthreatening manner.

Given that everyone wants the evidence to be on their side, the issue is not (merely) one of people selectively rejecting science, but also one of people manipulating evidence. In an environment where evidence talks but says different things to different people, "part of the battle is marshaling scientific evidence in favor of your point of view."[37] Ideologically motivated actors may undergo logical contortions to make it appear as though some evidence supports what they want it to. This can lead to bizarre interpretations of data, as well as sworn opponents appealing to the very same evidence to make their case.

Here's an example: the Heritage Foundation, a conservative American "think tank," released a report in 2010 called "Evidence on the Effectiveness of Abstinence Education: An Update." It concluded, "When considering effective prevention program [*sic*] aimed at changing teen sexual behavior, lawmakers should consider all of the available empirical evidence and restore funding for abstinence education."[38] The report cited seventeen studies that supposedly showed "significant results"—that is, evidence for the effectiveness of abstinence education; it also listed (presumably for the appearance of neutrality) five studies that showed "no significant results." The curious thing is that many of the studies cited as evidence for the viability of abstinence education are also used by proponents of CSE. How can this be?

It's possible that studies are inconclusive because the effects of different interventions on adolescent sexual behavior may be complex and contextual. With tens of millions of young people being guinea pigs in our convoluted educational experiments, there will occasionally be times when AOUME appears to have salutary effects along with the times when CSE seems successful—and even times where both appear to be true at the same time.

But shifty semantics and creative interpretations of data can make the ledger seem more balanced than it actually is. While purporting to tout the effects of AOUME education, for example, the Heritage Foundation report approvingly cites some studies that were actually about "virginity pledges," a practice in which young people make a public promise to remain virgins until they are married, sometimes during lavish events known as "purity balls."[39] It is true that such pledges have been found, in certain circumstances, to delay sexual debut among adolescents (while not guaranteeing the delay lasts until their wedding night!).[40] It is not true that school-based mandatory AOUME programs are the same as, or necessarily have the same effects as, voluntary—usually religious—chastity celebrations in local communities. One of the studies cited enthusiastically as evidence for the Heritage Foundation's preferred policies—a 1997 study by Michael Resnick et al. published in the prestigious *Journal of the American Medical Association* (*JAMA*)—deals with the importance of factors such as family connectedness to preventing all kinds of harm to adolescents and mentions abstinence only in the context of virginity pledges.[41] It does *not* provide evidence for the effectiveness of, or otherwise advocate, AOUME. Other researchers interpreted the Resnick article very differently from the Heritage Foundation. Beth Kotchick et al. noted that the positive effects of family connectedness applied, in Resnick et al.'s findings, only to *nonsexual* risk behaviors and had no impact on the likelihood of pregnancy by twelfth grade.[42] And anyway, family connectedness is not AOUME.

Other studies embraced by the Heritage Foundation have also been regarded more tepidly by researchers. For instance, another *JAMA* article was elevated for its modest finding that eleven-year-old African Americans were less likely than those in the control group to report having sexual intercourse three months after receiving an abstinence program.[43] This has been duly noted as an outlier study in more systematic surveys of the evidence.[44]

Then there are the papers described as reporting "no significant results" by the Heritage Foundation. Again, sometimes the evidence in this category pertains to virginity pledges rather than AOUME. But this hardly works in the foundation's favor. One of the "no results" studies found that virginity pledgers "transition to first sex later, have less cumulative exposure, fewer partners, and lower levels of nonmonogamous partners." This would actually appear to constitute "positive results" for the Heritage Foundation's position—unless you keep reading. The researchers go on to report that these "pledgers" have the same [STI] rates as non-pledgers and are *overrepresented* among adolescents having oral and anal sex.[45] This is not "no results." This is strong evidence that virginity pledges conceal hypocrisy and unmanaged risks. In fact, this is the very same study that made national headlines for showing that 88% of "virginity pledgers" have intercourse before marriage.[46]

The point here is not to place too much emphasis on one report penned by one ideologically motivated organization. The point is that we have a problem with attitudes toward evidence when nearly every study proffered as support for the AOUME position in a supposedly "evidence-based" report can simultaneously be used as evidence against AOUME and, in some cases, as strong evidence for CSE. In an environment in which most people are *not* researchers and depend on trusted messengers to simplify the scholarship on important issues, this kind of distortion can have enormous consequences. As we have seen, everyone filters information through their own psychological defense mechanisms. Sex education happens to be a topic on which those who are committed to abstinence-only approaches are more likely to be taken in by unscientific conclusions.

"On Our Side"? Public Opinion about Sex Education

Despite resistance to evidence of the impacts of AOUME, a different kind of evidence—public polling—shows that the majority of the North American public actually endorses most of the topics in CSE being taught in schools. For example, a 2018 report by the Sexual Information and Education Council of the United States (SIECUS) found that "public support for sex education in this country is overwhelming—regardless of political affiliation, religion, and/or regional demographics."[47] Likely voters surveyed prior to the 2018 midterms supported sex education in middle schools at a rate of 89% and in high schools at a rate of 98%, with support for individual topics also registering in the strong majority.[48] Republicans express lower rates of support for some topics in Comprehensive Sex Education than Democrats, but members of both parties still indicate clear majority support for sex education in schools that exceeds the harsh conditions of Title V.[49]

Advocates appeal to such polls to argue that CSE is justified, not (only) because scientists or "experts" recommend it, nor specifically because it can be correlated to desirable effects, but rather because a majority of the public believes it to be justified. In a democracy, the will of the majority is regarded as sacrosanct. The high levels of support for school-based sexuality education might be thought, just like the virtual consensus among researchers, to justify CSE policies all on their own. While encouraging to those who advocate for more sex education, however, this kind of evidence is not without its own problems.

First, the data yielded through public opinion surveys are susceptible to the kinds of framing biases and motivated reasoning we saw earlier. For example, a study conducted in 2014 found that 87% of Ontario parents agreed or strongly agreed that sex education should be taught in schools and rated each of thirteen sexual health education topics, from methods of contraception to media literacy, as "important" or "very important."[50] The provincial government appeared to be on very solid ground, therefore, when in 2015 it introduced the updated health curriculum covering all those topics. However, a renewed scuffle over provincial policy in 2018 appeared to confuse these same parents about their values and beliefs. A survey of five hundred parents conducted after the curriculum was repealed found that over half (51%) of them supported the abrupt policy shift, *even though their views on the necessity and age-appropriateness of items in the 2015 curriculum hadn't changed.* For example, 84% of them supported teaching about sexually transmitted infections, oral and anal sex, and the risks of "sexting" in seventh grade, all of which had just been struck from the curriculum. As Sean Simpson, vice president of the polling company, commented: "There's obviously a disconnect here."[51] How much faith can we put in evidence of public opinion when the public's opinions are manifestly self-contradictory?

There is a second reason to exercise caution when citing public opinion in support of educational policy perspectives. From a democratic standpoint, as much as we are obligated to defer to the majority, we also ought to rigorously defend the rights of the minority to express dissent. This is both out of deference to their individual rights as citizens and out of a concern, as expressed by John Stuart Mill, that simple democracy risks silencing better ideas through the tyranny of sheer numbers. We do not want to rule out the possibility that, at any given point in time, the majority of a civic body could be badly mistaken about what is in children's best interests. Indeed, as we have already seen, it was historically the defenders of school-based sexuality education who fought an uphill battle to turn the tide of public opinion toward their point of view. The fact that they now enjoy majority support should not embolden us to abandon the principle of listening to minority voices.

The value of evidence in public policy should not be equated with whatever a democratic majority, much less an ideological minority, thinks it is. The most reliable evidence comes from independent researchers who collect and analyze evidence professionally—including, as it turns out, evidence about how we interpret evidence, and evidence about the translatability of evidence into policy. Even though the notion of straightforward "evidence-based education policy" has been roundly critiqued by researchers themselves, the question is not *whether* evidence matters, but *how*. Those who find most of the evidence dissonant with their own preferences can't have it both ways: they can't try to win support by appealing to evidence when it appears to support their own position and then also misread the avalanche of evidence that contradicts it.

BUT WHAT IF THE ENDS DON'T JUSTIFY THE MEANS? EDUCATION AS EXPOSURE

What may appear to be opposing attitudes toward the validity or role of evidence in education could actually be a proxy for disagreement about the values underpinning different educational means. We were assuming in the previous section that rational people would support whatever means have been demonstrated to promote their shared aims (conservatively, reducing teen pregnancy and STI rates). At a certain point, however, some means may no longer be justifiable, whatever they accomplish. This harkens back to an age-old thought experiment in philosophy. If you tell me that shooting one person will save the lives of five others, I may refuse to shoot the one. The problem is not that I reject the evidence guaranteeing the outcome of my choice or that I don't care about the five people. The problem is that the ends don't justify the means. A charitable interpretation of some people's attitudes toward evidence would say that while they may accept the evidence, they think the ends don't justify the means.

The "means" of detailed sexuality education are enough to make anyone squeamish. Often a nonspecialist, such as a gym teacher, whose portfolio usually involves sports drills and square dancing, is tasked with sitting down embarrassed adolescents and running through some of the most intimate and stigmatized aspects of humanity in a few designated lessons—all without being judgmental, exclusionary, or inadvertently titillating. Even for the most committed educators, this kind of teaching can be daunting. Studies repeatedly show that teachers want more professional development and support to cover the full gamut of sexuality-related topics with accuracy and integrity.[52]

The awkwardness of sex education could be another area in which there is more commonality among opposing views than there is dissimilarity. Not only religious or conservative parents and teachers but also many otherwise liberal adults may be uncomfortable talking to children about sexuality, imagining their children having sexual desires and experiences, and answering questions about the ins and outs of birth control or safer sex. Indeed, many liberal parents welcome CSE in the schools precisely because they feel unequipped to have these discussions with their own children. To this extent, sex education really is *sui generis*: even for those who want their children to learn as much as possible, there is a stigma or anxiety that makes it different from other conventional school subjects. Most people would rather pass the buck.

But for some parents, the discomfort with frank education about sexuality goes far beyond embarrassment or limited expertise. The method itself already designates human sexuality as public, secular object of study, on par with math and languages. For conservative, especially religious, parents, the process of treating sexuality as a topic for school-based instruction is unacceptable from a moral perspective, whatever the outcomes. Mere exposure to detailed information about sex, even if empirically accurate, can already be corruptive of the worldview they wish to impart to their children. This may have to do with the sanctity of sexuality, the beauty of marriage, or other metaphysical commitments. The means of preventing teen sex and unwanted health outcomes therefore must meet some moral, as well as (or instead of) some empirical, bar. Evidence of its effectiveness is only part of the picture.

This apparent tension between educating according to evidence and educating for religion recurs throughout philosophy of education and is a thorn in the side of liberals. While liberals generally believe the purpose of education is to promote autonomy and expose children to more than just their parents' worldview, religious education has usually depended for its success on tight control over children's exposure to non-religious ideas, as well as ideological continuity between home, school, and religious community.[53] The purpose of AOUME, then, is not only to achieve some of the health outcomes that everyone can agree on (which the evidence shows it doesn't), but also to reinforce the bonds of religious belonging and a faith-based worldview that gives meaning to many people's lives (which it may well do).[54] Liberals have been charged with religious intolerance on the grounds that insisting on secular education could, for some children, be tantamount to arresting any possibility of transmitting their parents' religious beliefs.

Even if one is sympathetic to the case for religious preservation, Western societies are trending toward a degree of diversity that makes limiting children's exposure to secular or heretical materials increasingly unrealistic. As much as religious parents may wish for their children to encounter ideas about sex exclusively through the lens of faith, the crushing realities of globalization, cell phones, and pop culture will beat them to the punch every time.[55] Opponents of school-based CSE may argue that it merely contributes to the problem by drawing more attention to sex and validating these corrupt influences. The evidence shows that this is actually backward: trying to indefinitely shelter young people from "corrupt" influences only makes them more unprepared when they (inevitably) encounter them. The strategy of controlled exposure—as opposed to shelter—is more effective.

Once again, however, our picture of the disagreement tends to be oversimplified. Some conservatives endorse means that are strikingly similar to those of CSE; and some liberals would oppose the means of AOUME even if they were correlated with more desirable outcomes.

As an example of the former, Focus on the Family's web-based parental guidance for "Talking about Sex and Puberty" may astonish some CSE advocates with its no-nonsense, talking-beats-silence advice. The guidelines recommend using correct names for body parts from the beginning, avoiding confusing euphemisms ("making love") or myths ("storks"), and answering children's questions directly. Perhaps more significantly, parents are advised not to shame their children or overreact to normal incidents such as children showing each other their genitals. Masturbation is also dealt with more matter-of-factly than one might expect: "It is extremely likely that masturbation leading to sexual climax will occur at some point, especially for a male. If he is racked with guilt about it and repeatedly vows never to let it happen again, he will probably expend a lot of energy feeling like a moral failure and worrying unnecessarily about his spiritual welfare."[56]

While many parents and various advocates of CSE could object to the framing of these issues by Focus on the Family—for example, the undefended assumption that masturbation has any moral or spiritual stakes—they will also recognize in this advice echoes of what is considered best practice by non-religious professional sex educators. But the places where discrepancies persist are also informative. For instance, Focus on the Family, like most of its cousin organizations, defines sex exclusively in conventional heterosexual terms, dwelling on "boy-girl relationships" and the miracle of childbirth.[57] And within the parameters of these opposite-sex, marriage-oriented interactions, girls and boys play different roles: girls are gatekeepers and chastity defenders, while boys are desirers and pursuers.[58] This "complementarian" view of the sexes and its associated expression in traditional marriage is a nonstarter for many advocates of CSE.[59]

In fact, even if these AOUME-typical messages were highly effective at, say, preventing unwanted pregnancy and disease, many liberals would oppose them just as vehemently. Liberals, just like conservatives, have some moral ground rules. The ends do not automatically justify any means. Recall that some studies show that virginity pledges are correlated with later sexual debut and fewer partners. Even if this were considered an achievement, critics have argued that the practice of virginity pledging itself perpetuates harmful and regressive gender stereotypes, sexist attitudes about desire and control, discourses of sexual shame and guilt, naïvely optimistic views about the safety and pleasure of sex within marriage, fear of women's sexuality, and highly heteronormative understandings of what constitutes "sex," fulfillment, or love.[60] Much as some pro-chastity parents worry about the psychological harm that may come to children from being taught that premarital sex is a viable option, other adults are equally vexed about the damage inflicted when children are presented with sexual values that they regard as prejudicial or oppressive.

This brings us back to the bigger question of how to set public policy against the backdrop of incompatible worldviews and ethical paradigms. As we saw, nearly everyone agrees on the primary goals of reducing disease and teen pregnancy, even if they disagree on the means. But at the levels of both means and ends, a deeper controversy brews. Fundamental disagreement over sexual identity and gender roles probably accounts for most of the ethical dissonance between sex education opponents. Is the heterosexual, procreative gender binary the only legitimate model to offer kids?

IS HOMOPHOBIA PART OF MORAL PLURALISM?

The website True Tolerance was started in 2010 when anti-bullying initiatives in schools around the United States began to pick up steam. Sex and gender minorities are disproportionately represented among victims of bullying, which is often ignored or even perpetuated by school staff. Many believe that increasing tolerance of sexual diversity is the key to reducing bullying. The site has a different kind of "tolerance" in mind, however. The website contends that these new anti-bullying programs are actually a stealth way for "homosexual advocacy groups" to pursue "homosexual instruction" in multiple parts of school life, since parents can choose to opt their children out of sex education classes, where these groups first tried to spread their message. Among its many resources, the website provides a tip sheet with "7 ways parents can respond to homosexual activism in schools."[61]

The connection between AOUME and anti-gay attitudes is undeniable.[62] In the face of growing official protection for sex and gender minorities, some of the most influential AOUME advocates with the most virulent anti-gay beliefs have found ways of couching their moral framework in the more sanitized language of public health and risk, emulating the strategy of secular liberals.[63] National and local organizations, especially in the United States, have been tremendously successful at stalling educational policies that are perceived to normalize and validate sexual relations outside of conventional heterosexuality, often all while distancing themselves from the politically incorrect label of "homophobia."[64] They may view anything on the CSE spectrum as an endorsement of, or even recruitment mechanism for, what they regard as immoral "lifestyles."

In many writings about sex education within the broadly liberal philosophical tradition, the persistent divide over the moral status of homosexuality is regarded as another facet of pluralism that must be taken seriously. This means that even though liberals generally support gay rights, we shouldn't dictate what people should believe about human sexuality. While the term "homophobia" is obviously derisive (hence many people's understandable desire to dodge the label), being homophobic in belief or attitude is not forbidden—far from it. It is perfectly coherent within a liberal democracy for some of the population—even a majority—to sincerely believe that being gay is sinful or that particular sexual acts are not only distasteful but positively immoral.

Religion is often, but need not be, the framework for arriving at such beliefs and rendering them morally binding. Even without religious freedom, these are not attitudes that the liberal state could coherently police.

At the same time, people are free to identify and behave sexually however they choose, except where there is significant and demonstrable harm to others that could be fairly regulated. It is hard to reason that consensual sex between adults of any sex or gender is the kind of thing that reliably harms other people, much less warrants state interference. By contrast, non-heterosexual students are frequently harmed by others in a manner that is amenable to regulation, the same way we punish other types of assault. Much of the strategy of the gay rights movement has been to bring the force of law to bear on discrimination and violence on the basis of sexual orientation. You can think whatever you want about homosexuality, but you can't slam that kid into a locker because you think he's gay.

All of this creates quite a conundrum for the nominal liberal. The state is bound to protect individuals from undue harm and unwarranted interference, both the sexual minorities who face incessant discrimination and the anti-gay ideologues who are free to believe their interpretation of a holy book. It is supposed to be neutral between views of the good life and stay mum on inflammatory topics such as sexual morality; but it is also required to craft policy, including sex education in the schools, which can never hope to be neutral. The task for the liberal state, then, is not to force a consensus on questions of sexual values, but to justify public policy in a way that transcends specific worldviews.

Liberal philosophers have mostly been shy about teaching sexual orientation in schools. Michael Halstead and Michael Reiss argued that "schools should teach about homosexuality but should treat it as a controversial issue" and emphasize that teaching should be "balanced."[65] They insisted on parents' right to opt out of such lessons and conclude: "If a sex education programme of any sort proves highly divisive or unacceptable to a significant number of recipients, it needs amending."[66] In his 2000 essay on sex education, David Archard was clear that there is no liberal moral case against consensual same-sex relations, but he also stressed neutrality: "There is no reason to 'celebrate' homosexuality any more than there is reason to celebrate heterosexuality."[67]

These liberal assessments of how to approach sexual diversity in schools will probably strike us today as hollow. For one thing, the language is jarringly outdated. In an era where young people are identifying with an exploding diversity of orientations and identities, teachers are learning the etiquette of pronoun checks, human-rights cases are being fought over the exclusion of transgender students in schools, and well-meaning straight people can feel ashamed for not knowing the latest addition to the alphabet soup of queerness, to speak of teaching about "homosexuality" from a balanced liberal perspective is at best quaint and arguably harmful. Inclusive education in the twenty-first century requires contending with the lively and rapidly evolving conversation about queerness that extends far beyond the traditionalists' bogeyman of the "homosexual."

But updating the language to keep pace with the cultural moment may not be enough to rehabilitate this superficially liberal stance. We now know that the well-being of sex- and gender-minority students demands much more than a cool mention by a "balanced" facilitator; today's educational experts recommend far-reaching changes to curriculum and educational culture to dismantle the ingrained prejudices that have harmed LGBTQ+ students for so long.[68] Without robust recognition—indeed, "celebration"—of their identities, students who fall outside the prescriptive categories are at vastly increased risk of bullying, academic hardship, risky behaviors, and quiet suffering.[69] For example, the 2017 national School Climate Survey conducted by the Gay, Lesbian, and Straight Education Network (GLSEN) found that "59.5% of LGBTQ students felt unsafe at school because of their sexual orientation, 44.6% because of their gender expression, and 35.0% because of their gender," and an astonishing 87.3% of LGBTQ students "experienced harassment or assault based on personal characteristics."[70] Old-fashioned liberal education can be said to be complicit in the ongoing persecution of sexual minorities precisely because it protects homophobia as part of moral pluralism. It would be like saying, "Because some people are Islamophobic, we will treat Muslim identity as controversial in this class."

The fact that people disagree about sexual morality is indisputable, yet, as Jonathan Zimmerman and Emily Robertson note, "not every disagreement qualifies as a controversy."[71] There is a difference between a politically volatile issue and an issue that is truly indeterminate according to the basic political metrics of equality and liberty. Same-sex marriage was legalized by showing the underlying *consistency* of treating same-sex couples equally in a legal system where equality is supposedly enshrined. Therefore, while the ethics of same-sex relations remain controversial among some people, it is inconsistent for schools to go on pretending that our background political commitments are agnostic about sexual equality. We are fully justified in trying to change the *attitudes* of the locker-slammer as well as punishing the slamming.[72]

Inclusive sex education curriculum will obviously offend some conservatives, as well as perhaps others who believe the jury is still out on this issue. As we have seen, complete neutrality is unrealistic. Indeed, sex education cannot be divided into "moral" versions (such as religious approaches) and "amoral" (neutral or secular) ones. All sex education involves values, and the only way to ultimately defend some versions of sex education over others is to enter the ethical fray.

SEX EDUCATION AND MORAL EDUCATION

So far, we have established that sex education involves a combination of facts and values. Biology and social science should guide the facts, both about sexual health as such and about "what works" from a teaching perspective, insofar as we can draw conclusions from that evidence. But values enter sex education at multiple levels. There are the values that drive arguments for or against particular educational approaches. There are values embedded within the messages and information that students receive about sexuality, even when educators attempt to be neutral. And then there are the values that are self-consciously named and transmitted under the auspices of sex education. This latter phenomenon is where sex education meets moral education. Since conservative and (especially) religious voices have been the loudest ones moralizing about children's sexuality, we have been lulled into seeing moral education as intertwined with restrictive sex education and absent from, or irrelevant to, progressive or Comprehensive Sex Education. This distinction can work in conservatives' favor, allowing them to self-present as the true guardians of "family values" and "moral responsibility."

Indeed, moral education (or "character education," as some versions are called) has historically served fairly traditional purposes. In the United States, it has been used to assimilate immigrants and "civilize" racial minorities into middle-class white values. Currently, despite a lack of evidence for its effectiveness or social consensus about its contents, many schools continue to transmit a prescribed slate of character traits, such as perseverance, resilience, and courage, which may be more aligned with neoliberal[73] incentives than with philosophical conceptions of virtue.[74] In the case of AOUME, the prevailing values—such as chastity (abstinence), self-restraint, and gender-role conformity—smack of a Christian ethic that belies the supposed separation of church and state and cannot be defended in a multicultural democracy.[75]

It is therefore unsurprising that progressives may want to distance themselves from the aims of moral education so construed, and sexual morality education in particular. Without proper justification and implementation, moral education can be "directive" in a manner that has earned it charges of illiberalism.[76] For if, as many liberals and educational philosophers suggest, the guiding values of a liberal society ought to be autonomy and pluralism, then there is something suspiciously hypocritical about undertaking an educational program whose stated purpose is to tell young people what is right or wrong and how they ought to behave.[77]

Yet moral education is inevitable and ethically necessary. It is inevitable because "neutrality" is unrealistic, and it is necessary because the values of equality and liberty apparently require very explicit ongoing defense. However, moral education about sexuality can be done in less directive ways than the available models, without preselecting a set of sexual virtues or moral dogma through which to teach sexuality. We might prefer the term "ethics" here, meaning a systematic study of values and norms, instead of "moral," which implies that the correct answer has already been identified.[78]

An ethics-based sex education curriculum will not introduce morals in order for them to be merely absorbed by the students; instead, it will facilitate and scaffold inquiry into values as they relate to sexuality, culture, religion, and society. This requires the cultivation and promotion of critical thinking as well as knowledge of facts and conventions.[79] The "moral education" of AOUME is therefore not the same as moral education in an integrated CSE curriculum. It's roughly the difference between catechism and philosophy.

In the pioneering program Sexual Ethics for a Caring Society Curriculum (SECS-C), students are given the information and tools to openly discuss the multitude of messages that bombard them and to safely explore the meaning of sexual ethics.[80] As its designer, Sharon Lamb, explains in an influential article:

> This is a vision in which sexuality education is designed to educate the whole teen as a decision maker, a sexual citizen, and an ethical human being. Philosophical and practical discussions about individual rights, consent, human dignity, mutuality, respect, and even beneficence could and should be included in a sexuality education curriculum that has at its core moral development rather than prevention, restraint, or social skills development.[81]

The SECS-C curriculum—which consists of sixteen lessons and can be adopted within school curricula—gives educators room to explore some of the topics that are still taboo in conventional sex education, improving on both AOUME and CSE. The ethics approach includes attention to relationships, feelings, and obligations to others—a feature that has made AOUME programs attractive, even to some progressive educators, despite AOUME's narrow interpretation of sex in the context of heterosexual marriage.[82]

Putting ethics right at the center of sex education might therefore help to transcend some of the tensions caused by viewing sex education through mutually exclusive value systems. In fact, there is a normative framework—neither liberal nor conservative—that can accommodate and motivate such an approach. It is called the "ethics of care" and is attributed in large part to the eminent philosopher of education Nel Noddings.[83] The care perspective takes ethical questions to be inherently relational and contextual. It eschews predetermined solutions to ethical challenges and instead focuses on developing care as a kind of master value. Using care as a starting point, certain sexual behaviors are immediately morally condemnable, such as nonconsensual touching and dishonesty, while most are amenable to thoughtful assessment, including through various religious or secular lenses. Noddings provides hopeful possibilities for integrating moral education and sex education in novel and less divisive ways.[84]

CONCLUSION

Most of us presumably want to live in a society where disagreement is respected, maybe even encouraged, and where we accept that some issues elude scientific investigation. Yet we need baseline values, facts, and procedures to function as a stable society. Sex education starts to look different when we make judgments about which matters ought to be treated as settled in an advanced democracy and which are part of the diversity that we should respect. We can tolerate tremendous diversity of belief, but we cannot always expect our beliefs to find expression in school curriculum.

Policies about sexuality education must promote the norms of equality and liberty as well as comport with the evidence about how to pursue these ends, including the provision of accurate, inclusive, and comprehensive information about sexual health. Furthermore, rather than attempt to purify the curriculum of the controversy that surrounds it, educators should make ethics part of sex education itself. I will return to these components in chapter 6 in the description of Democratic Humanistic Sex Education.

In this chapter, I have sifted through competing viewpoints on sex education in order to map the disagreement and assess how well the reasoning stands up to publicly defensible benchmarks. This approach, which is common in liberal philosophy, nonetheless brackets the *sources* of the positions and their respective authority to make decisions about sex education. It considers the arguments on their own merits. Another way to decipher the battles over sex education is through the lens of educational authority. We are not always arguing over *what* children should learn about sex, but rather over *who* should decide. If it were uncontroversial who ought to be in charge, we could simply invest our stock in their judgment. But how ought we to identify the correct authorities? This is another philosophical question, to which the next chapter is devoted.

CHAPTER 5

Who's the Boss?

Clearly there is persistent disagreement about how schools should approach sex education, and only some of this disagreement can, or ought to, be dispelled. In the previous chapter, I argued that the norms of scientific evidence and democratic policy-making can help to narrow down the range of legitimate attitudes toward sex education, but the pluralism that remains is neither trivial nor undesirable: disagreement is not going away any time soon. Nonetheless, decisions have to be made. A liberal state may strive for education policies that are justifiable to the largest possible constituency and still face concerted blowback. So, when both neutrality and public consensus are elusive, and somebody has to make educational decisions, the question can shift from *what* sex education should be to *who* gets to decide. This is the idea of *educational authority*. Who has the right to override disagreement with other stakeholders and decide what children learn? Does the authority for sex education rest with different people than it does for other types of education? And are children the only ones whose interests matter in educational decisions?

As we saw in chapter 3, the AIDS crisis in the 1980s and 1990s had many Americans reconsidering their attitudes toward sex education. When the epidemic exposed the inadequacy of school curriculum, legions of fired-up students took up the mantle of sex education through peer-to-peer education and political activism, refusing to be a generation that suffered a cataclysmic disease because the adults in their lives were too prudish or incompetent to teach them safer sex. Until this period, responsibility for sex education had been volleyed between parents, schoolteachers, and policy makers, with the tacit assumption that young people depended on the adults in their lives to protect them from sexual harms or moral scandal. The student-led efforts that managed to earn considerable respect in the early 1990s have, alas, since been eclipsed again by the usual adult bickering. For the last several decades, decisions about sex education in most Western states have redounded to some combination of parents and politicians—for better and for worse.

State-supported universal education is one of the great achievements of the modern West. Children are born to parents, families, and communities who are usually strongly committed to their growth and well-being; but many of the goods we rely on for our individual and familial well-being cannot be provided by the small tribal groupings we live in. Without mandatory or universally accessible schooling, parents may keep their kids close, but most would find it impossible to educate their children privately as efficiently and comprehensively—or affordably—as state-organized schools do. Common schooling enables democracy and reduces inequalities between children.[1] But it depends on a division of authority that necessarily deprives parents of some control over their children. Given our liberal heritage, with its emphasis on individual freedom and pluralism, and the strong feelings aroused by the image of the innocent child, it is not surprising that schools should be the site of a persistent power struggle between the many adults involved in children's education. Adding sexuality to the mix only compounds the tension.

Many positions on sex education can thus be understood not only (or even primarily) as attitudes toward curriculum, but rather as statements about educational authority. The immediate questions about what constitutes appropriate sexual knowledge and behavior for young people are sometimes no more than window dressing for a more abstract question: Who's the boss?

AUTONOMY AND PATERNALISM

Let's begin with the basic premise. Why do kids need a "boss"? I use the term here with some deliberate cheekiness. What kids need is people to take care of them. But caregiving still requires the authority to make decisions on behalf of the child—to be the person in charge. In the first instance, that authority resides with the people who brought the baby into the world, or specific people they've designated.

The authority starts to spread out when children begin school. Now, teachers, principals, and others have the authority to make decisions about how children spend their time, what they can and cannot do, what they must learn; they can even mete out selected consequences. The authorities in schools are simultaneously educational professionals and, in the case of public schools, arms of the state. Curriculum and other educational policies frequently come down to educators through a pipeline of state policy and increasingly local layers of bureaucracy. And in a democracy, the state is supposed to represent all people—including the parents, who can in principle vote for the educational policies they support. In other words, the stakeholders mingle together to create a tangled web of authority, in which it's not always clear where one boss's purview ends and the next one's begins.

Meanwhile, children are growing up and likely getting impatient to exercise more control over their own lives. The kind of round-the-clock care that is required for a thoroughly helpless infant translates into adults having nearly complete authority over the child; but the seesaw tips precipitously over the next ten or fifteen years. Whoever the adults are, they will start to see their authority dwindle, eventually, in the face of children's growing maturity (or perhaps just teenage recalcitrance). After all, children will one day be adults themselves.

And there's the rub: children need a "boss" (or many "bosses") for their own good, but only until they're old enough to be their own boss. Whether we vest authority over children in their biological parents or in any other adults, the authority should always have been understood as provisional and time-limited. As the philosopher Eamonn Callan puts it, "*Any* credible theory of parental rights will entail that the right to govern the child's life shrinks to [a] vanishing point as the child grows up."[2] In principle, nobody should be the boss of anybody else as long as they are capable of looking after their own needs.

Governing another person's life is the opposite of autonomy, yet we recognize the necessity of limiting children's freedom as an inescapable part of caregiving. We act *paternalistically* when we force our kids to wear seat belts, no matter how much they object. According to the *parens patriae* doctrine, the state can sometimes treat adults paternalistically too, for example, in the case of severe mental illness.

Paternalism only requires justification insofar as we believe in autonomy. If we had no concern for autonomy, the control exercised by adults over children would be morally unremarkable; it would be no different from the control exercised over many competent adults in illiberal contexts, such as the disenfranchised and subservient, or over adults who have historically been regarded as literally the property of others, such as women and enslaved people. It is only because we believe that humans should eventually arrive at self-sovereignty that we must think carefully about how to shepherd humans from their newborn state of complete dependence to the realized state of autonomous adulthood. Parenting would look very different if we never had to prepare for a time when paternalism was off the table.

Liberalism, perhaps ironically, sees paternalism as a necessary route toward the ultimate aim of autonomy. The thought is that appropriate forms of paternalism actually *prepare* children to become autonomous. There is no abrogating the responsibility to exercise authority over children; there are only choices to be made about how to do it. In fact, this is another core idea on which adults of all ideological persuasions tend to converge. Children require adults to take charge of most aspects of their lives. The question of educational authority "is not *whether* paternalism in general is justified, but *who* has the right to determine its nature and aim."[3]

When assessing whether a specific instance of paternalism is justified, philosophers typically look at how well it satisfies the *interests* of the person whose autonomy is being curtailed. If the paternalistic agent isn't doing a better job than the person could do herself, it is nearly impossible to justify this unusual assignment of authority. Wrestling our toddlers into their car seats may feel to them like a rude violation of their interests, but as adults with knowledge of road safety, we rightly assert otherwise. When it comes to sex education, however, adults disagree about what is in children's best interests. Whether they're pro-abstinence, pro-sexual experimentation, or anything in-between, adults' attitudes toward sex education are conjoined to sincere beliefs about what they think is best for children. So we can't settle our differences just by saying which side is best for children. And to make things even muddier, parents' interests matter too, and it's not always clear where children's interests end and their parents' interests begin.

What is needed, then, is some account of who should get to be in charge of sex education, not because of what they believe, but because of who they are. This chapter is organized according to the stakeholders with potential authority over sex education. They are the state, parents, experts, and children. This crude breakdown is intended to recast recurring conflicts over sex education through the lens of authority. But it also highlights the slipperiness of distinguishing people by their roles and interests, which may help explain why educational battles can get so convoluted—for example, many, if not most, teachers are also parents; and all adults were once children. None of these groups can have exclusive authority over sex education. Instead, I argue that children's interests are best served when educational authority is distributed and when their own interest in sexual self-determination provides the litmus test for justified paternalism. This conclusion will feed into our conception of

Democratic Humanistic Sexuality Education and, specifically, the limits on parents' ability to unilaterally overrule it.

THE STATE

Education is a massive coordination challenge, and however much we may feel dissatisfied with contemporary schooling, the very fact of universal free schooling is a triumph of the modern state. For both ethical and logistical reasons, we should expect the government to have a lot of power over education. The logistical reasons are fairly obvious: if decision-making about every aspect of schooling were distributed, nothing would ever get done.[4] But there are also ethical reasons why the state, especially in a stable democracy, may legitimately use schooling to promote certain values, consolidate diverse identities, and equip all children with a shared foundation for responsible citizenship. Schooling is the most efficient—and perhaps the *only*—mechanism for shaping a generation that is otherwise fragmented along innumerable vectors.

The fear that an overzealous state would use its power over education to indoctrinate kids and prioritize the collective good over the good of the family goes back a long time: it's a key takeaway from Plato's *Republic*.[5] Liberalism developed as a response to the experience of overweening state power and constant unrest, which characterized all of the monarchies and theocracies and dictatorships that preceded it.[6] Liberals wanted to create a state that had the right amount of power, for the right reasons.[7]

Alas, this vision has been at times viciously betrayed. The Canadian Residential Schools system, for example, which operated from 1831 to 1996, used state power to take approximately 150,000 Indigenous children away from their families and communities and place them in Christian boarding schools, where their cultures, languages, and ways of life were systematically beaten out of them.[8] The state also forcibly adopted thousands of Indigenous children into non-Indigenous families in the 1960s.[9] All this was in the name of Canadian identity and the "well-being" of Indigenous children—that is, the state tried to play the paternalism card.

So let's not forget that we have never fully lived up to basic liberal ideals, and that the vision of state-coordinated education can be co-opted for truly grotesque purposes. We will therefore distinguish between the state in contemporary liberal theory and the state in reality. In contemporary liberal theory, the state has a crucial role to play in education, but only to the extent that it serves the broader liberal goals of freedom and equality.

Sex Education in the Liberal State

What kind of education will promote a peaceful society in which every person has dignity and as much liberty as possible without harming others? There are plenty of disputes at the micro level, but the broad strokes are pretty clear. Children have to be treated equally and learn to embrace the values of respect for diversity and cooperation with others. Children have to be taught in evidence-based ways that allow them to process and critique information and form their own views about contentious issues. Children have to be given a civic education that will allow them to participate as citizens. In short, a liberal education is an education for *autonomy* and for a society made up of equal, autonomous people. The state gets to wield considerable control over education only because it is best positioned to promote everyone's access to such a free society.

If these are our goals, then state authority over education will likely bump up against other authorities who may have different priorities—notably, parents. Maybe their children's autonomy is not so important to parents; it is often inconvenient, even hurtful, for example, when a child declares that they aren't attending church anymore. To be sure, autonomy is not the only value in childrearing, and a child's membership in cohesive families and communities can contribute immeasurably to his or her well-being. But the liberal state trades away some family immunity from state interference for the sake of children's self-actualization, and for the maintenance of a free society in which one's birth family is not synonymous with destiny.

Schools, as a branch of the state, therefore have an obligation to expose children to something more than what they might encounter if they were only educated at home, or within homogenous communities handpicked by their parents. You can find this intuition in the work of many philosophers, who use slightly different words to indicate the idea of a cleavage between home and school.[10]

In North America, the courts have usually ruled against parents who felt offended by their children's exposure to educational material that contradicts their personal values.[11] In *Chamberlain v. Surrey*, a Canadian teacher sued his school board for attempting to ban three books about same-sex families.[12] The school board complained that using the books would introduce an uncomfortable "cognitive dissonance" between the children's school and their more conservative homes. Chief Justice Beverley McLachlin, who wrote the majority decision, affirmed that dissonance is part of the point of education:

> The cognitive dissonance that results from such encounters is simply a part of living in a diverse society. It is also a part of growing up. Through such experiences, children come to realize that not all of their values are shared by others. . . . Children cannot learn this unless they are exposed to views that differ from those they are taught at home.[13]

No parents are so good that they can directly provide, or curate, all the information and ideas that their children need to grow and thrive in a diverse society; and without exposure to difference, children may compliantly assume that their parents' worldview is all there is. Such blind spots would spell trouble for peaceful democracy. Only the state can build diversity and critical thinking right into compulsory education. This means that parents can't object every time their children are exposed to something they personally disagree with. If parents' views and values are never allowed to be subjected to scrutiny, and the values of other groups are never encountered sympathetically, the whole edifice of liberalism falters: Children may become servile to their parents; diverse groups may be incapable of living harmoniously; oppressive ideologies may be legitimated. Schools can't be in lockstep with parents all the time.

This conception of education may smell suspiciously like state overreach—offensive books today, tyranny tomorrow!—until we recognize that the rest of liberal theory already allots enormous liberty to individuals in the raising of their children.[14] In a place like the United States, where the rights of individuals against their government are well enshrined, and Supreme Court decisions have repeatedly confirmed that schools cannot fully supplant parents' educational authority, there is at best a negligible risk that detached schools will become tyrannical and overtake the family.[15] As Meira Levinson argues, far from "imposing state tyranny, the detached school actually establishes a needed counterweight to the threat of parental tyranny."[16] In other words, the relatively large authority accorded to the state in liberal theory should never be confused with the Platonic dystopia that Amy Gutmann calls "the Family State."

Not everyone sees it that way. The basic detachment condition, shared even by liberals who disagree among themselves about the proper reach of the state, is not so popular among those with parochial values, for whom education and religion are inseparable.[17] In contrast to the detachment condition, some try to establish a seamless authority chain across educational settings. Children should receive the same messages at school as they do at home and in places of worship. As Pam, a nationally celebrated AOUME educator, says: "I want my kids to hear [my values] in school. . . . [T]hey need to get the same message from everyone."[18] Unsurprisingly, Pam and her supporters are inclined to abandon state education as soon as it strays from their message—precisely the opposite of how liberalism defines the state's duties. Whereas liberals see educational authority as a somewhat open chain in the service of autonomy, traditionalists see it as a closed chain in the service of particular adults' beliefs.

We will later discuss why this ideal of a closed loop is impossible from a practical standpoint, but it should also be recognized as antithetical to "education" in the true sense. It defines education as *omission* rather than *exposure*; it even prizes a certain kind of ignorance. It also depends on the faulty assumption that the only people who will be immediately affected by sex education are the children themselves, leading to the controlled and coordinated bubble that Pam describes. In fact, the state also has obligations to other citizens, who may never enter the educational authority equation as parents. It is not enough to prepare each child for a healthy life, whatever that may be; this must be done in a way that is compatible with the rights of others. When it comes to sexual relationships in particular, Vanessa's health may depend on Michael's education. Parents may not separate their own children from all their peers. Moreover, since being the parent of a school-aged child is not a prerequisite to voting, everyone of voting age in a democracy has a claim to express their interests in the society's approach to sexual health. This casts further doubt on parents' monopoly over sex education.[19]

The state, therefore, has an irreplaceable responsibility for bringing sex education into line with the values that sustain it. This translates into very concrete positions about things like putting a condom on a banana. A free and equal society demands that children be educated about their bodies and given tools for negotiating diversity and assessing their own values, whatever their parents' commitments. Only a democratic, non-denominational state can promote the autonomy of all young people.

Sex Education in the Actual State

Again, this is what liberal theory envisions following from its principles. Governments in many ostensibly liberal societies—notably the United States—have made sex education policy and related laws in ways that *don't* always cap parental authority, *don't* resist deference to one particular religion, and *don't* facilitate the development of sexual autonomy. The guidelines for federal AOUME funding, for example, withhold complete information about sexual health and safer sex, stigmatize or erase LGBTQ+ identities, and teach a conspicuously Christian brand of morality that valorizes chastity and procreation within marriage.[20] Such approaches not only defy the evidence about how to achieve better sexual health outcomes for teens; they also violate the terms of the legitimate exercise of state power in a liberal democracy. Therefore, while the state retains a great degree of educational authority, liberals would say that when it comes to sex education, the state often discharges that authority irresponsibly and in defiance of the liberal rationale for giving it so much power in the first place.

Florida policy in the early 2000s is a prime example of how federal and state actors collaborated to streamline funding and educational authority in the service of AOUME.[21] The state accepted all the available federal funding for AOUME and then some, including "from other federal programs designed to support families living in poverty," and more than matched it with state funds.[22] They used the money to develop a far-reaching abstinence-only campaign called It's Great to Wait.[23] Teachers who didn't stay on message were hit with lawsuits, in some cases leading to their termination, such as the teacher who dared to do a condom demonstration.[24] This use of state power to compel a uniform program of abstinence-only education makes it virtually impossible for other educational authorities to have an influence.[25]

Democracy, however, provides mechanisms for holding the state accountable when it strays from its own mission. In recent years, legal challenges have been mounted against governments around North America based on the unconstitutionality of sex education policies. Sex education advocates around the country celebrated when the Clovis United School District in California failed a "historic" legal challenge to its abstinence-only education program in 2015.[26] The ruling was made possible thanks to California's 2003 law that requires that sexual health education in schools be "medically accurate and objective."[27] Such unambiguous language may be necessary to protect sex education at the policy level, even if the written and unwritten norms of the liberal state ought to do so implicitly.

In a democracy, the boundaries between "the state" and the individuals and groups within it are meant to be porous—ideally, perhaps, non-existent. But the liberal state also has to abide by principles that are supposed to be impervious to political pressure. In a democracy that is *not* liberal, a majority of citizens could compel the government to discriminate against a minority without contradiction. But in a liberal democracy, discrimination is itself identified as an unacceptable use of state power. To this extent there is a good argument for the state to have broad authority over sex education that promotes, as Gutmann says, "non-repression and non-discrimination," even over the objections of other authority holders.[28]

PARENTS

But wait. Surely this line of reasoning is inexcusably dismissive of parents' rights to control their children's education. How can the law simultaneously enshrine parents' authority to educate their children as they choose and also override parental objections to state curricula?

Parents' Rights and Children's Interests

A formidable thinker once said, "The well educating of their children is so much the duty and concern of parents, and the welfare and prosperity of the nation so much depends on it, that I would have every one lay it seriously to heart."[29] That thinker was John Locke, one of the main originators of liberal theory, to whom contemporary libertarians are particularly indebted. You don't have to be a parent to sympathize with this view. Advocates of parents' rights tend to think that parents are the most important educational authority, and that their views should hold more weight than those of other stakeholders. The hyperbolic version of this view is what Gutmann calls the "State of Families" (in contrast with the "Family State"), which "places educational authority exclusively in the hands of the parents."[30]

If paternalism, or the interference in someone else's liberty for their own good, is associated etymologically with parenting, then presumably the justification for parental authority over their children is that it's good for children. The strongest arguments for parental authority are thus labeled "paternalistic" arguments. In this line of thinking, parents are best positioned to advance their children's interests because, for example, they know their children best, they have invested the most in their children, and children respond best to authority that is paired with love and attachment.[31] It is fair to say that most parents have their children's interests at heart and are reasonably adept at pursuing them.

The only reason the story doesn't end right here is because everyone can think of cases in which parents flagrantly violate their children's interests. This is why we have children's aid agencies: to rescue children from abusive families. Importantly, then, paternalist arguments show that sometimes it is best for children if their parents are constrained by other authorities. As we will see, sex education makes a particularly strong case for such constraints even in the absence of any particular abuse.

But there are also "non-paternalistic" arguments for giving parents broad authority over children under normal circumstances—that is, justifications for parental rights that aren't based only on children's interests.[32] For most people, parenting is a reflection of their *own* interests in living a certain kind of life. They are more than servants to the masters of their children's interests; they are full-fledged individuals for whom children may constitute an important part of a fulfilling life. This non-paternalistic rationale for parents' rights says that parents have the right to *express* themselves through their parenting just as free adults can express themselves in countless other ways without interference.[33] The "expressivist" argument has roots in the liberal ideal of individualism and also helps to check the threat of undue intervention into families.[34] For if the *only* criterion for allocating authority over children were the promotion of children's interests, then we might favor collective child-rearing or other non-parental models if they had some benefit to children's well-being.[35]

With the responsibility of parenting comes a significant amount of discretion to induct children into one's own way of life and to make choices that will close some of the doors in the vast hallway of human choices. We can't fault parents for (generally) wanting their children to embrace most of what they value, or for sometimes making parenting choices that redound most immediately to their own interests. If we care about freedom, then the interests of parents matter too, even if they are constrained by children's interests. Moreover, the two kinds of interests are interdependent: often, what is good for children *is* also good for their parents, and vice versa. But who is to decide when they come apart, and where to set the threshold for external intervention into that intimate relationship?

Some philosophers think that parents should have exclusive educational authority over their children; this group comes closest to endorsing the "State of Families" and was more prominent a generation ago.[36] Most philosophers in the last forty years, however, have endorsed some liberal interpretation of parental authority, according to which children's well-being is the limiting condition for parents' rights.[37] For example, Harry Brighouse and Adam Swift argue: "Parents' rights and duties . . . are entirely fiduciary. Parents have just those rights and duties with respect to their children that it is in their children's interests for them to have."[38] Others argue that it is inaccurate to use the language of "rights" at all in this context and that we should speak of parents having "privileges" or "interests" rather than rights with respect to their children, or speak only of children's rights.[39] Despite important differences between these views, the liberal intuition here is that parents' freedom to raise their children has to be defined in some relation to their children's present or future freedom.

This means that, while parents have *de facto* authority over their children's education according to most theorists, as well as international consensus,[40] parents can't use their children *simply* as a means to express or pursue whatever they think is good with no regard for their children's interests. We therefore need to ask: Are parents' choices about sex education aligned with children's interests?

Let's consider a few examples of parents' attitudes toward sexuality and sex education that may be consequential for young people's interests. Take abstinence. As we've seen, the promotion of abstinence until marriage permeates sex education (including Comprehensive Sex Education!) and commands the lion's share of available funding, but 97% of Americans have sex before marriage.[41] Are parents entitled to prefer and to communicate their expectation that their children stay virgins until they get married?

On the face of it, of course they are. Sexual behavior falls under the heading of moral and cultural upbringing, over which parents have dominion. In some communities, premarital sex or relationships bring shame not only on the young people involved, but also on the whole family. Having abstinent children may grant parents social status, religious satisfaction, less cause to worry about their children's safety and health, and plain old psychological comfort. Secular and liberal parents as well as their more traditional counterparts may find the prospect of their children being sexually active legitimately undesirable or unthinkable.[42] While it would certainly be wrong in a free society for parents to completely control their adolescents' movements or, say, spy on their relationships, communicating a strong preference for abstinence seems to fall squarely within parents' purview.

All these considerations may motivate parents to support AOUME and to echo the expectation of abstinence in their homes. (Even if they know the statistics, they can always hope to be in the lucky 3%!) Is this a case of justified paternalism? Some might say it depends on whether abstinence actually is the only right choice for teens. Let us grant for the sake of argument that it may be. Nonetheless, even if abstinence *were* ideal for all teens, we know that AOUME does not prevent teens from being sexually active.[43] It does, however, reduce the likelihood that they will use protection and seek sexual health care. This can't be good for them *or* their fearful parents. But authorities other than parents may be very well positioned to recognize these risks and perform a more accurate cost-benefit analysis. Parents' interests in abstinence may actually get in the way of what is best for their children, not to mention their own interests as parents.

Another highly sensitive topic in sex education is what is known as "porn literacy." At first blush it seems completely reasonable for parents to declare that no one should be allowed to discuss, or even acknowledge the existence of, sexually graphic material with their adolescent (or pre-adolescent) children.

But research shows that digital pornography has completely saturated kids' world, and many adolescents are accessing it, intentionally or unintentionally, by middle school.[44] Data from a large-scale survey in 2017 showed that "half as many parents thought their 14- and 18-year-olds had seen porn as had in fact watched it."[45] This is a generational divide that confirms just how much things have changed since young people's access to porn consisted of a *Penthouse* magazine stashed under a mattress.

Unsurprisingly, most parents don't want to talk to their kids about porn and don't want anyone else to either. Some parents insist that they have sheltered their children so thoroughly that such education can only be justified for *other* people's kids—the ones with smartphones and no curfew.[46] This isolationist stance is increasingly unrealistic in the interconnected world we live in: if your kid doesn't have a smartphone, one of his or her friends will. But even more cosmopolitan parents may bristle at the idea of porn education, which they see as a violation of children's innocence. Leaving aside the questionable trope of "innocence," this view is sadly out of touch. In reality, children are harmed by their parents' silence and the enduring taboos about an increasingly ubiquitous source of sexual misinformation.

On these and other important topics, parents' sincere preferences and children's interests can come apart.[47] There are legitimate debates to be had about the optimal time and manner in which to broach sexual topics, and these may vary slightly with each family or community. The upshot remains that parents are not as omniscient or benevolent on the topic of sex education as they may claim to be. Notice that there are at least two ways that parental decisions about sex education can fail the paternalism test. First, parents may think they know what is best for their children and strive to act out of genuine paternalistic regard, but lack the information to make good choices or be too distracted by wishful thinking to respond to evidence. Second, parents may have inadequate regard for their children's sexual and emotional health because they prioritize such factors as their own comfort, community judgment, or prudishness about sex. Either way, the risks to children's well-being are significant enough that parental authority over sex education should not go unchecked.

Religious Freedom

Some parents articulate their views about sex education not in terms of "parental rights" (which, as noted, is not a legal concept) but in terms of "freedom of religion." Religious commitments, after all, anchor many of the values that parents consult when forming opinions about their children's education and about sexual morality. Most liberal societies have robust commitments to the protection of religion, and for good reason.[48] As we know, however, religion is not always so liberal when it comes to sexuality. So what happens when a liberal freedom is invoked to exercise authority that may diminish children's freedom?

Independent people may subject themselves to all sorts of voluntary constraints in the name of faith. When religious parents make choices about their children's education, however, the lines between the parents' religious freedom and their children's sexual freedom may be blurred. In extreme examples, children may be held to rigid codes of abstinence-only conduct and segregated by gender for their entire upbringing, while also being deprived of any education about what to expect on their wedding night. Children in closed environments frequently lack any framework to recognize or report sex abuse, which thrives in hierarchical religious enclaves. Young people who are suspected of being LGBTQ+ may be subjected to conversion therapy and told their lives are unlivable. Girls can be raised to see themselves as baby-makers who have no choice about when or how often to reproduce. Child marriage and polygamy still continue in some communities. Parents who attempt to escape an extreme sect may have their children permanently taken away from them because of a legal preference for securing continuity in the children's environment.[49]

We should be alarmed by these phenomena and refuse to let adults' freedom of religion overshadow the right to sexual self-determination for those children born into such reclusive communities. For the most part, however, the relationship between parents' religious freedom and children's freedom is less cut-and-dried. Parents who seek to opt their children out of sex education, or endorse illiberal values about sexuality, may partially constrain their children's autonomy, but not to the extent that state interference is warranted.[50] Liberal philosophers disagree about whether the state can support religious schooling or religiously motivated homeschooling, and these debates have important consequences for sex education.[51] Moreover, the sensitive questions of religious upbringing can be compounded by the blurry lines between religion and "culture," to which there is no guaranteed right of free expression. This challenge surfaces especially among recent immigrants to the West, whose societies of origin may have comparatively restrictive attitudes toward sex education, and whose views may be challenged on racist grounds while the identical views when voiced by white people enjoy religious protection.[52]

As we saw in the last chapter, there is no way of thoroughly excluding religious or cultural views from decision-making about sex education, and the state would be wrong to try.[53] Yet while parents have the right to religious expression, they do not have additional rights as parents to deprive children of their own religious freedom, nor may they use religion as a shield from the general requirements of providing for their children's health and well-being. Religion is too easily used as an alibi for the perpetuation or exculpation of predatory and discriminatory behaviors. But religion can also be invoked to support the aims of sexual health education. As we saw in chapter 3, liberal religious groups such as Unitarians were among the first to implement the National Guidelines for CSE released in 1991. Many religious leaders and organizations have stood up for the rights of sex and gender minorities, denounced sexual abuse within their ranks, and defended the right to factual information and reproductive health care. They are important partners with families and schools.[54] Since parental authority over children's education is inevitably informed by religious authority, it is important to recognize these shared aims and the ability for religious cultures to change.

EXPERTS

Both the state and the family have obvious authority over aspects of children's education, but both are also flawed. They may misdiagnose children's interests or prioritize other interests at their expense. Where, then, is the authority that is "motivated solely, or at least predominately, by the interests of children"?[55] In many people's minds, the most neutral and qualified authorities on sex education are the "experts"—people who specialize in sexual health and sex education and have no conflicting investments in children being taught a particular curriculum or value system. Even if perfect neutrality is a myth, such professionals provide a necessary check against the obviously biased instincts of parents and publicly elected officials.

One kind of expert is the schoolteacher who has, presumably, been trained to provide sex education through both subject matter expertise and pedagogical certification. Teachers specialize in delivering curriculum in age-appropriate ways, mindful of different learning styles and sensitive to students' larger contexts. They spend more time with children than some of their parents do and perform many educational tasks that parents are happy to delegate. When it comes to most subjects, like math or Spanish, almost no one calls into question the teacher's authority to deliver the material. When it comes to sex education, of course, nothing is that simple.

Sex education is usually crammed reluctantly into another subject area, such as physical education, and many of the teachers charged with sex education have little to no specific training in that area. They may even still be working through the stigma and confusion about sex they inherited as students.

Studies of teachers have shown that many are woefully unprepared to cover sex education—in one British study, "three-quarters of respondents had not received up-to-date information regarding sexually transmitted infections"[56]—and this inadequate preparation makes them feel uncomfortable about teaching it, regardless of their views about its importance.[57]

Furthermore, however qualified and enthusiastic teachers may be, the adversarial climate we have been examining can be a major deterrent to wading into already touchy territory. Teachers are given their marching orders by multiple layers of educational bureaucracy and can face judgment or even professional sanctions for exercising too much discretion. (Remember the Florida teacher who was fired for doing a condom demonstration.) Teachers are acutely aware of these pressures and risks. As one teacher educator put it, "The interest is not in such potentially provocative issues as safer sex but in safer teaching."[58] When teachers feel muzzled, they cannot do whatever is necessary to meet children's best interests.

What about other experts? Traveling medical personnel like public health nurses can provide valuable assistance to overwhelmed teachers and are appropriate authorities for students to approach with health questions. But the definition of "expert" is distressingly flexible; in some schools, the outside "experts" are full-time abstinence-only preachers who bear the imprimatur of the state even as they disseminate scientifically inaccurate "information." For example, school boards can outsource sex education to avowedly religious groups that double as anti-choice "pregnancy crisis centers," such as Life Choices.[59] Because they are "experts," whereas the teachers are apparently not, it can be much harder to push back against the content of these presentations.[60] Nancy Kendall observed that teachers became extremely passive during these visits, "allowing everything said by all outside experts to pass without comment."[61] These kinds of stories only highlight the importance of ensuring that full-time teachers are themselves authorities on sex education. Without appropriate teacher capacity, schools can neither deliver essential health curriculum themselves nor confidently delegate it to anyone else.

In the last chapter, we looked at the role of evidence in designing sex education that will achieve common aims. Evidence comes from another kind of expert: researchers. Surely, scientists have the most authority on critical components of sex education such as the latest knowledge about contraception and sexually transmitted infections. Meanwhile, social scientists who study sex education—many of them referenced in these pages—provide crucial evidence about such topics as the effectiveness of educational programs, the sexual behavior of adolescents, and the dynamics of policy-making and school governance. Whoever else is involved in sex education, these experts are irreplaceable. Their authority, however, is usually recognized at the pleasure of policy makers, who may have vested interests in ignoring the evidence.

Put together, teachers, health care providers, and researchers are a locus of educational authority that can be easily sidelined by a system that concentrates power in the hands of selected parents and state officials.[62] From a paternalistic lens, these experts are much better situated to advance children's interests related to sex education than most other authorities for two reasons. First, in their professional roles, they are less likely to have motivations that may interfere with their assessment of what children need.[63] Second, even compared with other benevolent actors, they have a better foundation for covering this material and answering students' questions. Good sex education requires concrete knowledge and skills, not just good wishes and anecdotes.

CHILDREN

Our discussion of educational authority so far has focused on paternalistic agents who act in the putative interests of children.[64] In their best form, the battles between the state, the family, and educational experts proceed on this territory. Children's rights advocates have long asserted that children's interests comprise a discrete category of rights, which means that they are entitled to certain protections regardless of what other interests may conflict with them—including parents' interests.[65] A shining example of this conviction is the 1989 UN Convention on the Rights of the Child. It refers to the "best interests of the child" six times, making it the common reference point for all adults who might ever exercise authority over children.[66] The right to comprehensive and factual sex education has also been affirmed by medical, legal, and human-rights authorities around the world.[67]

Despite the centrality of children's interests in making sane decisions about sex education, adults' interpretations of their interests typically substitute for children's actual input. Researchers and children's advocates have pointed out that this oversight is impractical, if not also unethical. Michael Halstead and Michael Reiss argue: "If children tell us about the sexual understandings and values they have already picked up, this helps us to predict how they will experience and interpret the sex education they are given."[68] Even in a perfect paternalistic system, adult decision makers need information from children in order to best meet their interests.

But some advocates go further and ask why all of children's interests should be entrusted to the protection of adults. The point of education is to facilitate children's growth into autonomous adults who make their own decisions; there is no magical, abrupt transition from being a wholly dependent child to being a fully independent grown-up. At some point, then, children must be able to begin to assert their own interests, even in defiance of the adults who ostensibly protect them.[69] As children's rights advocate Howard Cohen argues, "The very adults who are engaged in the conflict are usually the adults who determine what the child's best interest is. And it is obviously in *their* interest to deny the conflict."[70] Such conflicts are not hard to imagine in the realm of sex education. Adolescent wants comprehensive and factual sex education. Adult objects. Adult wins, citing adolescent's best interests.[71]

So even if paternalism is the correct standard for most educational decisions, the argument falters as children approach adulthood. Philosopher Eamonn Callan asks, "Are students at all levels of schooling so egregiously immature that they are not even fit to be consulted about their own curriculum? I think the answer to this is obvious."[72] Adults' interpretations of children's best interests must yield to young people's own interpretations, or to what we have evidence to believe they would choose for themselves.[73] And when it comes to sex education, there is plenty of evidence for young people's preferences.

First, children around the world tell us that they want more school-based sex education.[74] While it is possible to dismiss some of these demands as false consciousness (children not knowing what is in fact good for them), salaciousness brought on by hormones, or knee-jerk youthful rebellion, the chorus becomes harder to ignore as it grows in size and age. When Ontario's Comprehensive Sex Education curriculum was repealed in 2018, a sixteen-year-old student organized a school walkout that drew forty thousand students from over one hundred schools. This wasn't an elaborate scheme to play hooky; students articulately explained the need for informed discussions in their schools about such topics as consent, LGBTQ+ issues, and contraception.[75] There is no reason to regard their civic action as any less legitimate than that of adults who have been failed by other state services.[76]

Second, kids have creative ways of resisting imposed ignorance. In one study, researchers separated students into an "intervention" (sex-educated) group and a "non-intervention" (not educated) group; they had their findings "contaminated" by the fact that the first group kept sharing what they had learned with latter.[77] Students have also been known to rip up the letters sent home to warn their parent of upcoming material, subverting the opportunity for parental opt-outs. These behaviors appear insubordinate only in a context that denies teenagers' ability to assert their own educational interests.

Some still consider it patronizing to consult young people about their interests in sex education and then expect them to be merely passive recipients of whatever adults decide on. The "student voice" movement sees "speaking out" as just the first step on a ladder of student participation that culminates in shared "decision-making" and "implementation" of educational actions, both at the level of school governance and curriculum design.[78] Indeed, as we saw in chapter 3, students have shown themselves to be capable of coordinating sex education without waiting for adults to grant it to them. It would be disingenuous and self-defeating to deny these students' efficacy as their own kind of educational authority.

Student authority is not a new concept. Experimental schools in early twentieth-century Britain and North America pushed the bounds of how much authority could be shared with—or completely ceded to—children. At the Summerhill boarding school in England, started by the radical reformer A. S. Neill, there were no exams of any kind, lessons themselves were optional, the afternoons were completely unprogrammed and unsupervised, and all school decisions were made strictly democratically, with each student and staff member having one vote. Neill wrote: "Every older pupil at Summerhill knows . . . that I approve of a full sex life for all who wish one."[79] Neill reported that there was never a pregnancy at his school, and that students left with healthier attitudes toward sex than any of their regularly schooled peers.

The image of hundreds of children running amok—and possibly having sex!—with little to no adult oversight steels most people against any proposal to increase "student authority" in schools; and to be fair, not all experiments are remembered as fondly as Neill remembers his. We need not go to such extremes, however, to correct for a restrictive bias in sex education. Our propensity to exclude children from meaningful participation in sex education says more about our own comfort than about children's interests and competence. It is significant that *almost no one* ever reflects, as an adult, that they wish they had been given *less* sex education.[80] The fact that many adults want to restrict children's sex education defies all reasonable predictions about what these children will later wish had been chosen for them when they were still hostage to adults' authority.

DISTRIBUTING AUTHORITY AND RESOLVING CONFLICTS

Let's recap. A state with too much educational authority can mean residential schools and forced family separation. Parents with too much educational authority can mean children who are prisoners to the family they happened to be born into. Teachers can flounder; experts may be disconnected from the pressures on policy makers; and children want power but still look to adults for education. The one conclusion that can be easily drawn here is that there should be no single "boss" when it comes to sex education.

Obviously, authority over sex education has to be distributed among the relevant stakeholders, but it is a separate question how this distribution ought to look.[81] One way of approaching this puzzle is to draw distinctions between the different roles each type of authority figure can play. We have been treating "authority" as a single category and focusing on how it can be deployed to serve different people's interests. But the notion of educational authority can be broken down into further types: the authority to teach is not the same as the authority to design curriculum, for example, and the authority to shape particular children's opportunities is not the same as the authority to determine educational policy for all children. The various stakeholders in children's education can occupy complementary roles in this picture.

Consider the authority to teach. When parents oppose school-based sex education by asserting their authority as parents, they frequently intend to position themselves as the proper *providers* of sex education as well as the ones who should decide what their children learn. Yet having someone's interests at heart doesn't necessarily make you the best person to fulfill them. Parents who withdraw their children from sex education at school, who homeschool, or who turn to resources such as Focus on the Family's "Talking about Sex and Puberty"[82] may promise to cover this subject, but research suggests they don't follow through.[83] Even well-intentioned parents may be ignorant of their children's actual exposure to sexually explicit material, the age at which adolescents become sexually active, the effectiveness of abstinence-only education, how various methods of contraception work, and other important topics.[84] These are not promising qualities in a sexual health teacher.

What parents *can* do is use their authority to teach children about the moral and cultural dimensions of human relationships, provide clear expectations, and learn along with their children from qualified sex educators and health care providers. In other words, they can supplement and contextualize sex education in accordance with their values. Experts recommend this complementary division of labor, and most schoolteachers embrace it.[85] This type of involvement honors parents' irreplaceable role in their children's education without allowing them to wield unilateral control over the provision or withholding of sexual health information.[86]

The authority to deliver school-based sex education should reside with various qualified teachers. Teachers are pedagogical experts who are trained in their subject areas and removed enough from students' family lives to provide disinterested guidance on sensitive issues. Unfortunately, as we've seen, teachers are not always as well prepared to provide sex education as they need to be, and medical experts are not always the best teachers. The authority to teach can only be effectively discharged when the appropriate structural supports are in place. Teachers need regular training and professional development on the full range of issues in sex education if they are to deliver the material; more importantly, perhaps, they need the political and institutional backing to meet their students' needs without fear of reprisal.

The authority to teach is different from the authority to make education policy. Curriculum is usually designed, not by teachers, but by a separate set of authorities who are either appointed by the state or hired by private companies. The proper stakeholders to fulfill this role are "experts"—researchers, health care providers, scientists, child psychologists, and other professionals who gather and interpret evidence about how to best promote children's sexual health and development.[87] But these experts do not have the authority to tell teachers how to teach, or parents how to parent. They have separate domains.

The state's role is to coordinate all these authorities and to ensure that sex education meets the basic standards required of a liberal democratic society. This involves training and funding teachers and experts; synthesizing different kinds of evidence; assessing legal and bureaucratic considerations that may be invisible to other stakeholders; evaluating and reviewing policies on a regular basis; delivering education in nonsectarian and nondiscriminatory ways; and ultimately ensuring the protection of sexual autonomy and public health, even when it may not be politically expedient.

Children—especially older ones—can be involved in all of these steps, but they shouldn't have to teach themselves the way the YELL kids did in the 1980s and 1990s. Although children are often capable of pursuing their own interests, effective sex education will preempt them most of the time, rather than leave them scrambling to fill in gaps and overcome shame or guilt. Adults may disagree on what is in children's interests, but we certainly know enough to get started. Children should become increasingly involved in the design and evaluation of sex education as they get older, without having to cut school and storm legislatures. Young people can also support each other as friends and direct each other to the most helpful adults.

In short, effective sex education is a team effort. Unfortunately, the team doesn't always want to play together. We may recognize that multiple people have some claim to being the boss, but sometimes there can only be one.

Before closing this chapter, let's look at a common conflict of authority: when parents oppose state-mandated sex education curricula.

Under ordinary circumstances, state curricula can be enforced without explicit parental permission. But to return to an ongoing theme, some may regard sex education as *different* in such a way that the normal reasoning just doesn't apply. Sex is the most intimate topic, and one need not be an opponent of state education in general to feel that it is properly dealt with by the people with whom a child is most intimate. Perhaps there are some areas that must ultimately be left to the discretion of children's first educators, even if others could theoretically do a better job.

Liberal principles advise a universal program of Comprehensive Sex Education that still recognizes parents as authorities, especially on anything that touches the no-fly zones of religion and morality. This intuition seems to underpin the widespread practice of granting exemptions to sex education, even in public schools, for children whose parents oppose the curriculum.[88] Selected absences from discussions about sexuality are an exception to every norm of school attendance and academic completion; imagine a parent saying, "My child will be skipping today's lesson on fractions because it offends my sensibilities." Yet courts have repeatedly accepted the same rationale for exempting students from sex education.[89]

Liberal philosophers may also favor the provision of opt-outs for pragmatic reasons. When parents feel their values cannot be fairly accommodated in the public system, they are more likely to switch their children to private systems or homeschooling, which defeats the liberal goal of common education altogether. Many view exemptions as a reasonable trade-off for keeping the children of very traditional or illiberal parents in common schools most of the time.[90] This is not the same as agreeing that parents really ought to have the last word on sex education, however; it is a compromise view that attempts to resolve an otherwise never-ending tug-of-war between authorities.

While the standard move here is to defer to parents, if sex education really is a special category, we could just as easily reason in the other direction. I have argued that parents are not necessarily more legitimate educational authorities than others; their hopes for their children's sexuality and cultural or religious identity may in fact disqualify them from properly assessing what is in their children's best interests. The discrepancy between children's interests and parents' interests may be wider here than on most issues. Furthermore, parents, unlike detached schools, have the possibility of exclusively indoctrinating children into worldviews that are sexually harmful. Consequently, all else being equal, the authority question should be ruled *against* parents in case of conflict: an appropriately constrained state should ensure mandatory sex education that prioritizes children's developing autonomy.[91] Such policies already prevail in places like Germany, Denmark, and Finland.

CONCLUSION

Children are owed a basic minimum of sex education. No authority figure—including their parents—should have the ability to deprive them of the opportunity for sexual health and sexual autonomy. Our vision of Democratic Humanistic Sexuality Education, elaborated at the end of the next chapter, is one in which young people learn from a variety of formal and informal educators, and their interests are nurtured with the help of caring others. School curriculum is the most obvious way to guarantee that everyone is exposed to some evidence-based sex education. But that is a far cry from concluding that we should put all our sex education eggs into the school curriculum basket. What are schools for, anyway?

CHAPTER 6

What Are Schools For?

One would be justified in assuming that a book about "sex education" would focus on formal schooling, and, indeed, our focus throughout this book has been on the effort to introduce sex education into schools and the ensuing debates about what belongs on the curriculum. But the nature of schooling itself is often assumed within discussions of sex education. We sometimes forget that schools are contingent institutions. Historically, education has not been transmitted only, or even primarily, in schools, and schools have not been the whirlwind of ringing bells and high-stakes standardized tests that we know today.

We have already discussed how one key aspect of ethical controversy over sex education, the question of authority, doubles as a battle over location: some conservative-minded people believe that sex education is the purview of parents, and therefore it belongs not in schools but at home. Yet it is not only more traditional critics who have raised questions about the compatibility of sex education and schooling.[1] To equate "education" with "schooling" already presupposes certain views about the meaning of education and where it happens. The aims of schooling itself are as much a question for philosophy of education as the aims of any particular subject or teaching method. We should not take for granted that everything worth learning can be optimally delivered within the idiosyncratic institution of contemporary schooling.

The phrase "sex education" also implies that we know what sex is and what it would mean to teach it. This, too, is a peculiarly modern, culturally specific, conceit. The clashing positions on sex education obviously hinge on sexual values. But the problem goes deeper than that. Sex is not a set of propositions that can be committed to memory, much less a predictable process that can be learned in a laboratory. So what do we think we are doing when we design school-based sex curriculum? And how is "sex" taught in schools alongside, or even in spite of, the official curriculum?

In this chapter, I frame some of the controversies over sex education as a question of what we can, and ought, to expect of schools in the world we live in. Attitudes about the aims of schooling have implications for when, where, and how we teach sex education. I begin with some healthy skepticism about sex education as a school-based enterprise, with help from the theorist Michel Foucault. The lesson is not to give up on schools, but to reflect critically on both their potential and their limitations as sites of sex education. The next section reviews six ideas about the aims of schooling: democratic citizenship, humanistic or individual flourishing, economic success, social reproduction, social transformation, and public health and population control. Each aim corresponds to certain recommendations about sex education. In the third section, I look at the informal sex education that young people are receiving outside of school, focusing on four paradoxes in the contemporary cultural landscape: porn/purity, feminism/post-feminism, failing boys/toxic masculinity, and bad media/good media. I argue that these features of young people's lives and educational experiences ought to instruct us about the purpose of schooling as it relates to sexuality.

At the end of this chapter, I outline our vision of Democratic Humanistic Sexuality Education (DHSE). This framework elevates the democratic and humanistic aims of schooling over other possible aims and responds to both historical lessons and contemporary realities. Rather than arguing for some permanent or universal curriculum, DHSE stresses the importance of sex education that is informed by evidence and promotes freedom and equality for all. Furthermore, it requires changes to the place of sex education in the curriculum, assessment practices, school policies, and teacher training.

STUCK IN *SCIENTIA SEXUALIS*

A standing red herring about sex education in schools is that what might be taught is *sex* as we usually employ the word—the act of physical intimacy in pursuit of pleasure. Laughable though it may seem, some particularly mistrustful parents have worried that mentioning "masturbation" on a curriculum means that children will actually be invited to masturbate in class. (At least, this is *usually* laughable; one saucy exception is covered later in the chapter.) More abstractly, many opponents of school-based sex education contend that learning about sex in class will encourage students to try it outside of class. (It doesn't.)

In fact, what is taught as sex education in most Western schools today is everything *but* sex. We teach about biology, about health and disease, and in the more ambitious curricula perhaps about media and ethics. As noted in chapter 4, the political poles on sex education remain strikingly aligned on the aims and framing of the material: sex education is information about things surrounding actual sex acts, with the intention of reducing harms and pregnancy, if not sex itself. This is not how we normally teach. Abstinence-only education is particularly paradoxical in this sense; it is akin to teaching Spanish by saying, "Some people speak Spanish, and perhaps one day you will, but right now stay as far away as possible from all things Spanish."

These ideas about the meaning of "sex education" are all derivative of the paradigm that Michel Foucault, in his influential book *The History of Sexuality*, dubbed *scientia sexualis* (literally, "the science of sex"). This modern European take on human sexuality came of age during massive scientific and political revolutions. Sex was codified, medicalized, and monitored in newfound institutions, like clinics and prisons, and subjected to Christian protocols of confession and penitence.[2] The "truths" of sex were defined and circulated very differently in most human civilizations both before the Enlightenment and outside of Europe. In other cultures, "truth is drawn from pleasure itself, understood as a practice and accumulated as experience."[3] Foucault calls this approach *ars amoris* (literally, "the art of love"). Sex "education" here has nothing to do with blackboards, priests, or lab coats. Think Kama Sutra and *Fifty Shades of Grey*. Needless to say, no matter how sex-positive it may be, school-based sex education makes no sense in this paradigm.

In *scientia sexualis*, by contrast, schools and other institutions are the essential condition for managing young people's sexuality, and this management is at least as much the purpose of the institution as its ostensibly educational aims. In secondary schools of the eighteenth century, "one can have the impression that sex was hardly spoken of at all," Foucault writes. "But one only has to glance over the architectural layout, the rules of discipline, and their whole internal organization: the question of sex was a constant preoccupation."[4] Specifically, they were obsessed with stopping onanism—an old-fashioned word for masturbation.

Foucault's genealogy helpfully reframes important questions about sex education today. He shows that schools can be preoccupied with sex even when they aren't explicitly talking about it, and that children are constantly receiving messages and admonitions about their sexuality through a variety of indirect cues. This is what we now call the "informal curriculum" or the "hidden curriculum."[5] He also pushes us to think about what kind of "knowledge" sex education purports to supply, and to what ends. When we look at these questions more carefully, it turns out that our settled attitudes about the meaning of sex education could be very different.

In schools, students listen to teachers and demonstrate their mastery of information through various assessments. Since the defeat of Family Life Education in the 1970s, sex education has survived by adhering to the least controversial, "just the facts" approach. Sex is sanitized by making the body into an object of study, as in the biological sciences, which meet the gold standard of "truth." There is little to no room for "ambiguity,"[6] confusion, vulnerability, or affect of any kind.[7] In a marked contrast with *ars amoris*, pleasure is conspicuously avoided in this construction of sexual knowledge, even as it is the specter that gives sex education its *frisson* of the illicit. Critics have been complaining for decades about this gap. The omission of pleasure in sex education is thought to be particularly detrimental for girls, who are already discouraged from expressing their desires and are shamed for acknowledging that they have sexual appetites, which can lead to unsatisfying and nonconsensual sexual encounters.[8] But these worries are beside the point if the purpose of sex education is to prevent students from having it.

The focus on memorizing the risks of sexual activity is wrong for another reason, too: it assumes a direct line from knowing facts to behaving certain ways. But this is patently false: young people who earn good grades in health class may still experience unwanted pregnancy, sexual violence, and the spread of disease. If sexual health were a simple matter of applying factual knowledge to real life, sex education could virtually eradicate these outcomes. This could be why many young people turn for knowledge about sexuality to their friends, slightly older youths, or popular media, even though they acknowledge the prevalence of misinformation in these sources.[9] They also ask for information about pregnancy, parenthood, and abortion,[10] all of which are taboo as long as out-of-wedlock pregnancy is construed as socially unacceptable and rationally preventable.

Another conceit of formal curriculum is that everything has to be standardized. Curriculum theorists note that standardized education leads to problematic exclusions and naturalizes particular organizations of knowledge ("in history we study this . . . in science we study this . . ."). Furthermore, we group students into grades based only on their biological age, as though this made them identical as learners. This type of categorization is particularly ludicrous in the realm of sex education, since any given group of adolescents at the same age will likely include sexually precocious students as well as those who are disinterested, embarrassed, or sexually atypical compared to their peers. No set of guidelines for sex education at the bureaucratic level will pitch it just right for everyone.

Cramming sex into the logic of schools therefore distorts realities about both sex and learning. Our contemporary notions about the meaning of sex education are steeped in a European knowledge paradigm that enshrines particular ways of doing business. And as we saw in the first chapter, sex education was initially designed to protect racist and classist conceptions of heterosexual virtue. Although our stated aims have evolved, studies find that sex education continues to alienate and misrecognize students who were not included in this original circle of concern, especially Black, Hispanic, Indigenous, non-Christian, and queer students, as well as students with disabilities, many of whom already have an ambivalent relationship to formal institutions.[11]

There is one other major strike against school-based sex education that deserves special mention. As noted in previous chapters, some schools have themselves been used as vehicles for sexual abuse. The same institutional features that enable coordinated education can also be exploited by those who desire access to children, and such access has been sickeningly systematized in certain places, especially at schools with religious missions or colonial agendas, resulting in an intergenerational cycle of trauma and, in some cases, justified wariness regarding state schooling of any kind.[12] Now, there are many steps we can and must take to minimize the risk of such abuses, but even after doing our best to make today's schools safe and salubrious, the trauma of past atrocities that took place in schools cannot be designed out of existence. For some communities, the promise of "culturally sensitive" sex education is nothing short of insulting.

POSSIBLE AIMS OF SCHOOLING

This quick Foucauldian analysis reveals a paradox. "Sex education" is taken to be virtually synonymous with standardized curriculum delivered in mandatory schooling. But we arrange curriculum and schooling to be completely at odds with sexual development, experience, and pleasure. Not only traditional stakeholders, such as religious parents and homeschoolers, but also the most critical researchers and progressive sex educators have expressed doubts about the compatibility of sex education and formal schooling. It's possible we've been going about this all wrong.

In the last chapter, I argued that the distribution of authority over sex education requires the involvement of the democratic state and of trained teachers.

This doesn't yet tell us what specific role schools should play in the delivery of sex education—especially when sex education occurs in myriad other venues as well. What are the distinctive goods that schools make possible, and what are their distinctive responsibilities? What are the proper aims of state-organized education? These are ethical questions to which the popular answers evolve over time. Schools cannot do everything for all people. But if we have a clearer idea of what they ought to aim for, we can narrow down what it is reasonable to expect of them and how to avoid the pitfalls they present with respect to sex education specifically.

Philosophers have had a lot to say about the aims of education over the centuries.[13] By "aims" I mean the larger values and goals toward which education is oriented.[14] Aims are not declarations of specific learning outcomes, curricular content, or pedagogical choices; but they provide frameworks that can be used for choosing them.

Here I review the six best candidates for the aims of schooling and see what sex education might look like if it took each aim as primary: (i) democratic citizenship, (ii) humanistic or individual flourishing, (iii) economic success, (iv) social reproduction, (v) social transformation, and (vi) public health and population control.

i. Democratic Citizenship

One of the most prominent views of the aims of schooling in the last century has been the democratic conception.[15] For many contemporary proponents, the overarching justification for schooling is the nurturing of democratic citizenship, and this ideal provides the skeleton of what should happen in schools.[16] This includes civics education—learning political procedures and national history, developing an appreciation for the law and the division of powers—but it extends to all aspects of curriculum.[17] Formal education should aim to cultivate citizens who critically assess information, form and revise their own opinions, exchange ideas in civil ways, and respect the rights of others.[18] Schools, like public life, should be participatory—and emancipatory.[19]

The democratic ideal has influenced much of contemporary educational theory, so much so that its originally provocative qualities may now be invisible. In fact, living up to democratic ideals in education is no easy feat, even if "democracy" now has a breezy ring to it. Critics worry that the values of democratic education have been appropriated by neoliberalism (more on this in a moment), which can make it seem that "freedom" is the state teaching people to be responsible for themselves.

If schools ought to be cultivating citizens who will be able and inclined to participate in a democratic society, then sex education must be oriented toward applying these values to sexual behavior and including sexuality as an essential aspect of responsible citizenship.[20] This framework is endorsed by many sex educators and researchers, and, as we saw in our discussion of the liberal state in chapter 5, it handily justifies the principal tenets of Comprehensive Sex Education.[21] Most sex education in the English-speaking world falls considerably short of this democratic conception.

ii. Humanistic or Individual Flourishing

A similar account of schooling, but one that is worth elaborating in its own right, may be called the humanistic aim. In this view, the primary aim of schooling, like that of education more broadly, should be "the self-fulfillment of the individual," "living a more distinctively human life," "opening visions to new meanings and understandings and (possible) ways of life," or, simply, human "flourishing."[22] More than providing students with skills and content knowledge, education should "attempt to make sense of what it is to be a person, of how one might live a life that is personally fulfilling, of what kind of life is worth living."[23] It is consistent with contemporary movements like "whole-child education" or "holistic education" and resistance to standardized testing.[24] Like the democratic conception, the humanistic one will in practice support liberal arts education and promote critical thinking. The main difference is that if schools' aims are ultimately humanistic, these endeavors are valued as good in themselves, not only as a means of sustaining democracy.[25] For example, philosopher Alasdair MacIntyre defends critical thinking in education because "the critical ability which ought to be the fruit of education serves nothing directly except for itself, no one except those who exercise it."[26] A more modest humanistic aim would be to ensure that schooling helps to "further the development of an individual qua human being" and not violate anyone else's humanity in the process.[27]

The humanistic conception may be linked up with quite diverse attitudes toward sex education. Having no fixed political agenda, the aim of promoting individual flourishing leaves a lot to interpretation. Avoiding sexually transmitted infections may be relevant to flourishing, as is developing loving, fulfilling relationships. As we've seen, conservative proponents of sex education across the decades have often justified their preferences for sex education by talking about what makes for a happy life overall (albeit usually in the context of a heterosexual marriage). Rather than just focusing on abstinence, this humanistic aim can justify the inclusion of topics that go even beyond standard Comprehensive Sex Education, such as the pleasure of sexual intimacy and the wonders of parenthood, or whatever matters to particular students' life aspirations. Humanistic education feeds naturally into some of the more progressive and experimental models of sex education, but it is not exclusive to them.

iii. Economic Success

By far the most familiar aim of contemporary schooling, and the one that provides the starkest contrast with humanism, is the aim of economic success. This discourse has both individual and societal dimensions. On the societal level, schooling is viewed as the great engine of economic growth, the training ground for a generation of productive workers and innovators who will keep their nation competitive and earn money with which to consume more products. In the United States, the rhetoric of international competition took off during the Cold War and is now abetted by the obsessive rankings developed to compare countries according to educational attainment. Although characteristic of the political Right, this is less of a partisan discourse than a globalization discourse, embraced by Democrats and Republicans alike.[28] Schooling is for national success.

At the individual level, schooling can also be envisioned as preparation for each student's economic success. While some humanists and democratic theorists worry about instrumentalizing education in this way, people eventually need livelihoods, and schools are well equipped to help them with that. Much of the philosophical literature about educational aims contrasts humanistic or liberal arts education with "vocational" education (sometimes referred to as "training").[29] This dichotomy is surely oversimplified; we can expect schools to help students learn valuable things *and* secure a future with a livable wage.

The "functional education" trend described in chapter 2 shows how sex education in the midcentury tried to prepare young people for middle-class family life. Under the current economic and cultural model, sex education emphasizes responsible decision-making and self-sufficiency. Following this logic, good sexual subjects, like good employees, manage themselves and absorb the consequences of their actions.[30] In theory, this may include Comprehensive Sex Education, but it has been linked much more clearly with AOUME. As Lauren Clark and Sarah Stitzlein explain, "AOUM [*sic*] proponents argue that abstinence is the only completely safe method of avoiding pregnancy and STIs. . . . Students who choose to have sex have made a wrong, irresponsible decision, and such decisions should not be enabled through publicly funded interventions teaching them how to practice bad decision-making."[31] This attitude has been criticized for blaming victims of sexual assault and further marginalizing racialized and poor youths, who have more social inequalities to overcome in the exercise of "self-sufficiency."[32]

iv. Social Reproduction

What is taught in schools? Things that are already known and valued, of course. Regardless of time and place, schools are concerned with transmitting to a younger generation whatever the older generations have determined to be essential to their civilization. Schools thereby represent, and reproduce, the society into which children are born.[33] This is by no means inherently nefarious. Learning—including in humanistic and democratic accounts—requires being inducted into the wealth of knowledge that has gotten our society to where it is now. Education is "to pass on and develop those ways of knowing and understanding which are the common heritage" and to make this legacy relevant to the new generation.[34] More conservative schooling, however, reproduces this heritage uncritically, along with its unequal distribution of advantages and disadvantages. On the economic side, this is not so much articulated as a conscious aim as it is imputed by critics who think it should be otherwise.[35]

On the values side, reproduction is a very conscious aim. For social conservatives, schools should be in the business of reinforcing traditional beliefs. They are highly skeptical of using schools to promote critical thinking—an exercise that is thought to breed moral relativism and encourage rebellion against the family. In fact, the Texas Republican Party took a stand against it in their 2012 official platform:

> We oppose the teaching of Higher Order Thinking Skills (HOTS) (values clarification), critical thinking skills and similar programs that are simply a relabeling of Outcome-Based Education (OBE) (mastery learning) which focus on behavior modification and have the purpose of challenging the student's fixed beliefs and undermining parental authority.[36]

Because of the perceived incompatibility of current educational trends with the aim of social reproduction, many conservatives believe that schools have lost their way. Hence arises a great deal of advocacy for school choice, homeschooling, and attempts to gird children of religious conservatives for the tests of faith they will face in common schools.

Ironically, despite conservatives' sense that the educational tides are moving against them, we have a pretty good idea of what school-based sex education looks like for this group, because they have been winning the battle for sex education in the United States since about 1981. The AOUME model epitomizes the aim of social reproduction as applied to sex education, with its emphasis on (some might say romanticization of) the patriarchal nuclear family and condemnation of extramarital sex.

v. Social Transformation

In contrast to the aim of social reproduction, many people in the education sector like to think of schools as agents of social transformation. There are more and less radical versions of this view. Historically, compulsory schooling was designed to transform a highly stratified classist society, such as Renaissance England, into one of more equal opportunity. Universal literacy was revolutionary in itself. These days, improving access to quality public education remains one of the best ways to alleviate poverty and inequality, especially in developing countries, and to reduce the gap between rich and poor nations.[37] It helps to reduce suffering for girls and women in particular, boosting health and life expectancy for all. This kind of "transformation" is not especially controversial.

Within affluent nations, however, mandatory schooling as such is no longer enough to transform society. In order to tackle pervasive inequality, school-based education must challenge received ways of thinking, even, perhaps, subverting the institution itself. This kind of cultural transformation is very controversial, as evidenced by fights between educators who see themselves as advancing social justice and critics who say they're "brainwashing" children into radical left-wing politics.[38] So-called "social justice education" goes beyond liberal and democratic aims in education because the existing structures and values are thought to be in need of significant revision.[39]

The connections between sex education and social transformation are obvious to many who advocate more politically inflected versions of the birds and the bees.[40] Through sex education, we can radically revise the way young people think about their bodies and relationships, ushering in a "culture of consent," ending sex-based discrimination and oppression, and even upending failing social institutions like marriage, welfare, and health care. These aims may be pursued by combining the nuts and bolts of regular Comprehensive Sex Education with critical analyses of power and culture, delivered via antiracist, feminist, and decolonial pedagogies. While there is no gold standard for socially transformative sex education, the sentiment is that schools should be doing much more than grudgingly explaining how to use a condom. Rather, sex education should be a form of political education, in which some perspectives are upheld as correct while others are shunned.

vi. Public Health and Population Control

A final aim of schooling to consider is one that may have little to do with education at all. In 2019 the US Centers for Disease Control and Prevention reported that chlamydia cases were up 18%, gonorrhea cases were up 63%, and syphilis cases were up 71% since 2014.[41] Most of these cases were in people aged 15–29. If you want to stop an epidemic of preventable infections among young adults, you naturally look for a place where you can reach all of them efficiently, preferably before too much hanky-panky has occurred. That place is, obviously, schools.

This aim of schooling has a long history. As we saw in chapter 1, sex education was reluctantly introduced into schools because it seemed like the best way to advance "social hygiene" on a population level. Since the early twentieth century, "the public debate in sexuality education has largely centered on the role played by the public schools in the battle against venereal disease."[42] Panic over out-of-wedlock births could be handled through the same means. Notice that this aim can be understood as distinct from the humanistic or liberal aims of schooling, which may promote disease control and planned parenthood as a precondition for self-fulfillment; the aim here is strictly epidemiological. The only problem is our approach doesn't seem to work. In the "battle against venereal disease," venereal disease is winning.

More comprehensive models of sex education, as we saw in chapter 4, are better at disease control. Furthermore, schools can be used as hubs to promote sexual and public health using plain old medical treatment. For example, the HPV (human papillomavirus) vaccine, which immunizes young people against the most virulent strains of the cancer-causing STI, has been offered in schools around the world for over a decade, significantly reducing the incidence of HPV.[43] This is the sexual health equivalent of routine dental exams and lice checks for schoolchildren. Some countries go even further. British schools have experimented with a "Clinic-in a Box," set up next to the school building, run by nurses and offering birth control and pregnancy tests.[44] In Norway, schools are connected with sexual health clinics, where students can access confidential counseling, emergency contraception, gynecological exams, and hormonal birth control—free of cost and without parental permission.[45] Ironically, these direct health care interventions are the least obviously *educational* things that schools do. Yet they may accomplish more of the agreed-upon aims of "sex education" than any curriculum does. Schools provide a natural platform for reaching a whole cohort of people in particular risk categories; this is the public health promoter's dream.

Multiple Aims

Foucault postulated that the treatment of sexuality in schools reflected broader social mandates. He asked whether "all this garrulous attention which has us in a stew over sexuality" was not "motivated by one basic concern: to ensure population, to reproduce labor capacity, to perpetuate the form of social relations, in short, to constitute a sexuality that is economically useful and politically conservative?"[46] There are actually several basic concerns mentioned here, corresponding to aims iii (economic success), iv (social reproduction), and vi (public health), if not others as well.

In fact, it is very difficult to articulate an account of the aims of schooling, and almost no one is likely to claim that the purpose or justification of schooling can be encapsulated in any one of them alone. Most sophisticated accounts of the aims of education or educational practices refer to multiple norms.[47] In the case of sex education, as I will argue, the broader aims, such as democratic citizenship and humanistic flourishing, can incorporate and provide an ethical rationale for the narrower ones, such as promoting public health.

SEX EDUCATION OUTSIDE THE CURRICULUM: THE CULTURAL LANDSCAPE

Does this leave us back where we started? It seems that almost any attitude toward school-based sex education can be derived from some recognizable story about the aims of schooling. Since people hold different legitimate views about a range of matters, including the purpose of schools, we should not expect or try to enforce a consensus. Yet, as I have argued throughout, not all positions on sex education are equally tenable—and some are entirely spurious—in light of other things we know and supposedly care about. There are facts about young people's lives today, and especially their experiences of sex education *outside* of school, which put considerable strain on the conservative conceptions of the aims of schooling. Sex may not change over time from a biological standpoint, but it evolves constantly from a cultural one. As dynamic, situated institutions, schools must adjust their purposes and methods to respond to the actual world. Before we start drawing conclusions about the role of schools in sex education, let's take a quick inventory of the major extracurricular influences on young people's sexuality.

Young people in the West today are living in a time of unprecedented sexual freedom and information, alongside some of the most persistent and pernicious forms of sexual repression and gendered discrimination in modernity. We've come a long way, baby, except where we haven't. The sexual culture of young people can be described as a series of overlapping contradictions. I will focus here on four: porn/purity, feminism/post-feminism, failing boys/toxic masculinity, and bad media/good media.

Porn/Purity

The first contradiction is the coexistence of porn culture and purity culture. In the previous chapter, we noted that parents are apt to underestimate their children's exposure to pornography, which has become increasingly ubiquitous in the last decade. Some cultural researchers have referred to a "pornification" of Western culture, in which not only has regular pornography become vastly more accessible, but pornographic tropes and norms have also infiltrated supposedly non-pornographic forms of culture, including advertising, mainstream media, fashion, and music.[48] The concern here is that some of the harms and distortions associated with mainstream pornography—the sexual objectification of women, the invisibility of consent, the artificially constructed bodies—are smuggled into youth culture in detrimental ways before kids are even old enough to identify them. Through mainstream cultural engagement, kids learn that presenting oneself as sexually available is part of overall attractiveness. On Instagram and other social media platforms, girls learn from a young age how to pose for selfies and curate their appearance, wearing skimpy clothing and heavy makeup, to maximize sexual approval. So-called "self-sexualizing" behavior is intended to be socially rewarded with "likes" and other forms of attention,[49] but social media use is strongly correlated with depression in girls.[50]

We also shouldn't underestimate the direct effects of actual pornography consumption on young people's developing sexual norms. Girls and boys alike learn from sexually graphic materials about what bodies are supposed to look like and what they are supposed to do with them. It is thanks in large part to porn that young men experience insecurity about their penises and performance anxiety in sex, and an exploding number of girls as young as *nine* are requesting labiaplasty for purely cosmetic reasons.[51] Then there are the worrying effects of learning about sexual relationships from a media form that is typically devoid of narrative or any nonsexual intimacy.[52] Under the tutelage of adult entertainment, young people learn that "pleasure" is whatever big business markets to straight men—which often involves violence and aggression.[53] One content analysis of best-selling pornography videos found that 96% of the time—in over three thousand separate instances—women in the videos responded to aggression with pleasure or neutrality.[54] In interviews, young women and girls report feeling inadequate or prudish because they "should have enjoyed" certain sex acts, such as anal sex, which are rendered as mutually pleasurable in pornography.[55] Sex education—wherever it occurs—must be part of the response to these trends.[56]

In fact, researchers have argued that pornography has already displaced schools and other venues as the premier site of sex "education."[57] Psychotherapist Mary Anne Layden explains why pornography is a more effective educator: "we learn better using images than words," and "we also learn better when aroused."[58] It is no wonder that so many young people are riveted by pornographic teachings. Layden concludes: "You couldn't have come up with a better, more perfect learning environment than Internet pornography. With the exception that everything it says is a lie."[59]

Alongside the pornification of young people's culture sits an opposing, yet similarly powerful and harmful, cult of "purity."[60] In direct contrast to porn culture, purity culture is "sex-negative," moralizing, anti-pleasure, and pro-marriage. Whereas popular culture may reward young people—especially girls—for being sexually experienced and "up for it," purity culture promises rewards for being inexperienced and closed.[61] There are several interrelated sources of purity culture, not all of which affect young people to the same extent. First, there is abstinence-only education—especially the aggressive federally funded version long promoted in the United States—where "purity" by another name is promoted through the emphasis on abstinence and virginity.[62] Teens who are not abstinent, especially white girls, are compared to "chewed gum," used tape, and "dirty shoes," whom no one would want to marry.[63] Second, these expectations may be tirelessly repeated by parents and informal educators outside school. Young people may be inducted into purity culture through ritualized purity balls or virginity pledges, which are scandalously ineffective and hypocritical, not to mention patriarchal and sexist.[64] "Purity" euphemistically establishes sexual hierarchies along predictable lines of class, gender, and race, effectively separating "good" middle-class white girls from "hypersexual," "irresponsible" minorities and poor people, and charging girls with protecting their bodies against helpless lustful males.[65] The pervasive stigma around STIs, unwed mothers, and abortion are all part of this culture. Third, and related to the first two, Christian evangelism is extremely influential in the United States, where it sponsors much organized sex education and also perpetuates its own forms of slut-shaming and sexual redemption through religious and pseudo-religious teachings.[66]

Young people may thus be genuinely caught between the seemingly incompatible poles of pornography and purity, with both cultures masquerading as complete and emancipatory sex education. Women and girls lose big either way.

Feminism/Post-feminism

A second contradiction in contemporary culture relates to the vexed status of feminism, especially on questions of sexual agency. Millennials in affluent Western countries have grown up reaping the benefits of earlier feminist activism without having any memory of how they came about. The backlash against feminist advances of the 1960s and 1970s, most famously documented by Susan Faludi, has succeeded in convincing many Westerners that the aims of feminism have been achieved, therefore any further activism is whiny, exaggerated, or vindictive—a form of "reverse sexism."[67] This mood is described as "post-feminist,"[68] though it shades from conspicuously anti-feminist movements (such as "Men's Rights Groups" and "incels"[69]) into more subtle forms of false consciousness among young women. Students encounter some of these messages in school even before they are cognizant of sexual politics: educational research has trumpeted the academic success of girls and made a gender-equality project of helping "struggling boys" who are threatened by girls' runaway success.[70] This reinforces the message that girls have achieved equality (if not more) and "have it all," despite persistent gender-based barriers in their real lives.[71] Hand in hand with neoliberalism, the post-feminist mentality rules out structural or coercive explanations for women's individual circumstances, appropriating everything girls do as a triumphant product of "choice."[72] Supposedly emancipatory trends like pole-dancing and porno-chic fashion are all predicated on the idea that anything a woman does sexually is voluntary and liberating because, feminism's goals having been achieved, the only possible reason for still opposing these trends would be prudishness.

This mentality helps to explain the pressure girls apparently feel to participate in sexual activities that could otherwise be described as degrading or not in their own interests.[73] Sending sexually explicit pictures of themselves ("sexting"), performing casual oral sex, lap-dancing, and other behaviors that serve boys' interests may be coded as "empowering" on a loosely liberal interpretation of feminist agency.[74] The discourse of "empowerment" has been co-opted from its original usage and arguably deployed to manipulate young women into doing precisely what heterosexual men have always wanted them to do anyway. This is the kind of thing that would make second-wave feminists roll over in their graves.

But feminists also want to avoid deciding in advance what sexual activities women can enjoy. Kids' sexual behaviors have caused a moral hysteria among adults who may fail to differentiate between consensual sexual exploration that they find shocking and nonconsensual or morally ambiguous activities.[75] It's difficult to tease apart the various elements here, which many researchers consider to be entangled with racism and classist sexual morality. There are real child pornography and sex trafficking rings that suck in children and girls, especially those who are already marginalized and vulnerable, and receive comparatively little attention.[76] There is also reportedly an uptick in middle-class girls voluntarily trading sex for cash, taking on much older "sugar daddies," and doing pornography work as a side hustle while finishing high school, seemingly oblivious to the exploitative nature of their activities.[77] All of these phenomena may horrify feminists and non-feminists alike, if not for the same reasons. One clear takeaway from the recent studies of young people's sexual behaviors is this: they have been sold a story about girls' empowerment that may blind them to a host of perils and nuances.

At the same time, feminism—and especially its critique of heterosexual relations—is undergoing a veritable renaissance in mainstream culture. Alongside the backlash against feminism and a pornographic, post-feminist Zeitgeist that licenses victim-blaming, the #MeToo generation is reinvigorating longstanding feminist concerns about sexual harassment and gender-based violence and has even been critiqued for going too far. Indeed, the feminism of their mothers and grandmothers has not been so much rejected by young people as updated and recharged: young feminists embrace more recent iterations of "intersectional" or "fourth-wave" feminism, which include anti-racist and anti-colonial analyses along with less focus on "women" as a gendered class. Young women may be conversant with these discourses and express strident views about the effects of patriarchy, the ubiquity of sexism alongside various other forms of oppression, and the diversity of women, trans, and nonbinary people. This renewed feminist consciousness has surely affected how the generation now coming through school thinks about sex and gender.

The confluence of forceful post-feminist and new feminist messages produces a contradiction that bears directly on the aims of sex education. In some studies, the same girls describe themselves as empowered and agentic, while simultaneously reporting that they have been coerced into sex.[78] This is certainly a lot to sort through.

Failing Boys/Toxic Masculinity

Evolving attitudes toward feminism and gender have impacted boys as well. Once more or less invisible as a gendered category, boys are now considered subject to suffocating gender norms and pressures, simultaneously beneficiaries and victims of the patriarchy. "Masculinity studies" has emerged as a field alongside women's studies, and educational scholarship has exploded with gendered explanations for boys' academic performance. The advancements of feminism helped to make schools more equitable for girls and draw attention to the educational plight of boys, who were seen to be falling behind and losing interest due to such factors as the "feminization" of teaching, emasculating environments, and the advent of video games.[79] The trope of "failing boys" has been taken up by both conservatives and by feminists, each explaining the emerging "gender gap" in terms of some hitherto unrecognized dimensions of gender.[80]

While the relationship between gender and boys' academic performance is debatable,[81] one thing is certain: boys encounter fierce pressures to prove their masculinity. From "cool boys" to "party animals" to many derogatory characterizations of boys who are lower on the social hierarchy, the options are thickly coded and communicate expectations about studying, socializing, and sex.[82] These pressures are far more pervasive and coercive than any norms a teacher can communicate through formal sex education—and frequently at odds with them. In what Michael Kimmel refers to as "Guyland," masculinity is implicitly understood as the repudiation of all things feminine or "gay" and epitomized in heterosexual conquest.[83] When asked to explain what it means to "be a man," adolescent boys consistently trot out antiquated stereotypes about muscles, money, and not crying.[84] Loyalty to other boys—crassly referred to as "bros before hos"—is the price of admission into the orbit of masculinity, and deviations from "bro culture" are policed and punished. Ironically for a culture that is partly predicated on homophobia, Kimmel argues that "masculinity is largely a 'homosocial' experience: performed for, and judged by, other men."[85] Boys often don "masks" to hide their real feelings, experiencing depression and isolation as a result, and many turn to substance abuse or violence to cope[86]—providing further data for the thesis that boys are "failing" and need to be punished and/or rescued.

There's a place for both accountability and compassion when we witness the extremes of masculinity. Boys are neither simply misogynist egoists nor hapless pawns. There's gender infrastructure here, which boys have to figure out how to negotiate at every turn. For example, the sexist and aggressive tendencies associated with masculinity run rampant in pornography, and, alongside the migration of so much human communication to digital platforms, dating apps and "hook-up culture" amplify the opportunities for disconnected, self-serving sexual exploits. Post-feminism, as just described, may incentivize girls to go along with these trends. At the same time, boys have clearly internalized the ideal of gender equity that their grandparents' generation may have regarded as radical. Despite the ubiquity of homophobic and misogynistic epithets as casual putdowns in their social groups, Peggy Orenstein found that many of the boys she interviewed held relatively egalitarian views, had gay friends, and were literate about gender diversity; some even "spontaneously offered up their 'pronouns' when asked how they identified."[87] Boys may recognize these contradictions and still struggle to live up to the standards of both the locker room and *Queer Eye*.

Parallel to the contradiction of feminism and post-feminism, traditional masculinity has been stretched to polar extremes in recent public culture. Clearly, the norms of old-fashioned masculinity are alive and well. Indeed, they have been supercharged by porn culture, attacks on LGBTQ+ rights, and the glorification of ultra-rich men and unrepentant sexual predators. There is abundant evidence of "toxic masculinity."[88] However, the fact that phrases like "toxic masculinity" or "rape culture" register at all in mainstream vocabulary represents a startling advancement over earlier ways of thinking about men's behavior. Even "jocks" refer to these phenomena as givens.[89] Masculinity is arguably as toxic as ever, but for the first time, its toxicity is a recognized object of public discussion. This has bewildering and contradictory effects. There are now far more positive alternatives to traditional masculinity, as well as stubborn and sometimes violent pushback against attempts to shed light on it.

Many boys are caught between these influences, wanting to be "good guys" and wanting to fit in, needing validation for their whole selves while being reduced to sexual caricatures. Sex education often casts them in deterministic sex roles, even as mainstream culture has called on them to interrogate and defend their gender in a way that no previous generation has ever been called to do.

Bad Media/Good Media

A fourth tension in young people's sex lives relates to the evolving nature of education itself. While most young people still attend conventional schools, where the information offered by the formal curriculum may be tightly controlled, never before has a generation had access to such an infinite menu of human knowledge and artifacts. Any pretension of limiting children's access to supplemental information, however plausible it may have once been, is now beyond farcical. A 2019 survey by Common Sense Media found that 53% of American children have their own smartphone by age eleven; the number goes up to 69% by age twelve, and 91% by age eighteen—and that just represents one of multiple devices to which most kids have access. The same study found that teens use screen media for purposes *other than school or homework* an average of 7 hours 22 minutes *per day*—and that was before COVID-19 sent us into lockdown.[90] The media and the Internet are largely driven by profit, which can be fiercely at odds with the aims of education. We have already reviewed some of the misinformation and harmful messages kids encounter when they turn to their smartphones for sex education, especially when it comes from the porn industry. But digital media such as Planned Parenthood's birth control apps can also swiftly counteract misinformation.[91]

Education also occurs through entertainment, and some new media are producing the most comprehensive, forward-looking, and engaging sex education ever created. Consider the Netflix series *Big Mouth* and *Sex Education*. The first is an animated, raunchy comedy about suburban American adolescents coming of age, and the second is a drama about British teens trying to compensate for poor sex education. In just a couple of seasons, these shows each blew through all the taboo subjects in official curriculum and hit every comprehensive note in the book: consent, abortion, contraception, pornography, sexting, sexism, bullying, menstruation, masturbation, STIs, internalized homophobia, gender identity, slut-shaming, alcohol and drugs, oral sex, heartbreak, religion, female orgasm, and, appropriately, the shocking inadequacy of school-based sex education, just to name some of the most obvious.[92] Even better, both shows (including the silly cartoon) make it clear when they're presenting objective information—for example, debunking myths about the transmission of STIs and reminding viewers that "sexting" is illegal. The academic studies aren't out yet, but it's not too soon to predict that kids who watch these shows are learning more relevant and accurate sex information than any curriculum planner could dream of.

To return to the argument that schools are actually an obstacle to sex education, these examples may be further proof that thorough, engaging sex education can't thrive in the classroom format. The Netflix shows, unburdened by scholastic mandates, lure viewers with compelling narratives, likable and relatable characters, arresting visuals, clever dialogue, and humorous asides. They can be watched in private or with others, on command, and reviewed at leisure, any time. The viewers are not watched while they watch, and hence not at risk of public embarrassment like students in a real classroom. They don't have to posture for others or take tests. They can just learn and enjoy.

It would be nice if we could just leave it at that. Forget school-based sex education; prescribe mandatory viewing of pre-vetted television series! Alas, that won't work, and not only because of the minor complication of parental objections. The same devices that provide lifelines to young people who are starved of real sex education can also open portals to oceans of miseducation. Looking up sexual information online, or surfing random television and movies with the hope of finding quality sex education, will readily turn up factual misinformation and radically distorted fantasies of sex. And porn is not the only culprit. One study that analyzed 177 *sexual health websites* found that "46 per cent of those addressing contraception and 35 per cent of those addressing abortion contained inaccurate information."[93] And as we have repeatedly noted, adults are not, for the most part, talking to young people constructively about what they are finding online.

Then there is the whole issue of social media. Psychologists of adolescence have described "not having a social media profile . . . as 'social death.'"[94] The ways that young people interact online are absolutely essential to their sexual development and knowledge, even if "sex education" never appears in the mission statement of Instagram. Oh, the world of delights and horrors that await the adolescent as she types in her password! This is not your average schoolyard. Sex-positive researchers and educators remind us not to jump to prudish outrage here; these are, after all, merely new and sometimes liberating vehicles for doing what adolescents have always done anyway.[95] Still, the novel features of digital life can compound the harms of sexual coming of age. Pocket technology has enabled the effortless, spontaneous filming of drunken escapades or clumsy hookups. And unlike in past generations, when social traumas could at least be contained geographically or temporally, the Internet indelibly records these moments, following students from home to school, from college to the job market.

Sex education was installed in schools on the presumption that the information in schools would be more accurate and beneficial than what kids learned about sex elsewhere. That calculation is more complicated now. Kids are certainly getting sex education outside schools, mostly away from the organized supervision of adults, and some of it is excellent. A lot of it is appalling. Schools have to step up and redefine their role in sex education.

AIMS REVISITED: WHAT SCHOOLS CAN AND SHOULD DO

We began this chapter by exploring the often overlooked limits and harms of schooling. We then discussed, on the other side, the positive aims of schooling and their implications for sex education. Sex education must have transparent aims and respond to students' real needs. Now that we have a snapshot of the sexual landscape in which young people come of age, and consequently what they might need from sex education, we can reevaluate our expectations of schools. Of the six possible aims surveyed above, four of them turn out to be unjustifiable or unnecessary as frameworks for contemporary sex education. The two that remain—democratic and humanistic aims—form the backbone of our vision for sex education.

Let's start by revisiting the aim that is used to support most opposition to CSE, the aim of social reproduction (iv). Recalling traditional attitudes toward gender and the family, advocates of this conservative aim stress that schools should not discuss sexuality in any depth or express approval of any adolescent sexual activity.[96] This position follows from convictions about both sexual ethics and the proper aims of schooling. As discussed in chapter 4, it is important to wrestle with moral pluralism about sexuality, but it is not realistic to search for moral consensus at the level of policy. We need to design common sex education without waiting for an agreement about matters that will never be settled.

Convictions about the purpose of schools may be more amenable to evidence and debate, however. Conservatives may endorse AOUME because they believe that schools ought to be used as a mechanism for limiting the spread of bad ideas and shoring up traditional morality. But can they? Even if we espouse this aim, it depends on the belief that schools can tightly control what students learn. As we saw in the previous chapter, this view corresponds to the "closed loop" view of educational authority, in which schools cooperate with parents and sometimes religious communities to deliver a univocal message while sheltering students from all other perspectives that they see as potentially corrupting.

Yet this understanding of schooling can't be defended in the present landscape, even if it once could. The idea that schools can sustain conservative values by controlling sex education is belied by all the sex education that bubbles up between and outside the curriculum, not to mention the massive failure of AOUME to meet its stated goals. The "closed loop" never really worked, and in the age of cell phones, it can only be regarded as an exercise in futility. Likewise, the faith in prescriptive pedagogies of sex education ("Don't have sex. Or you will get pregnant and die."[97]) on which AOUME curricula depend simply doesn't check out. People don't robotically follow rules and admonishments, especially when it comes to sex, and especially when newer media platforms are so much more captivating.[98]

If we can't micromanage sex education in the manner necessary for conservative aims to be achieved (a good hunch), then perhaps we should just keep mum. This solution also fails the litmus test of common sense. Precisely because students are living in this world of stimulus overload and cultural contradictions, schools have to engage with their questions, anxieties, and misconceptions. Even without a formal curriculum or designated time for talking about sex, these issues will emerge of their own accord, whether in other classes or in the guidance counselor's office, in the hallways or in the schoolyard. Sex can't be bracketed out of schooling. Besides, as Foucault illustrated, schools are teaching sex all the time, even if it is never named. The question is not *whether* to teach about sex, but how to integrate the teaching into the educational ecosystem. This has to be done explicitly and with top-down guidance, or else we're sure to end up with an even bigger mess. Teachers and administrators who are deprived of formal curriculum documents and policies are put in an untenable position.

These realities mean that, even if conscience militates against so-called liberal curricula, schools simply can't assume the role that they would need to in order for the conservative aims to be upheld. Furthermore, the strain on schools' control of the sex discourse will only be exacerbated with time. Each year (or week, or day) brings new controversies in the public sphere related to sexuality, new information about health and human behavior, new shifts in demographics and changes in political power, and—you can bet your bottom dollar—new apps. The aim of conservation (iv) by definition tries to ride out the changing times by repeating a consistent and absolute message. Sex education of this type goes stale pretty fast.

The democratic (i) and humanistic (ii) aims, by contrast, are less vulnerable to the vicissitudes of culture. There is ample room within them for moral disagreement and religious pluralism, for evolving public discourses, and for students' self-identified concerns. Furthermore, they are compatible with, indeed demanded by, the technological changes that continuously encroach on traditional education. Democratic education helps to equip students to negotiate a complex world full of misinformation and diversity. Humanistic aims help students to figure out what it means to live a good life. Both categories fuse the kind of learning that schools can offer with the realities of young people's lives; neither requires trying to keep the lid on sexuality or insisting on impossible standards of sexual conduct. Given what we know about the wider context, this is the only approach that puts schools in a potentially constructive position.

When school-based sex education is organized around democratic and humanistic aims, some of the other things we may want from schools are likely to follow. The economic aims of schooling (iii) are legitimate in principle, but the neoliberal, restrictive sex education they seem to inspire is precisely the wrong way of achieving them. In fact, people are more likely to be financially stable and professionally successful if they can control their fertility and enjoy autonomy in their private lives (just look at women's history). The public health aims (vi), too, will best be achieved by programs that are comprehensive and complemented by reliable health care services for young people, such as those in Norway, especially in places where such services are otherwise hard to access. If our aims are democracy and human flourishing, the STI boxes will already be checked.

The aim of social transformation (v) is more complex. It is arguably inseparable from the project of truly comprehensive school-based sex education and already embedded within democratic or humanistic aims.[99] Nonetheless, directly aiming at radical social transformation through schools is hard to justify. For one thing, it has proven strategically flawed, at least in North America; ambitiously progressive sex education programs, like all large-scale social justice education efforts, elicit enormous backlash and can be impossible to legislate. At the level of principle, it may also be criticized, irrespective of one's own political views, because it uses (some might say subverts) policy to expedite certain social causes before they've cleared the usual democratic processes.[100] There is plenty of obvious work to be done just to bring sex education into line with basic norms of equality and fair opportunity, without overextending the political significance of schools. Making sex education truly democratic and humanistic would not require us to build everything from the ground up. Done properly, however, it would in fact be transformative.

DEMOCRATIC HUMANISTIC SEX EDUCATION

So, what are schools for? They can be for many things, and we need not settle on a list of aims for all time. In the realm of sexuality, however, the aim of schools must be to set students up for a healthy and fulfilling lifelong relationship with their bodies and their world. Schools cannot avoid this responsibility when students' lives are already saturated with contradictory, and sometimes harmful, sexual influences, and when no other actors are reliably positioned to reach all children. The democratic and humanistic accounts of schooling indicate some pedagogical techniques and priorities that can be translated into the teaching of sex education: critical thinking skills, participatory dialogue, cross-disciplinary exploration, and so on. Like civics and humanities education more generally, sex education must be approached in a social and political context and be informed by, but not reducible to, science and empirical evidence. Students need a place to critically unpack the influences of media and technology, learn to compile and assess information, and think about the meaning of ethical relationships. These criteria amount to a program of sex education that is at least as comprehensive as existing curricula that boast the label, as well as including the recommendations of many health organizations and researchers who study the effects of school-based sex education.[101] Lisa Andersen and I call it Democratic Humanistic Sexuality Education (DHSE).

What is proposed by DHSE is not a curriculum or set of universal standards and topics. Rather, it is a philosophically grounded approach to designing sex education that will result in somewhat different expressions when applied in different contexts. As such, it will be able to better adapt to the needs of particular groups of students than can the kind of predetermined laundry list into which CSE is often reduced. Still, this is only a partial vindication. To return to the Foucauldian analysis with which we began the chapter, school-based sex education is inherently flawed. It proceeds from a narrow account of knowledge and learning, and it operates via an institution that has been used to discipline and marginalize students as much as to emancipate them. What can be said about these enduring critiques?

It may be impossible to dispel every worry about the awkward marriage of school and sex, but DHSE can mitigate most of them. While this approach still proceeds from a modern Western understanding of both "sex" and "education," promotes some conspicuously Western values like individual autonomy, and reproduces certain medical and scientific discourses, it need not recapitulate the sins of *scientia sexualis*. It is not limited to "plumbing and prevention" and does not assume a dualistic, hierarchical account of mind and body. It does not seek to catalog, prescribe, or punish sexual types, and has no use for confession. It is not entirely dictated by educational authorities and received unquestioningly by docile students. It does not treat young people as idealized rational economists who maximize their interests by acting on abstract knowledge. It celebrates the benefits and complexities of sexual relationships as well as noting the risks.

Further adjustments will also enhance the efficacy of sex education and reduce the dissonance between material and venue. Four particular recommendations emerge from the preceding discussion: the place of sex education in the curriculum, assessment, school environment, and teacher education.

Place of Sex Education in the Curriculum

As noted earlier, Western curriculum tends to separate subjects into discrete academic categories, with sex education usually awkwardly housed in physical education, biology, or a kind of integrated careers and personal development curriculum. Sex education should not be contained in an embarrassed corner of a single course, where it is allocated only a few tense hours per year. This practice compounds the message that sex is a shameful thing to be contained and managed. This makes no sense pedagogically, and it renders the flimsy sexuality content even more vulnerable to erasure.[102] Other models exist. For example, the Canadian province of Quebec treats sexuality education as a cross-curricular priority for which all teachers are responsible, as does Norway.[103] Schoolteachers have found productive ways to incorporate sex education into other courses, such as language arts and social studies, in addition to or even in defiance of the stated curriculum.[104] The cross-curricular approach should be cultivated and encouraged, as the reformers in the 1920s intended.

Assessment

Another wrinkle affecting the integration of sex education into formal schooling is assessment.[105] The subservience of curriculum to neoliberal aims in education typically chains teachers to cookie-cutter assessment models that are supposed to quantify and track student learning. There is something particularly ludicrous about this requirement if we are imagining a fluid democratic and humanistic path for sex education. The kinds of learning we have been talking about are hard to measure by almost any conventional metric. Tests and assignments underscore the sterile institutionalism of school, ironically inhibiting meaningful learning for many students. More importantly, the value of quality sex education will play out in students' lives, not in "book knowledge"—we might as well give students grades on their intimate relationships. Here's a radical idea: leave summative assessment out of sex education. The important thing is that students show up.[106]

School Environment

We also reviewed concerns about the informal curriculum in schools—unofficial learning, institutional policies, and material conditions that perpetuate sexual norms and even undermine the official curriculum, no matter how progressive. We are not helplessly beholden to these either. DHSE requires bringing a number of other aspects of schooling into line: policies and practices that oppose gender-based discrimination and take a strong stand against sexual harassment, inclusion of diverse forms of embodiment and identity, resistance to racist and classist expectations, and so forth. Fortunately, the more that the formal curriculum welcomes sex and related topics as legitimate aspects of students' lives, the less power the informal curriculum has to interfere with it.

Teacher Education

You may have noticed that the more we cram into these ambitious plans for DHSE, the more we are expecting from teachers. As it is, the teachers responsible for sex education are characteristically underprepared and overburdened. The Sexuality Information and Education Council of the United States (SIECUS) reports that "only 61% of colleges and universities require sexuality education courses for health education certification and nearly one-third of teachers responsible for sexuality education report receiving *no* pre-service or in-service training in this area."[107] And that's just for those with a health education certification! Much so-called "sex education" is taught by teachers without any health education background. No wonder teachers crave more professional development.[108] A review of teacher preparation classroom outcomes found that "teacher training is the most significant indicator in determining the comprehensiveness of the sexuality education instruction and the number of sexuality topics taught within any curriculum."[109] The content of a curriculum is only as good as the capacity of teachers to teach it. So, if we're going to add to the depth and breadth of topics to be covered in sexuality education, we had better have a plan for teacher development.

Teacher training varies by region, and there have been numerous initiatives worldwide to enhance teacher education as a condition of enhancing K–12 sex education. As with the more comprehensive curricula, of course, most of these complementary teacher-training plans have not been implemented at scale.[110] However, they provide encouraging data about the positive correlation between improved teacher training and classroom outcomes.[111] Still, on the more holistic model we recommend, in which sexuality recurs throughout the curriculum, *all* teachers will need to participate in the teaching of challenging topics related to sex as they arise in various subjects. Revamping teacher education and professional development for DHSE is thus a weighty task. But it's not unfeasible: every revolution in K–12 curriculum subjects has demanded changes to how teachers prepare for and perform their jobs.

Does this vision ask too much? Although the democratic and humanistic aims of schooling will never be perfectly realized, progress in schooling over the last century shows how much can change when there is political will. Not that long ago, girls were required to learn "home economics" while boys learned "shop"; now, there are national government and nonprofit organizations devoted exclusively to recruiting girls to science, technology, engineering, and mathematics (STEM). Racist materials have been banned, dress codes have been relaxed, and, even in the face of sweeping neoliberal policies, K–12 education has increasingly encouraged students to think for themselves. Most countries have also made great strides in delivering useful sex education. In spite of the understandable skepticism toward schooling expressed by critical theorists, marginalized communities, people with traditional values, and frustrated practitioners, sex education belongs in schools. It should be pursued via democratic and humanistic aims in a manner that counteracts the features of schooling that inhibit real freedom and equality. This would make many students and teachers much happier. Evidence suggests that it would also lower STI and teen pregnancy rates—the holy grails of sex education—as well as potentially the rates of sexual violence. Hopefully, very few people would argue with these results.

CONCLUSION

The autonomous Extremadura region of Spain is a true pioneer when it comes to school-based sex education: in 2009 it introduced masturbation workshops into its high school curriculum. The addition was rationalized as part of a larger commitment to reducing pregnancy and promoting safer sex. Reflecting on this bold turn in sex education, Spanish cultural critic Mario Vargas Llosa mused, "How many things have changed since my childhood when the Salesian Fathers and the La Salle Brothers . . . scared us with the idea that 'improper touching' produced blindness, tuberculosis and madness. Six decades later we have jerking-off classes in schools. Now that is progress."[112]

Vargas Llosa was being sarcastic, of course. It doesn't follow from a commitment to sexual liberation that schools should become masturbation laboratories. Nor should "progress" in sex education be measured simply by the successive addition of taboo topics, or the degree to which a curriculum outrages the clergy. Not everything about sex is made more fulfilling, more just, or more democratic by being placed under the bright glare of fluorescent classroom lights. This insight could have been gleaned from Foucault's description of *ars amoris*, in which "there is formed a knowledge that must remain secret, not because of an element of infamy that might attach to its object, but because . . . it would lose its effectiveness . . . by being divulged."[113] Translation: exhaustive sex education kills sex.

The kind of sex education that young people need, and that schools can provide, is comprehensive without trying to be exhaustive, factual without being heartless. It should not strive to approximate the intimate education of *ars amoris*, but nor should it emulate the *scientia sexualis* of a nineteenth-century clinic. Rather than try to teach young people everything there is to know about sex and sexuality as though in preparation for some cosmic multiple-choice test, schools should focus on equipping young people to be literate members of the sexual world and ethical participants in all their relationships.

The details of such an education will depend on the time and place, but it is increasingly obvious that an integrated approach is necessary. There may have been a time when schools could leave most of the heavy lifting of sex education to someone else, or get through all the key points in one afternoon. In our current reality, characterized by globalization, unlimited access to unvetted information, and contentious conversations in the public sphere about sex, gender, and power, it is naïve to think that sexuality can be either isolated from schooling or neatly contained within it. Among the aims of education in the twenty-first century has to be the cultivation of critical thinkers who can negotiate the sea of unfiltered information at their disposal. Nothing we may legitimately hope for our children will be achieved through ignorance or blind obedience.

Advocates of comprehensive school-based sex education need not deny that there are very real limits to what can be accomplished in schools. Recall that, from the beginning, classroom-based sex education was reformers' second choice, a bargaining point, and a compromise. Schools are convenient ways of reaching entire cohorts of young people, but they are not the whole story. We need schools to offer the sex education they are best positioned to offer and for other actors to do the same.

Conclusion: We're Out of Touch

Audrie Pott committed suicide on September 10, 2012, at the age of fifteen. A few days earlier, she'd woken up naked, with green marker all over her body, after a debauched coed all-night party in a wealthy California suburb. She had no memory of what had happened, but "friends" told her that she had gotten very drunk and made out with several boys before being carried to a bed, where she was undressed, graffitied, and fondled by three male acquaintances. They had taken pictures. On Facebook, she received messages declaring: "honestly like really no joke everyone knows . . ." and "u were one horny mofo." After desperately trying and failing to get her peers' assurance that images of her violated body would not be shared, Audrie hanged herself in her home bathroom.[1] Among her last Facebook messages to friends, she wrote, "I can't do anything to fix it. I just want this to go away. The whole school knows. My life is ruined and I don't even remember how."[2]

There are far too many examples with which we could have opened. Amanda Todd, fifteen, hanged herself after a protracted saga of sexual extortion, abuse, and bullying, which even moving to a new city failed to solve.[3] Rehtaeh Parsons, seventeen, killed herself after being dogged by pictures of her being gang-raped at fifteen.[4] Grace McComas. Channing Smith. The list goes on.

From all the ugly permutations of social media and teen sexuality that lead to harm, patterns are starting to emerge. In one scenario, a girl sends explicit images to her boyfriend ("sexts") or engages in consensual porn production, which is later shared or posted to humiliate the girl and congratulate the boy ("revenge porn").[5] Many victims of this kind of crime contemplate suicide.[6]

In a variation, a boy (or man posing as a boy) extorts sexual images from a girl, later posting them on social media or using them as blackmail. In an even more horrific version, a perpetrator or group of perpetrators films a live sexual assault, often while the victim is unconscious, and the footage is circulated. Sometimes, such footage serves to further bully the victim, rather than rally people to come to her aid.

Girls and queer kids are most vulnerable to sexual cyberbullying, but violence of this type can afflict anyone. At one all-boys Catholic school in Toronto, known for its exceptional athletics, a video emerged in 2018 showing a boy being gang-raped with a broomstick in an apparent hazing ritual. The subsequent investigation surfaced at least five more videos like it.[7]

When these cases come to light, well-meaning people exhibit similar reactions. Outrage and sadness bridge divides both partisan and religious. These tragedies have led to new laws, charitable foundations, and a national day to stop cyberbullying.[8] The victims become heroic symbols and cautionary tales; after Amanda Todd's suicide, more than one million Facebook users "liked" her Facebook memorial page. Depending on the details of the story, journalists and activists may give it a different top spin: Audrie Pott's story is also one of an eating disorder; Todd had struggled with untreated depression for years; the Catholic boys' school was a hotbed of toxic masculinity. The stories are simultaneously evidence for excessive underage drinking, the misuses and surprising benefits of technology,[9] the inadequacy of child pornography laws, a precipitous rise in mental illness among young people, and parents' increasing remoteness from the social world of their teens.

But as much as the legal, psychological, and technological dimensions of this phenomenon deserve attention, the obvious connections to sex education hardly get airtime. "Comprehensive" sex education, as it is typically practiced, still teaches about sexual health in generic rather than contextual terms, avoids topics like sexting except to issue blanket condemnations, and reduces the time horizon for potential action to the moment before a pregnancy or an assault occurs—not everything that comes after. Although we can't know which specific interventions may have saved the young people mentioned here, we know there is a lot more we can do. Students like Audrie Pott need an integrated curriculum that treats sexuality as a part of human identity across the life span and understands students' lives in a particular time and place. It should affirm, as many feminists have insisted, that sexual activity should be mutually pleasurable, while at the same time speaking candidly about the messiness of pleasure, desire, and consent. It should address social media and cyberbullying, as many curricula already do, but it should be frank about the role of pornography, slut-shaming, and "bro culture" on these platforms. It should identify the physical and emotional risks of sexual activity but also assure young people that their future is recoverable after something goes wrong—something that Pott obviously didn't believe. And if she had received a sex education that was localized and specific, maybe Pott would have known about services such as crisis counseling in the area, and perhaps what state laws her assailants had violated.

Pott was part of a culture that mocks vulnerability and frequently reduces complex ethical or emotional issues to eighty-character judgments. What were her friends thinking that night—like the girl who helped the three boys carry her upstairs nearly unconscious? How could they have responded in the aftermath? Sex education has been inordinately concerned with telling young people—especially girls—to simply avoid risk. The focus on responsibility, which we earlier connected to neoliberalism, may increase the likelihood of victim-blaming. What if, instead, sex education taught young people to care about and work through harm? Friends should know how to comfort each other and support people undergoing trauma, as well as how to rebuild relationships after a breach of trust. Sex education can facilitate more open communication between young people and their parents and caregivers, making teen sex less of an open secret. The peers who circulated nude images should have felt accountable to communal norms, not protected by a teen code of conduct that was beyond the reach of family and school authorities. Indeed, these young people will very likely be parents instructing their own children someday. What might have Pott's assaulters have done differently if they had ever been asked to reflect on how to raise a daughter? Were they ever prepared to think about how to vote on policies related to sexual harm, or how to serve on a jury?

There are important gaps in young people's sexual knowledge, but they're not the ones we tend to dwell on. These stories illuminate the ridiculousness of stale debates—often touchstones of AOUME vs. CSE conflicts—about how explicit anatomical drawings should be in curriculum materials or whether a teacher should demonstrate how to use a condom. The same cell phones that record sexual assault and torment its victims make anatomical drawings and condom demonstrations readily available. What young people need to know about sex may be different at this historical moment than in the past, emphasizing the information and skills for which no simple search terms exist. Adults tend to assume that their own experiences are what make them sex education authorities, and perhaps that their children should have only the information that they would have needed at that age. In the new cultural and technological landscape, this attitude is not only misguided: it puts young people in serious danger.

What young people know and believe about sex matters more than almost anything else they may learn in school. Both conservative activists and progressive sex education advocates are right about that. It's worth fighting to get it right.

We have argued in this book that the nature of this fight is often misunderstood. Ironically, the broad aims of sex education are less controversial than people think they are, in part because conservative approaches to sex education have had a stranglehold at the federal level for thirty years. The political dance floor has accordingly moved to the right: after many frustrated efforts to make inroads against the conservative fortress, there are some fundamental battles that progressives long ago stopped picking. For example, the organizations that eschew "abstinence-only"—like Planned Parenthood—still cleave to a clear message of "abstinence first." In most curricula, contraception and safer sex are introduced primarily as damage control for the inevitable failure of abstinence. What to do if one has an unplanned pregnancy—raising an infant, having an abortion, securing parental and child support—is hardly referenced; conception remains the conventional stopping point. In younger grades especially, non-heterosexual activity is mentioned obliquely, if at all; although respect for diversity is enjoying more recognition in recently updated curricula, "safer sex" for non-heterosexuals is still taboo, in part because it would require explaining sexual positions, a historical bogeyman. So, there is consensus about some big topics in sex education, but consensus is not proof that we're on the right track. Among policy makers and public office holders, almost no one can be found who publicly disputes the conception of a sexually healthy young person as "the abstinent heterosexual."[10]

How can people who agree so much spend so much time locked in bitter conflict? The history of sex education is defined by two pathways: a school subject developing in tandem with America's expanding educational system and corresponding to academic research; and a battered arena for countless other issues related to the fitful diversification of American society through the twentieth century. The culture wars since the 1970s have problematically solidified the associations between particular views on sex education and political identity, meaning that the second pathway has become more important than the first. By portraying opponents as radical, immoral, or out of touch with reality, mainstream players crowd out discussions about where we actually agree and disagree. Political expediency advises that some ideas are untouchable, and instead we must continue to ride the merry-go-round of CSE vs. AOUME.

We share grief over the fate of Rehtaeh Parsons, but woe betide anyone who suggests discussing revenge porn in a classroom. There is some comfort in the simplistic narrative that modern societies like the United States simply cannot agree on sex education. Perhaps we are lazy, to the extent that we would rather tolerate conflict than go through the awkwardness of substantial deliberation across political lines.

Against this defeatist attitude, we have argued in this book that the broader principles related to sex education are derivable from the basic liberal conception of a free society. We are all embodied, and we are all entitled to use our bodies for consensual sexual pleasure. We all have beliefs about values related to sex, and we are entitled to them as long as we respect others' sexual identity and autonomy. Citizens of twenty-first-century democracies should make education policy in response to the best available evidence and the evolving realities of a digital globalized world, which requires updating curriculum often. These propositions should not be controversial if we actually believe in freedom and equality.

We cannot let the sensitive nature of sexuality be used as an excuse to give up on these commitments. We've learned through painful trial and error that denying young people information about sex, or substituting unabashed moral rules for sex education, doesn't work. Trying to keep the birds and the bees under wraps until young people are married was indefensible one hundred years ago, and today it is utterly unthinkable. Teaching sex either exclusively in the context of character education or exclusively in the context of biology leaves gaps in young people's understanding and still doesn't satisfy all stakeholders. Abdicating responsibility for teaching about sex and relationships imposes an unjustifiable burden on young people. Telling young people to just keep their pants on, as American federal policy has done for decades, is demonstrably self-defeating.

Moreover, in all cases, the failures of sex education have startlingly disproportionate effects. Without appropriate sex education, heterosexual men—especially those who are also in other privileged groups—usually muddle through. But girls and minorities are particularly vulnerable. Young women are at risk of unintended pregnancy, which can change their entire life trajectory, especially when stigma, economic inequality, and restrictions on abortion are added to the mix. Women are more susceptible than men to both contracting sexually transmitted infections and suffering long-term health consequences because of them.[11] Women, sex and gender minorities, racial minorities, and people with disabilities are more likely to be victims of sexual assault, harassment, and discrimination. And young queer people are vastly more likely than their peers to find school alienating or flat-out dangerous because of their sexual identities.[12] Everyone needs and deserves good sex education, but good sex education is also an equity issue of paramount importance.

A society committed to freedom and equality of opportunity should not tolerate preventable disparities and discrimination on the basis of sex, any more than we should simply give up when confronted with difficult problems. We have the resources within our political traditions and legal institutions to demand sex education that serves the needs of all young people. We have the knowledge and the means to choose sex education programs that are more likely to accomplish shared goals and elevate the well-being of the most disadvantaged. What we need is political will.

Not all of the sniping between liberals and conservatives is superficial showboating, however. Some of the controversy dredged up by sex education reflects the enduring challenges of pluralistic societies, such as how to separate church and state without denying the role of religion in many people's lives. For some parents, it is incoherent to teach about sex outside the parameters of God and chastity.[13] The state cannot and typically should not try to enforce a public narrative about sex that takes a stand on such metaphysical claims. Religious views about sex and schooling may be particularly powerful in the United States due to the primacy of religious freedom and freedom of conscience in American history and political culture. The United States also has higher rates of homeschooling and a much stronger tradition of allowing parents to opt out of controversial school programs than most liberal democracies. Societies that interpret the separation of church and state to require proactive secularism and uniform civic education have favored more comprehensive mandatory sex education, albeit not without their own contradictions.[14]

Another aspect of American culture that may account for its idiosyncratic experience with sex education is the emphasis on individual responsibility. Whereas all Western democracies espouse the importance of public health and individual opportunity, they accord different levels of responsibility to the state for coordinating social goods. In the United States, the ideals of self-sufficiency and state non-interference carry greater currency than in Europe and many other democracies.[15] While conservatives may decry the high rates of STIs and teen pregnancy, therefore, they may attribute responsibility for these outcomes to individual teens and their families, who should have made better choices. The redistribution of resources toward elaborate education and public health programs will seem unjustified from this perspective. In contrast, many liberals, like their counterparts outside the United States, see individual responsibility as at most a partial explanation for disparities in sexual health outcomes and insist on systemic responses to young people's health education needs.

While sex education is usually defined, and explicitly pursued, only as a sub-subunit in a packed school curriculum, these debates reveal it to be of cross-cutting educational and cultural importance and, for some, monumental moral significance. The topics of sex and education independently invoke profound questions of human value; together they reveal some of the deepest fault lines between members of the same polity. These questions should be raised squarely *within* sex education rather than used to limit and spin it. We do not need to agree on everything in order to prepare young people for peaceful coexistence. Indeed, if we already agreed on everything, such preparation would be redundant. This is why ethics and democratic education are the appropriate pedagogies for teaching about sensitive and controversial issues. Precisely because diverse societies will always encounter ideological conflicts about sex and human values, sex education cannot be resolved in the confines of a ninth-grade health unit. It must confront the political, emotional, scientific, moral, and social dimensions of human sexuality.

Democratic Humanistic Sexuality Education (DHSE), the approach that we argued for in the previous chapter, is best positioned to prepare young people for responsible and healthy sex lives in a complicated world. It begins with the factual information that already characterizes the most comprehensive aspirations for sex education, unfolding a sequence of topics in ways that track students' physical and mental development, and spiraling back to add depth and nuance as students mature. DHSE treats young people as already sexual beings and as future adult citizens. It thus values skills that support students' increasing autonomy, while also making them aware of their obligations as friends, civic actors, and possible parents. Drawing from the democratic aims of schooling and a long tradition of democratic education, this form of sex education teaches critical thinking alongside scientific knowledge and encourages students to formulate their own views, rationally consider topics of political significance, and respect others as equals. If we assume that education ought to prepare students to live alongside people different from them, anti-discrimination and attention to systemic inequalities must be built into the treatment of all topics, not merely added as an afterthought. Embedded in a democratic and humanistic approach to sexuality is the recognition that health priorities and life plans may legitimately vary between communities and individuals. DHSE welcomes perspectives on sexuality from the arts and humanities, opening up the methods and concerns of religion, philosophy, and literature, among other influences. Most importantly, it provides moral education in the mode of a liberal arts ethics education, rather than by choosing a prescriptive moral doctrine or vainly attempting to avoid questions of value altogether.

By definition, such an education cannot reside with a single teacher or even a single course. The concept of sex education as an exercise in democratic and personal growth illuminates the problems arising when a small and homogenous group of adults sets the standards for young people's sexual behavior and knowledge. Parents can and ought to complement school-based sex education in their capacity as primary caregivers, but some "detachment" is necessary and desirable, as we saw in chapter 5. No child should be denied accurate and inclusive information about sex because of who their parents are. Authority for sex education is a collective responsibility, with specific tasks distributed among the people in a child's life according to their competence and investments, and young people themselves playing a consulting role. DHSE requires cross-curricular attention that should begin in the first year of school and continue until graduation.

Our specific philosophical framework has not guided the implementation of sex education in any North American school districts to our knowledge, but it synthesizes the recommendations of countless educational experts, researchers, theorists, and students themselves.[16] Educational decision makers need not start from scratch; many best practices already express the ideal of DHSE even if they were not consciously grounded in this paradigm. Versions of it have thrived in community-based programs, peer-education modules, international NGOs, and, increasingly, online resources. These modes of sex education will no doubt proliferate and should be nurtured. Yet schools are the irreplaceable locus of any type of curriculum that aims to reach all members of a generation. Most children spend many hours of most days in a physical school until the age of eighteen. To support DHSE, we need to reject the definition of sex education as something that can be taught in a few hours in a conventional classroom. We must pursue bold change at the level of curriculum design, school policies, and teacher education.

The single most important feature of sex education going forward, therefore, will be its responsiveness to the evolving needs of young people. The bewilderment of the adult world at the news of Audrie Pott's suicide indicates that we are missing the boat. It is unfair to hold schools, or any particular stakeholder, responsible for the tragic phenomenon of teen suicide. But we would have less to answer for if formal education were more proactively responding to the technological and cultural situation of young people—and not shying away from the realities of teen sexuality.

One of the benefits of studying sex education through historical and philosophical analysis is that it allows us to track "progress" in this highly fraught area and thereby begin to break out of our contemporary rut. What was once unthinkable is now common sense; what was controversial in the early twentieth century emerges under a new guise in the twenty-first. History shows that things change due to a confluence of efforts and contingencies, and philosophy shows that what counts as controversial in any given time period reflects our evolving moral and political presuppositions. To return to a question we posed in the first pages: Is there progress in sex education?

PATCHY PROGRESS

Sweden is often regarded as the beacon of progressive sex education worldwide. A leader in the response to AIDS in the early 1990s, Sweden pioneered human-rights-based sex education and was the first country to implement UNESCO's 2009 *International Technical Guidance on Sexuality Education.*[17] In Sweden, as well as in other northern European countries, sex education is non-denominational, mandatory, comprehensive, and sex-positive. To many liberal onlookers, this part of the world represents the gold standard of a sexually healthy society, with record-low teen pregnancy rates, few if any conflicts over school curriculum, social acceptance of LGBTQ+ people, and apparently high levels of consensual and pleasurable sexual relations. As one op-ed in the *Los Angeles Times* advertised, "Worried about your teenage daughter? Move to the Netherlands."[18]

It may seem appropriate, if these characterizations are correct, to model North American sex education on what has worked so well in northern Europe. And to a great extent this may be true. But regarding sex education as a final product that can be copied in different contexts sidesteps the more nuanced work of defining what counts as progress in a given culture or state, and seeing what levers are realistically available to advance sex education in light of other constraints and priorities.

American ideas about sex, gender, and education have certainly come a long way since the dawn of the twentieth century. The Mosher wives knew nothing about sex and would have been scandalized to lose their virginity before marriage. Early textbooks used in Family Life Education portrayed the "socially adjusted" woman as a middle-class wife and mother who was sexually satisfied by the family patriarch. Decades later, these attitudes came to be widely regarded as quaint, or coercive. Nonetheless, it is evident that "traditional" family values—the view that sex belongs in a heterosexual marriage sanctioned by God; the belief in essential gender differences and the naturalness of male dominance—continue to thrive alongside significantly updated ideas about sex and gender.

How ought we reconcile these points of reference? It is important to acknowledge the very real tensions between these attitudes without overstating their solidity. Traditional views, derived from ancient scriptures, are alive and well in the contemporary West, perhaps even growing in some evangelical communities and among traditional religious minorities, whose numbers are on the rise. Still, cultural and legal norms have been moving, clumsily yet unmistakably, toward interpretations that are regarded as more "progressive." Today's attitudes toward women's role in society are very different from the norms of mid-twentieth-century America. Even those who still believe in "complementarianism"—the view that men and women are naturally suited to different, complementary roles—are obliged, by public precedent if not personal conviction, to espouse the standard of equal opportunity. If traditionalists want to teach that girls should aspire to conventional, even subordinate, roles in heterosexual relationships, they must at least pay lip service to women's legal equality and the knowledge that women are not exclusively homemakers.

One measure of progress, therefore, is the evolution of language: what is sayable or unsayable about sex and gender, what premises are permitted or forbidden in sex education classes. It is no longer acceptable to say that women should be dependent on their husbands to learn about sex, or that one gender is inherently superior or, for that matter, that all homemaking moms are secretly miserable. We may cynically dismiss these developments as the work of "political correctness," but economic and other data over the last half century show that our view of women's roles in particular has in fact shifted precipitously, and for the better. As much work as there is left to do, such hard-won progress should not be discounted. To the extent that sincere debates still rage over the ethics of same-sex marriage and transgender identity, we are nonetheless in a "tipping" period where public opinion has shifted drastically in just a few years.[19]

Another metric by which some measure sex education's "progress," and for which sex education should get some credit, is a straightforward summary of the concrete health outcomes it is intended to influence. For example, teen birth rates have fallen in the United States from 59.9 births per 1,000 girls aged 15–19 in 1990 to just 18.8 in 2017.[20] This is progress, almost everyone would agree. But in Sweden the birth rate in 2018 was just 5 per 1,000 girls in the same age range.[21] Is progress a measure of how far you've come, or of where you are relative to others? As we've seen, these numbers also eclipse other aspects of sexuality that matter greatly to young people, and a fixation on predetermined public health outcomes invites a techno-rationalist approach to sex education that can be incompatible with democratic and humanistic values. In other words, we want to improve the numbers, but we want to do it without coercion or force, or as part of some weird eugenics fantasy.

This brings us to the question of means. Is there progress in *how* we deliver sex education? Again, some things have changed since sex education first tiptoed its way into the formal school curriculum in the early twentieth century, but there is little consensus on how much improvement there's been. As we well know, "comprehensive" these days signals "progressive" because it is more popular with the political Left, and more different from older approaches, than its rival, "abstinence-only" is. But we must not mistake the number of topics in a curriculum for a critical or boundary-pushing take on sex. Indeed, the laundry-list approach to sex education, to which additional topics can always be appended, belies some of the very problems that progressive educators have sought to rectify, such as the risk of decontextualization and lack of attention to the emotional and social valences of sexuality. Yet there is consensus among researchers and educators that a parsimonious curriculum is both unlikely to achieve its stated goals and also unlikely to promote an agenda of equity. In order to be "progressive," a curriculum has to be fairly hefty, or "comprehensive" in terms of content, but not just a long series of facts—nor, for that matter, should it offer something akin to Spain's absurd experiment in masturbation workshops.[22]

When politically liberal school reformers talk about "progressive" sex education, they sometimes use this term as a synonym for "secular." The conflation of liberal attitudes toward sexuality with hostile attitudes toward religion is a recent one, however, dubbed "sexularism" by some researchers.[23] Eschewing religion often means eschewing moral education altogether, and sex education that earns high points for "secularism" may look like nothing more than a glorified biology class. Both progressive secular critics of sexuality education *and* many religious educators have derided the tendency to present sexuality as a set of cold facts that can be mastered; in the Family Life Education of the mid-twentieth century, Christian-inspired family values allowed more discussion of pleasure and intimacy than most "liberal" curricula allow today. We are probably more likely to find heteronormative conceptions of relationships in a religiously inspired sex education curriculum and to find gender-inclusive conceptions in a secular one, but the relationship between religion and progress is more complex than that.

The countries touted for having the most "progressive" sex education are also more likely to make it mandatory. In the United States, parents can usually opt out of a curriculum they consider to be unconscionable. In most of the European Union, they can't. Of course, these factors could come apart: there could be cases where conservative sex education is strictly mandatory. But most advocates for sex education think there is a better chance of all students in a diffuse system receiving important instruction if the curriculum is statutory. At the same time, the notion of locally developed, responsive, culturally appropriate, and open-ended pedagogy has been central to the theories of anti-racist and inclusive education. And preventing opt-outs from public school curriculum has been seen as self-defeating, since some families will simply redirect their children to private schools that share their values, or homeschool them instead.

"Progress" implies "change," and there has been change in sex education over the years, whether measured in attitudes toward gender roles, declining teen pregnancy rates, curriculum content and delivery, or on other metrics. Yet progress as a *normative* ideal remains contentious, not only because we lack consensus about some of the aims we're striving for, but also because political benchmarks are always moving. There is nothing inherently "progressive" about sex education that is secular, comprehensive, or mandatory. These are just the markers that correspond to the state of sex education politics today.

Sweden is more "progressive" than the United States in all these dimensions, but it has been argued that Scandinavia's greater ethnic homogeneity and strong social safety net have advanced sexual politics in a way that North American societies cannot. The Nordic countries' relative insulation from the diversity of southern Europe and Asia facilitates a focus on sexual inclusion to the point that any expression of homophobia or prudishness about sex may be viewed as cultural invasion. This smugness about sexual progress and its racist underbelly have been described as "a discourse of sexual imperialism," even by those who share liberal sex education goals.[24] Unfortunately, then, "progressive" attitudes toward sex education may mask other agendas. Far-right xenophobic political parties have risen precipitously across Europe in recent years, tracking the influx of non-white, and especially Muslim, immigrants. Some, like the Alternative für Deutschland in Germany, also defend traditional and restrictive sexual paradigms, but in Scandinavia, the supposedly forward-thinking values behind sex education are viewed by some as explicitly Islamophobic.[25] Likewise, when Ontario experienced backlash to its "progressive" curriculum in 2015, some of the curriculum's defenders played on stereotypes about the Muslim and Asian protesters being ignorant and "backward," literally in the wrong place.[26] "Progress" invokes geography as well as history. We must be vigilant about how the politics of sex education affect other social aims.

WHAT'S NEXT?

In light of all this, what kind of progress should we strive for? We have argued that authentic progress does not mean fitting sex education into preexisting labels and political shorthand, nor is it change for its own sake. Progress requires ensuring that sex education meets the evolving needs of young people as much as possible, not doubling down on some prefabricated conception. Our preceding discussions have already indicated some of the content areas that sex education must urgently incorporate to meet this obligation. We saw in the last chapter that teens are far more influenced by pornography, technology, gender politics, and clashing sexual extremes than even so-called "comprehensive" sex education currently admits. Researchers have sounded the alarm on these oversights, but the uptake is too little, too late. Even pointed discussions about social media and sexting that may have been appropriate in 2015 would need to be updated today. In the last few years alone, students have watched the unanticipated phenomenon of #MeToo recast cultural attitudes toward sexual harassment and consent.

Consent appears to have been the fatally missing ingredient in the experiences of the teens we named at the beginning of this chapter. They are not alone. A survey of six thousand American youths found that 18% of girls and a smaller number of boys have been sexually assaulted *by a peer* by the age of seventeen.[27] Inspired by cultural momentum, students are sometimes leading the charge to take teen assault more seriously. For example, students from Los Gatos, California, which is adjacent to where Audrie Pott lived in Saratoga, organized a rally after one student's Instagram post about her assault inspired a petition and a new senior's hashtag: @metoolghs. Sheila Pott, Audrie's mother, was one of the speakers.[28] A new student group, From Survivors For Survivors, proposed a two-tier plan, including "detailed and public Title IX investigation process and reporting protocol . . . four year sex education curriculum teaching about healthy relationships, consent, body image, and sexual assault/harrasment [*sic*], [and] sexual assault awareness and recovery resources on school grounds."[29]

The question of *how* to teach for consent is no small nut to crack, however. Since the 1990s, post-secondary guidelines have evolved from "no means no" into "affirmative" consent, which requires that consent be voluntary, enthusiastic, and ongoing. However, as many experts have pointed out, the ethics of sexual agency and consent are blurrier than the black-and-white poles of "yes" and "no" negotiated by equally powerful parties.[30] It is not enough to instruct young people to declare their sexual boundaries confidently and unambiguously; our desires and modes of communication are shot through with social and psychological influences. It is also not enough to raise consent only toward the end of a high school program: consent education should also begin very early, before sex as such becomes the contentious focal point, as soon as children start learning about bodies and relationships (for example, consent to hugging, consent to tickling).[31] And even then, some children have already been victims of sexual abuse before they set foot in a classroom. In some cases, the very people to whom we normally refer children with private questions—parents, babysitters, coaches, older siblings—have been their violators. As children move through the school system, greater numbers experience sexual or other forms of trauma, which is known to impact their personal boundaries and agency, with drastic implications for sexual consent.[32]

The practice of teaching for consensual relationships will require much more nimble and interdisciplinary teaching than sex education has typically featured. Sexual health will have to fuse with media studies, social studies, mental health, and civic education; schools will have to prepare to address controversial and emerging discussions about gender and power, not only in abstract terms, but on their own school grounds. Students will need support from counselors, nurses, and social workers as well as teachers, parents, clergy, politicians, and their peers. Consent education is just one emerging topic that highlights the limits of our existing education paradigms. The world is always changing. In 2020, COVID-19 ripped through the world and instantly confounded our norms for touching, learning, and even leaving our homes. The ethics and logistics of sexual experimentation changed overnight. This is why we think that DHSE provides the proper framework for ongoing school-based sex education, but not a table of contents that will survive the tests of time. Sex education has always been, and must remain, a work in progress.

A SUBJECT APART

We have noted that sex education might, compared to other topics in education, be *sui generis*—a category until itself. Some of the hoopla over sex education apparently grows from this sense. It is not that the arguments for comprehensive school-based sex education are irrational, or that the evidence is irrelevant, some will say; rather, sex just isn't the kind of topic about which we can reason in this manner. Sex is physical, sex is irrational, sex is private. Education—at least, in modern Western schooling—is intellectual, rule-bound, and public. Sex is something we *do* more than something we *learn*. It is about who we are, what we believe, and what we aspire to. It's no accident that no other area of school curriculum is so radioactive.

The historical and philosophical perspective we have offered confirms that in many ways, the very concept of "sex education" is a paradox. Over the years and across ideological groups, reformers have encountered the inherent challenges of fitting teen sexuality into the straitjacket of formal education. We dream that the right policy, the right curriculum, or the right teacher can magically "domesticate the wildness of sexuality."[33]

Still, rational curriculum policy is our best collective weapon against the worst sexual outcomes, as well as our best bet for getting basic information into the minds of all young people. It may even help students realize healthy and happy relationships. Almost all North Americans agree that CSE belongs in schools—just perhaps not in the same way that math belongs in schools. It's about helping young people take the first steps in awkward conversations and find their way into responsible intimacy. It requires wading into some of the heaviest topics in all of education—disease, birth, death, violence—while affirming that sex can be immensely pleasurable, not to mention pretty hilarious. Sex education is a profound form of education that no standardized test could ever possibly chart.

In these respects, sex education *is* different from other subjects. It's a touchy subject, but one we can't let go.

ACKNOWLEDGMENTS

We owe special thanks to Jonathan Zimmerman and Randy Curren, the series editors, who introduced us and nurtured the development of this manuscript. Their feedback helped us to stretch beyond the confines of discipline and academic scholarship, hopefully resulting in a book appealing to a broad audience.

Lisa Andersen extends special thanks to the Liberal Arts Department and the Academic Writing Workshop at The Juilliard School. Early versions of this material were presented at the American Educational Research Association, John Jay College, the Southern California Sex Education Summit, the Center for Sex Education's National Sex Education Conference, the University of Toronto, the International Standing Conference for the History of Education, and the podcast *The Longest Shortest Time*. Parts of this book are published with permission from my article "'Kids Know What They Are Doing': Peer-Led Sex Education in New York City," which appeared in *History of Education Quarterly* 59, no. 4 (November 2019), © 2019 by the History of Education Society. Thanks to Zoë Burkholder for many commiseration sessions, to Abigail Karlin-Resnick for lending professional insight, to Jon Zimmerman for copious advice, and to Matthew J. Perry for reading, rereading, and general tolerance. A special shout-out to Mrs. Patricia Novak of St. Simon School for her dedication to Family Life Education, and to Mom and Dad for some good stories. The kids and the dog were, as always, welcome distractions during the writing process.

Lauren Bialystok thanks the many students and colleagues who welcomed her brash entrance into sex education scholarship. Special mention is owed to Jen Gilbert, Sarah Flicker, Jessica Wright, Sharon Lamb, and the Touchy Subject team. Some arguments in this book were presented at the Philosophy of Education Society, the Ontario Institute for Studies in Education, the University of Western Ontario's Department of Women's Studies and Feminist Research Annual Research Conference, the American Educational Research Association, the Association for Moral Education, and the Canadian Society for Studies in Education; thanks are due to colleagues for valuable questions and feedback. Shout-out to the Bay Centre for Birth Control and Planned Parenthood Toronto, where Lauren learned the challenges, urgency, and rewards of educating for sexual autonomy. Thanks to Randy Curren for his confidence, incisive feedback, and lightning-quick responsiveness on email. Deep thanks to Matt Ferkany for tapping Lauren for the job and for general support and wonderfulness. And to Mom and Dad, as always.

Thank you to Zoom, for making collaboration possible in the most unlikely of circumstances. Lisa received financial support from the Elmer L. Andersen Research Scholarship (no relation) at the University of Minnesota's Department of Archives and Special Collections.

Our editor, Elizabeth Branch Dyson, has carefully shepherded the manuscript. Thanks also to the anonymous peer reviewers whose comments illuminated problems and possibilities.

NOTES

INTRODUCTION

1. Matthew Rodriguez, "Watch Omaha Parents Rage Because They Think Planned Parenthood Influenced School Sex Ed," Mic, October 24, 2015, https://www.mic.com/articles/127307/watch-omaha-parents-rage-because-they-think-planned-parenthood-influenced-school-sex-ed; Ed Mazza, "Omaha Parent Claims Sex Education 'Rapes Children of Their Innocence,'" *Huffington Post*, January 6, 2016, https://www.huffpost.com/entry/omaha-sex-education_n_568c862be4b0a2b6fb6dd505.

2. Joe Dejka and Erin Duffy, "Psst. Have You Heard What They're Teaching Kids about Sex in Omaha Public Schools? What You Heard, It Turns Out, May Not Be True," *Omaha World-Herald*, February 12, 2017.

3. John Lynch, "The 10 Actors Who Americans Like the Most," *Business Insider*, April 26, 2018, https://www.businessinsider.com/most-popular-actors-in-the-us-2018-4; José Gabriel Navarro, "Share of Consumers Who Have a Favorable Opinion of Selected Star Wars Characters in the United States as of December 2017," *Statistica*, August 21, 2021, https://www.statista.com/statistics/790398/star-wars-characters-opinion/.

4. Omaha Public Schools Research Division, *Human Growth and Development Curriculum Review*, 2015, 6. See https://district.ops.org/Portals/0/PUBLIC_INFORMATION/HumanGrowthContentStandards/1-HGD%20Parent%20Survey%20Results.pdf.

5. Centers for Disease Control and Prevention, *School Health Policies and Practices Study: Health Education Fact Sheet*, 2014, http://www.cdc.gov/healthyyouth/data/shpps/pdf/2014factsheets/health_education_shpps2014.pdf.

6. Lacey Merica, quoted in Mazza, "Omaha Parent."

7. Katja Bigalke, "Was Sexualkunde Heute Leisten Muss," *Deutschlandfunk Kultur*, February 26, 2018, https://www.deutschlandfunkkultur.de/aufklaerungsunterricht-an-schulen-was-sexualkunde-heute.976.de.html?dram:article_id=411678; Gilda Sedgh, Lawrence Finer, Akinrinola Bankole, Michelle Eilers, and Susheela Singh, "Adolescent Pregnancy, Birth, and Abortion Rates across Countries: Levels and Recent Trends," *Journal of Adolescent Health* 56 (2015): 223–30.

8. Sexual Information and Education Council of the United States (SIECUS), "State Profiles Fiscal Year 2017: Nebraska," 2018, https://siecus.org/wp-content/uploads/2018/07/NEBRASKA-FY17-FINAL.pdf; KETV, "Report: STD Rates Surge in Douglas County," February 28, 2015, https://www.ketv.com/article/report-std-rates-surge-in-douglas-county-1/7650795#.

9. Nathan Lo, Anita Lowe, and Eran Bendavid, "Abstinence Funding Was Not Associated with Reductions in HIV Risk Behavior in Sub-Saharan Africa," *Health Affairs* 35, no. 5 (2016): 856–63.

10. A-B-C stands for "Abstinence, Be faithful, and use a Condom."

CHAPTER ONE

1. See Catherine Cocks, "Rethinking Sexuality in the Progressive Era," *Journal of the Gilded Age and Progressive Era* 5, no. 2 (April 2006): 96–97.

2. Carl Degler, introduction to *The Mosher Survey: Sexual Attitudes of 45 Victorian Women*, by Clelia Duel Mosher, James MaHood, and Kristine Wenburg (New York: Arno Press, 1980); Carl Degler, "What Ought to Be and What Was: Women's Sexuality in the Nineteenth Century," *American Historical Review* 79, no. 5 (December 1974): 1467–90; Steven Seidman, "Sexual Attitudes of Victorian and Post-Victorian Women: Another Look at the Mosher Survey," *Journal of American Studies* 23, no. 1 (April 1989): 68–72.

3. Alice B. Stockham, *Tokology: A Book for Every Woman* (Chicago: A. B. Stockham & Co., 1898), 28.

4. John Harvey Kellogg, *Plain Facts for Old and Young* (Burlington, IA: Segner & Condit, 1881), 57.

5. Margaret A. Cleaves, in *Transactions of the American Society of Sanitary and Moral Prophylaxis* (New York: American Society of Sanitary and Moral Prophylaxis, 1906), 114. See also Helen Lefkowitz Horowitz, *Rereading Sex: Battles over Sexual Knowledge and Suppression in Nineteenth-Century America* (New York: Vintage, 2002).

6. Mosher, MaHood, and Wenburg, *The Mosher Survey*, 123, 219.

7. Evelyn Brooks Higginbotham, *Righteous Discontent: The Women's Movement in the Black Baptist Church, 1880–1920* (Cambridge, MA: Harvard University Press, 1994).

8. Vicki Ruiz, "The Flapper and the Chaperone: Cultural Constructions of Identity and Heterosexual Politics among Adolescent Mexican American Women, 1920–1950," in *Delinquents and Debutantes: Twentieth-Century American Girls' Cultures*, ed. Sherrie A. Inness (New York: New York University Press, 1998), 58–61.

9. Kathy Piess, *Cheap Amusements: Working Women and Leisure in Turn-of-the-Century New York* (Philadelphia: Temple University Press, 1986); Eileen Suárez Findlay, *Imposing Decency: The Politics of Sexuality and Race in Puerto Rico, 1870–1920* (Durham, NC: Duke University Press, 1999); Glenda Gilmore, *Gender and Jim Crow: Women and the Politics of White Supremacy in North Carolina, 1896–1920* (Chapel Hill: University of North Carolina Press, 1996); Wilma King, "'Prematurely Knowing of Evil Things': The Sexual Abuse of African American Girls and Young Women in Slavery and Freedom," *Journal of African American History* 99, no. 3 (Summer 2014): 173–96; George Peffer, *If They Don't Bring Their Women Here: Chinese Female Immigration before Exclusion* (Urbana: University of Illinois Press, 1999); Harriet Jacobs, *Incidents in the Life of a Slave Girl* (Boston, 1861), 83.

10. Cocks, "Rethinking Sexuality in the Progressive Era," 101.

11. Mosher, MaHood, and Wenburg, *The Mosher Survey*, 382.

12. Edith Wharton, "Life and I," in *Novellas and Other Writings*, ed. Cynthia Griffin Wolff (New York: Library of America, 1990), 1069–96.

13. Gloria C. Erlich, *The Sexual Education of Edith Wharton* (Berkeley: University of California Press, 1992), 27–30.

14. Wharton, "Life and I," 1087–88.

15. Mosher, MaHood, and Wenburg, *The Mosher Survey*, 251, 286–87.

16. Mosher, MaHood, and Wenburg, 412.

17. J. Riddle Goffe, in *Transactions of the American Society of Sanitary and Moral Prophylaxis* (1906): 118; Jennifer Burek Pierce, *What Adolescents Ought to Know: Sexual Health Texts in Early Twentieth-Century America* (Amherst: University of Massachusetts Press, 2011), 82–83.

18. Prince Morrow, *Social Diseases and Marriage: Social Prophylaxis* (New York: Lea Brothers and Company, 1904), 349–50.

19. Orrin Giddings Cocks, *Engagement and Marriage: Talks with Young Men* (New York: Association Press, 1913), 39.

20. Prof. and Mrs. J. W. Gibson and W. J. Truitt, *Golden Thoughts on Chastity and Procreation Including Heredity, Prenatal Influences, Etc., Etc.: Sensible Hints and Wholesome Advice for Maiden and Young Man, Wife and Husband, Mother and Father* (Atlanta: J. L. Nichols & Co., 1903), 301, 103. The two "etc." in the context of a twenty-eight-word title is a bit much. Still, this is a fascinating primary source, containing really interesting illustrations of African American families by African American artists.

21. E. Anthony Rotundo, *American Manhood: Transformations in Masculinity from the Revolution to the Modern Era* (New York: Basic Books, 1993), 31–74, 124–26.

22. On refutation of the double standard, see Thomas Walton Galloway, *The Sex Factor in Human Life: A Study Outline for College Men* (New York: American Social Hygiene Association, 1921), 120–21. Someone with access to the Harvard Library scribbled out "college men" in this title, replacing it with "grammar school boys." This graffiti was made hilariously permanent through the Hathi Trust: https://babel.hathitrust.org/cgi/pt?id=hvd.32044012769311&view=1up&seq=6.

23. Cocks, *Engagement and Marriage*, 28–29.

24. Ferdinand C. Valentine, in *Transactions of the American Society of Sanitary and Moral Prophylaxis* (1906): 100.

25. On the history of LGBTQ+ people during the Progressive Era, see George Chauncey, *Gay New York: Gender, Urban Culture, and the Making of the Gay Male World, 1890–1940* (New York: Basic Books, 1994); Lillian Faderman, *Odd Girls and Twilight Lovers: A History of Lesbian Life in Twentieth-Century America* (New York: Columbia University Press, 1991); and Jen Manion, *Female Husbands: A Trans History* (New York: Cambridge University Press, 2020).

26. Julie Malnig, "Apaches, Tangos, and Other Indecencies: Women, Dance, and New York Nightlife of the 1910s," in *Ballroom Boogie, Shimmy Sham, Shake: A Social and Popular Dance Reader*, ed. Julie Malnig (Urbana: University of Illinois Press, 2009), 79–85.

27. On the New Woman, see John D'Emilio and Estelle B. Freedman, *Intimate Matters: A History of Sexuality in America*, 3rd ed. (Chicago: University of Chicago Press, 2012), 188–94;

Martha H. Patterson, *Beyond the Gibson Girl: Reimagining the American New Woman, 1895–1915* (Urbana: University of Illinois Press, 2005); and Jean V. Matthews, *The Rise of the New Woman: The Women's Movement in America, 1875–1930* (Chicago: Ivan R. Dee, 2003).

28. Hugh Cabot, in *Report of the Sex Education Sessions of the Fourth International Congress on School Hygiene and of the Annual Meeting of the Federation, at Buffalo, New York, August 27th and 29th, 1913* (New York: American Federation for Sex Hygiene, 1913), 41.

29. Jeffery Moran, *Teaching Sex: The Shaping of Adolescence in the 20th Century* (Cambridge, MA: Harvard University Press, 2002), 30. The capacity of each mature generation to assume that each new generation of young people is horrible remains one of the few constants in American history.

30. Vicki L. Ruiz, "Nuestra América: Latino History as United States History," *Journal of American History* 93, no. 3 (December 2006): 664.

31. Susan Stryker, *Transgender History: The Roots of Today's Revolution*, rev. ed (New York: Seale Press, 2017), 53–54. For examples of transgender people and organizations in this era, see Stryker, 45–78; and Manion, *Female Husbands*, 139–257.

32. Pierce, *What Adolescents Ought to Know*, 1.

33. D'Emilio and Freedman, *Intimate Matters*, 234.

34. "Brieux Play Acted," *New York Times*, March 15, 1913; Pierce, *What Adolescents Ought to Know*, 66–79.

35. Eric Schaefer, "Of Hygiene and Hollywood: Origins of the Exploitation Film," in *Hollywood: Critical Concepts in Media and Cultural Studies*, ed. Thomas Schatz (New York: Routledge, 2004), 1:165–68.

36. Upton Sinclair, *Damaged Goods: The Great Play by Brieux* (Pasadena, CA: John C. Winston Company, 1913), 12, 7–8.

37. Alan M. Brandt, *No Magic Bullet: A Social History of Venereal Disease in the United States since 1880* (New York: Oxford University Press, 1987), 31.

38. I'm here thinking about the "Reproduction" number in *Grease 2*, which probably deserves its own article-length explication. Susan Zaeske, "The 'Promiscuous Audience' Controversy and the Emergence of the Early Woman's Rights Movement," *Quarterly Journal of Speech* 81, no. 2 (1995): 191–207.

39. Cocks, *Engagement and Marriage*, 39–40.

40. Peggy Pascoe, *Relations of Rescue: The Search for Female Moral Authority in the American West, 1874–1939* (New York: Oxford University Press, 1993); Timothy J. Gilfoyle, *City of Eros: New York City, Prostitution, and the Commercialization of Sex, 1790–1920* (New York: W. W. Norton, 1992); Ann R. Gabbert, "Prostitution and Moral Reform in the Borderlands: El Paso, 1890–1920," *Journal of the History of Sexuality* 12, no. 4 (October 2003): 575–604; Courtney Q. Shah, "'Against Their Own Weakness': Policing Sexuality and Women in San Antonio, Texas, during World War I," *Journal of the History of Sexuality* 19, no. 3 (September 2010): 458–82.

41. David J. Pivar, *Purity Crusade: Sexual Morality and Social Control, 1868–1900* (Westport, CT: Greenwood Press, 1973).

42. Piess, *Cheap Amusements*, 51–57, 108–14; D'Emilio and Freedman, *Intimate Matters*, 194–97.

43. Cocks, *Engagement and Marriage*, 31; R. Marie Griffith, *Moral Combat: How Sex Divided American Christians and Fractured American Politics* (New York: Basic Books, 2017), 79.

44. Galloway, *Sex Factor in Human Life*, 62.

45. Moran, *Teaching Sex*, 15, 37; Tracy L. Steffes, *School, Society, and State: A New Education to Govern Modern America, 1890–1940* (Chicago: University of Chicago Press, 2012), 95–117.

46. Venkatraman Chandra-Mouli, Lucia Gómez Garbero, Marina Plesons, Iliana Lang, and Esther Corona Vargas, "Evolution and Resistance to Sexuality Education in Mexico," *Global Health: Science and Practice* 6, no. 1 (March 2018): 139.

47. Benjamin C. Gruenberg, *The Teacher and Sex Education* (New York: American Social Hygiene Association, 1924), 16.

48. Maurice A. Bigelow, *Sex Education: A Series of Lectures Concerning Knowledge of Sex in Its Relation to Human Life* (New York: Macmillan Company, 1916), 94–95.

49. Wayne Urban and Jennings Wagoner Jr., *American Education: A History* (New York: McGraw-Hill, 1996), 209–10; James W. Fraser, *Between Church and State: Religion and Public Education in a Multicultural America*, 2nd ed. (Baltimore: Johns Hopkins University Press, 2016), 137.

50. Jeffery P. Moran, "'Modernism Gone Mad': Sex Education Comes to Chicago, 1913," *Journal of American History* 83, no. 2 (September 1996): 504–5.

51. Newell W. Edson, *The Status of Sex Education in High Schools* (Washington, DC: Government Printing Office, 1922), 9.

52. Herbert M. Kliebard, *The Struggle for an American Curriculum*, 3rd ed. (New York: Routledge, 2004), 229.

53. Thomas M. Balliet, "Points of Attack in Sex Education," *Journal of Education* 79, no. 4 (January 1914): 88.

54. Prince A. Morrow, *Instruction in the Physiology and Hygiene of Sex for Teachers* (New York: Society of Sanitary and Moral Prophylaxis, 1913), 11–13.

55. See Brandt, *No Magic Bullet*; and Alexandra M. Lord, *Condom Nation: The U.S. Government's Sex Education Campaign from World War I to the Internet* (Baltimore: Johns Hopkins University Press, 2010).

56. Moran, *Teaching Sex*, 73–75.

57. Moran, 105.

58. Michael Imber, "Analysis of a Curriculum Reform Movement: The American Social Hygiene Association's Campaign for Sex Education, 1900–1930" (PhD diss., Stanford University, 1980), 104.

59. Maximilian P. E. Groszmann, *A Parent's Manual: Child Problems in Health and Illness* (New York: Century, 1923), 2:193.

60. Imber, "Analysis of a Curriculum Reform Movement," 66–69; Gruenberg, *The Teacher and Sex Education*, 27; Charles W. Fender, "Some Experiments in the Teaching of Sex Hygiene in a City High School," *School Science and Mathematics* 14, no. 7 (October 1914): 573–78; American Social Hygiene Association, *One Year's Activities of the American Social Hygiene Association* (New York: ASHA, 1914), 3; "No Sex Hygiene for Montclair," *New York Times*, February 1, 1914; "Teacher Suspended over Hygiene Talk," *New York Times*, April 5, 1922.

61. Robin E. Jensen, *Dirty Words: The Rhetoric of Public Sex Education, 1870–1924* (Urbana: University of Illinois Press, 2010), 63. Young suggested that other schools follow Chicago's lead; "Divided on Sex Hygiene," *New York Times*, March 22, 1914.

62. Mabel M. Wright, *Journal of Proceedings and Addresses of the Fifty-Second Annual Meeting of the National Education Association of the United States* (Ann Arbor, MI: National Education Association, 1914), 697–701.

63. Timothy Walch, *Parish School: American Catholic Parochial Education from Colonial Times to the Present* (New York: Crossroad Publishing, 1996), 108–11.

64. Moran, "'Modernism Gone Mad,'" 506.

65. Leigh Ann Wheeler, *Against Obscenity: Reform and the Politics of Womanhood in America, 1873–1935* (Baltimore: Johns Hopkins University Press, 2004), 116; Jensen, *Dirty Words*, 36–66.

66. Marjorie Murphy, *Blackboard Unions: The AFT and the NEA, 1900–1980* (Ithaca, NY: Cornell University Press, 1990), 82.

67. For a list of Young's accomplishments, see Dana Goldstein, *The Teacher Wars: A History of America's Most Embattled Profession* (New York: Doubleday, 2014), 83.

68. Here, I must note that "truthiness" is a new word but an old practice. Thank you, Stephen Colbert. For further information, see https://www.merriam-webster.com/words-at-play/truthiness-meaning-word-origin.

69. James E. Peabody, *Sex Education in the Home and High School* (New York: American Social Hygiene Association, 1916), 4, 7–9.

70. Geraldine J. Clifford, *Those Good Gertrudes: A Social History of Women Teachers in America* (Baltimore: Johns Hopkins University Press, 2014), 21.

71. Bigelow, *Sex Education*, 110–11.

72. On gender's role in shaping teaching as a semi-profession, see Murphy, *Blackboard Unions*, 12–16. On the ensuing desirability of professionalization, see Steffes, *School, Society, and State*, 35–36.

73. Diana D'Amico Pawlewicz, *Blaming Teachers: Professionalization Policies and the Failure of Reform in American History* (New Brunswick, NJ: Rutgers University Press, 2020), 64–70.

74. Edson, *Status of Sex Education in High Schools*, 6.

75. Thomas M. Balliet, in *Report of the Sex Education Sessions of the Fourth International Congress on School Hygiene*, 30–31.

76. On civics being distributed throughout the curriculum, see Steffes, *School, Society, and State*, 171.

77. Thomas M. Balliet, *Introduction of Sex Education into Public Schools* (New York: American Social Hygiene Association, 1927), 5.

78. David Tyack and Elisabeth Hansot, *Learning Together: A History of Coeducation in American Public Schools*, rev. ed. (New York: Russell Sage Foundation, 1992), 224–27.

79. "Sex Education Is the Most Popular Course at Howard Summer Session," *New Journal and Guide* (Norfolk, VA), June 29, 1929.

CHAPTER TWO

1. See also Jeffery Moran, *Teaching Sex: The Shaping of Adolescence in the 20th Century* (Cambridge, MA: Harvard University Press, 2002), 98–99.

2. Benjamin Gruenberg, *High Schools and Sex Education* (Washington, DC: Government Printing Office, 1939), xiii; Frances Bruce Strain, *Sex Guidance in Family Life Education: A*

Handbook for the Schools (New York: Macmillan 1942), 263; John F. Cuber and Mark Ray, "Reflections on Sex Education in the High School," *Marriage and Family Living* 8, no. 1 (February 1946): 14.

3. Phyllis B. Dolloff and Miriam R. Resnick, *Patterns of Life: Human Growth and Development* (Columbus, OH: Charles E. Merrill Publishing, 1972), iii.

4. Stephanie Ventura and Christine A. Bachrach, "Nonmarital Childbearing in the United States, 1940–99," *National Vital Statistics Report* 48, no. 16 (October 18, 2000): 1, https://www.cdc.gov/nchs/data/nvsr/nvsr48/nvs48_16.pdf; R. Marie Griffith, *Moral Combat: How Sex Divided American Christians and Fractured American Politics* (New York: Basic Books, 2017), 30–34; Kristy L. Slominski, *Teaching Moral Sex: A History of Religion and Sex Education in the United States* (New York: Oxford University Press, 2021), 178–81; Lee G. Burchinal, "Research on Young Marriage: Implications for Family Life Education," *Family Life Coordinator* 9, nos. 1–2 (September–December 1960): 6–24.

5. Courtney Q. Shah, *Sex Ed, Segregated: The Quest for Sexual Knowledge in Progressive-Era America* (Rochester, NY: University of Rochester Press, 2015); Mary Ransom, "Panel on Venereal Disease Held by Women's Interracial Council," *New Journal and Guide* (Norfolk, VA), November 13, 1948.

6. Alexandra M. Lord, *Condom Nation: The U.S. Government's Sex Education Campaign from World War I to the Internet* (Baltimore: Johns Hopkins University Press, 2010), 98.

7. Lord, 108.

8. Ventura and Bachrach, "Nonmarital Childbearing in the United States, 1940–99," 17; Lord, *Condom Nation*, 109.

9. My interpretation builds upon Jeffery Moran's work, which connects the decline in STIs to the rise of Family Life Education, viewing the latter as a means of re-professionalizing the field. I am asking why this *particular* form of re-professionalization was so appealing.

10. Moran, *Teaching Sex*, 94–95. See also Nathan G. Hale Jr., *The Rise and Crisis of Psychoanalysis in the United States: Freud and the Americans, 1917–1985* (New York: Oxford University Press, 1995).

11. Frances Bruce Strain and Chester Lee Eggert, *Framework for Family Life Education: A Survey of Present Day Activities in Sex Education* (Washington, DC: American Association for Health, Physical Education, and Recreation, 1956), 73. On the mental hygienists' classification of inhibited children as "maladjusted," see Sol Cohen, "The Mental Hygiene Movement, the Development of Personality and the School: The Medicalization of American Education," *History of Education Quarterly* 23, no. 2 (Summer 1983): 131.

12. Lester A. Kirkendall and David S. Brody, "The Arousal of Fear—Does It Have a Place in Sex Education?" *Family Life Coordinator* 13, no. 1 (January 1964): 14. Kirkendall was one of Maurice Bigelow's students.

13. Omnia El Shakry, "Youth as Peril and Promise: The Emergence of Adolescent Psychology in Postwar Egypt," *International Journal of Middle East Studies* 43, no. 4 (November 2011): 591–610, esp. 600.

14. Wang Ning, "The Reception of Freudianism in Modern Chinese Literature, Part I (1920–1949)," *China Information* 5, no. 3 (Spring 1991): 62; Mei Fong, "The Misconceived One-Child Policy Lives On," *Current History* 115, no. 782 (September 2016): 241–42.

15. Ralph G. Eckert, "Highlights of a Marriage Course," *Marriage and Family Living* 8, no. 2 (May 1946): 39; Beth Bailey, "Scientific Truth . . . and Love: The Marriage Education Movement in the United States," *Journal of Social History* 20, no. 4 (Summer 1987): 725.

16. Slominski, *Teaching Moral Sex*, 134–35, 215–16. I'm here using "mainline" to describe Protestants who interpret the Bible's meaning through a historical lens and aspire to use reason to apply biblical teachings to a modern context.

17. Alma Long, summarized in Oliver Erasmus Byrd, ed., *Family Life Sourcebook* (Stanford, CA: Stanford University Press, 1956), 136.

18. On the biblical inferences that Christian conservatives made to explain racial segregation, see Griffith, *Moral Combat*, 85–89.

19. Rebecca L. Davis, *More Perfect Unions: The American Search for Marital Bliss* (Cambridge, MA: Harvard University Press, 2010), 104; Bailey, "Scientific Truth . . . and Love," 724–25; Eckert, "Highlights of a Marriage Course," 39.

20. Slominski, *Teaching Moral Sex*, 156–57.

21. Elmer N. Witt, *Life Can Be Sexual* (St. Louis: Concordia, 1967), 43–45, quoted in John H. Phillips, *Sex Education in Major Protestant Denominations* (New York: National Council of Churches of Christ in the U.S.A., 1968), 9–10.

22. Eric W. Johnson, *Sex: Telling It Straight* (Philadelphia: J. B. Lippincott, 1970), 73–74.

23. Alessandra Aresu, "Sex Education in Modern and Contemporary China: Interrupted Debates across the Last Century," *International Journal of Educational Development* 29 (2009): 532–35.

24. Sarah R. Arvey, "Sex and the Ordinary Cuban: Cuban Physicians, Eugenics, and Marital Sexuality, 1933–1958," *Journal of the History of Sexuality* 21, no. 1 (January 2012): 93–120.

25. Curtis E. Avery and Margie R. Lee, "Family Life Education: Its Philosophy and Purpose," *Family Life Coordinator* 13, no. 2 (April 1964): 31.

26. Murray Maughan, Loye Painter, and Richard Sackett, "Logan Junior High Program of Sex Education," folder: Reports on Programs, box 37, National Council on Family Relations Records, Social Welfare History Archives, University of Minnesota Archives and Special Collections (hereafter NCFRR).

27. Lester Kirkendall, *Sex Education* (New York: Sex Information and Education Council of the U.S., 1965), 11.

28. Henry A. Bowman, *Marriage for Moderns* (New York: McGraw-Hill, 1942), 214.

29. For examples of these pamphlets, lesson plans, films, and sample kits, see folder: Ed.-Family Life and Sex Edu., Teach Aids—Elem. and H.S. Combined, box 93, NCFRR. On feminine hygiene, see Susan K. Freeman, *Sex Goes to School: Girls and Sex Education Before the 1960s* (Urbana: University of Illinois Press, 2008), 85–91; Joan Jacobs Brumberg, "'Something Happens to Girls': Menarche and the Emergence of the Modern American Hygienic Imperative," *Journal of the History of Sexuality* 4, no. 1 (June 1993): 99–127.

30. Helen Manley, *A Curriculum Guide in Sex Education* (St. Louis: Slate Publishing, 1964), 22, folder: Ed.-Family Life and Sex Edu., Teach Aids—Elem. and H.S. Combined, box 93, NCFRR; Helen Manley, *Family Life and Sex Education in the Elementary School* (Washington, DC: NEA, 1968), 12, 14–15; Lester V. Smith, quoted in Winnipeg School District Report on Sex Education, section B10 on University City, Missouri, folder: Reports on Programs, box 37, NCFRR; Gayle Dale and George C. Chamis, *Sex Education Guide for Teachers* (Flint, MI: Flint

Community Schools, 1967), 5, folder: Reports on Programs, box 37, NCFRR; Kirkendall, *Sex Education*, 5; Midwest Project on In-Service Education of Teachers, *Strengthening Family Life Education in Our Schools* (New York: ASHA, 1955), 46.

31. TAMA Division of Professional Productions, *Human Sexuality Education . . . Materials and Teaching Aids for an Effective School Program* (1966), folder: Ed.-Family Life and Sex Edu., Teach Aids—Elem. and H.S. Combined, box 93, NCFRR.

32. Katrina Karkazis, *Fixing Sex: Intersex, Medical Authority, and Lived Experience* (Durham, NC: Duke University Press, 2008), 31. On sexual "normalcy," see also Julian Carter, *The Heart of Whiteness: Normal Sexuality and Race in America, 1880–1940* (Durham, NC: Duke University Press, 2007).

33. Student quoted in Laura Winslow Drummond, *Youth and Instruction in Marriage and Family Living* (New York: Bureau of Publications, Teachers College, Columbia University, 1942), 67; Esther E. Prevey, "Family Life Education in the Kansas City, Missouri Public Schools," *Coordinator* 6, no. 4 (June 1958): 55; Dale and Chamis, *Sex Education Guide for Teachers*, 18.

34. Manley, *A Curriculum Guide in Sex Education*, 59.

35. Bowman, *Marriage for Moderns*, 4.

36. "Bennett Girls Told How to Get and Hold 'Boy Friends,'" *Atlanta Daily World*, April 23, 1941.

37. Winston W. Ehrmann, summarized in Byrd, *Family Life Sourcebook*, 19.

38. Midwest Project on In-Service Education of Teachers, *Strengthening Family Life Education in Our Schools*, 89.

39. Tim Wall, "Rocking Around the Clock: Teenage Dance Fads from 1955 to 1965," in *Ballroom, Boogie, Shimmy Sham, Shake: A Social and Popular Dance Reader*, ed. Julie Malnig (Urbana: University of Illinois Press, 2009), 186–94.

40. Robert D. Herman, summarized in Byrd, *Family Life Sourcebook*, 151.

41. Midwest Project on In-Service Education of Teachers, *Strengthening Family Life Education in Our Schools*, 148.

42. Byrd, *Family Life Sourcebook*, 1.

43. Gladys Hoagland Groves, summarized in Byrd, 20.

44. Meyer F. Nimkoff and Arthur L. Wood, summarized in Byrd, 5.

45. Marvin C. Dubbe, "What Teen-Agers Can't Tell Parents and Why," *Coordinator* 4, no. 3 (March 1956): 4–5.

46. Judson T. Landis and Mary G. Landis, *Personal Adjustment, Marriage, and Family Living: A High School Text* (New York: Prentice-Hall, 1950), 102.

47. Christina Simmons, "'I Had to Promise . . . Not to Ask "Nasty" Questions Again': African American Women and Sex and Marriage Education in the 1940s," *Journal of Women's History* 27, no. 1 (Spring 2015): 114, 115, 118.

48. Agnes Elizabeth Benedict and Adele Franklin, *The Happy Home: A Guide to Family Living* (New York: Appleton-Century-Crofts, 1949), 20; William G. Kornegay, "Family Life Education and the Junior High School," *High School Journal* 40, no. 6 (March 1957): 262; Jonathan Zimmerman, *Too Hot to Handle: A Global History of Sex Education* (Princeton, NJ: Princeton University Press, 2015), 50, 68.

49. Lawrence S. Bee, "Evaluating Education for Marriage and Family Living," *Marriage and Family Living* 14, no. 2 (May 1952): 101.

50. Melinda Chateauvert, "Framing Sexual Citizenship: Reconsidering the Discourse on African American Families," *Journal of African American History* 93, no. 2 (Spring 2008): 198–99, 207.

51. "Raise Academic Level at Tuskegee Institute in Fall," *Tri-State Defender* (August 26, 1961); "Mrs. Streat Appointed to New Bennett Post," *New Pittsburg Courier* (October 13, 1962).

52. Slominski, *Teaching Moral Sex*, 142, 148, 163; Phillips, *Sex Education in Major Protestant Denominations*, 1–11.

53. W. Dean Belnap and Glen C. Griffin, *About Life and Love: Facts of Life for LDS Teens* (Salt Lake City, UT: Deseret Book Company, 1970), 11.

54. Phillips, *Sex Education in Major Protestant Denominations*, 6–8; "Religious Queries: Should the Church Supplement Sex Education," *Chicago Defender*, February 5, 1966.

55. Moran, *Teaching Sex*, 147–48, 168–69; John F. Cuber, "Can We Evaluate Marriage Education?" *Marriage and Family Living* 11, no. 3 (August 1949): 93–95; Leland H. Stott, "The Problem of Evaluating Family Success," *Marriage and Family Living* 13, no. 4 (November 1951): 149–53.

56. Lester Kirkendall, interview by Yvonne Loso, February 19, 1984, Portland, Oregon, College of Home Economics Oral Histories, Special Collections and Archives Research Center, Oregon State University Libraries, http://scarc.library.oregonstate.edu/omeka/exhibits/show/oralhistory/item/33761.

57. Donna J. Drucker, "'A Noble Experiment': The Marriage Course at Indiana University, 1938–1940," *Indiana Magazine of History* 103, no. 3 (September 2007): 236–37.

58. Patricia A. Smith, "Some Observations on Family Life Education at the Secondary Level," *Coordinator* 6, no. 4 (June 1958): 51–53.

59. See Diana D'Amico Pawlewicz, *Blaming Teachers: Professionalization Policies and the Failure of Reform in American History* (New Brunswick, NJ: Rutgers University Press, 2020), 110–11, 126–27.

60. Anna M. Laitala, "A Sex Education Unit in the North Target Area Experimental Junior High School," 9, speech presented at the Tenth Biannual Governor's Conference on Children and Youth (1966), folder: Reports on Programs, box 37, NCFRR.

61. Cecelia E. Sudia to Donald Durman, February 1, 1966, folder: Ed—Family Life–Sex Education, Opposition and Controversy, 1945–1974, box 36, NCFRR.

62. Freeman, *Sex Goes to School*, 51.

63. Laitala, "A Sex Education Unit in the North Target Area Experimental Junior High School," 9.

64. Curtis E. Avery, "Toward an Understanding of Sex Education in Oregon," *Coordinator* 5, no. 1 (September 1956): 8–9.

65. Freeman, *Sex Goes to School*, 44.

66. Anne M. Valk, *Radical Sisters: Second-Wave Feminism and Black Liberation in Washington, D.C.* (Urbana: University of Illinois Press, 2008), especially chapters 2 and 5.

67. Susan Stryker, *Transgender History: The Roots of Today's Revolution*, rev. ed (New York: Seale Press, 2017), 117.

68. Adrienne Rich, "Compulsory Heterosexuality and Lesbian Existence," *Signs* 5, no. 4 (Summer 1980): 650–53.

69. Lester A. Kirkendall, "Two Issues in Sex Education," *Family Life Coordinator* 15, no. 4 (October 1966): 179.

70. Muriel W. Brown, quoted in Avery and Lee, "Family Life Education," 34.

71. Moran, *Teaching Sex*, 159.

72. Mary S. Calderone, "Special Report: SIECUS in 1969," *Journal of Marriage and Family* 31, no. 4 (November 1969): 674–76.

73. National Education Association's Commission on Professional Rights and Responsibilities, *Suggestions for Defense Against Extremist Attack: Sex Education in the Public Schools* (Washington, DC: NEA, 1970), 2, folder: Opposition and Controversy, 1945–1964, box 36, NCFRR.

74. Janice M. Irvine, *Talk about Sex: The Battles over Sex Education in the United States* (Berkeley: University of California Press, 2004), 35.

75. It would be difficult to overstate my indebtedness in this section to Natalia Mehlman, "Sex Ed . . . and the Reds?: Reconsidering the Anaheim Battle over Sex Education, 1962–1969," *History of Education Quarterly* 47, no. 2 (May 2007): 203–32. Natalia Mehlman Petrzela's most recent book is *Classroom Wars: Language, Sex, and the Making of Modern Political Culture* (New York: Oxford University Press, 2015).

76. Irvine, *Talk about Sex*, 38; Moran, *Teaching Sex*, 172; Mehlman, "Sex Ed . . . and the Reds?," 204.

77. Esther D. Schulz and Sally D. Williams, *Family Life and Sex Education: Curriculum and Instruction* (New York: Harcourt, Brace, and World, 1968).

78. Kirkendall, "Two Issues in Sex Education," 178.

79. Irvine, *Talk about Sex*, 48. This is a summary of Irvine's 1997 interview with Eleanor Howe.

80. Adam Laats, *The Other School Reformers: Conservative Activism in American Education* (Cambridge, MA: Harvard University Press, 2015), 14, 21–24; June Melby Benowitz, "Reading, Writing and Radicalism: Right-Wing Women and Education in the Post-War Years," *History of Education Quarterly* 49, no. 1 (February 2009): 89–111.

81. Slominski, *Teaching Moral Sex*, 170, 173–76.

82. This flyer's story was circulated by several different organizations, the ostensible incident being placed in at least five different cities—a contradiction that did not seem to bother the rumor's perpetuators; Irvine, *Talk about Sex*, 54–55.

83. Tim LaHaye, *A Christian View of Radical Sex Education* (San Diego: Family Life Seminars, c. 1969), in *Jerry Falwell and the Rise of the Religious Right: A Brief History with Documents*, ed. Matthew Avery Sutton (Boston: Bedford / St. Martin's, 2013), 74.

84. I'm here envisioning a meme reading "When wild oats have raw sex . . ."

85. Parents Opposing Sex Education in Public Schools, Inc., flyer, "What Parents Should Know! About Sex Education in the Public Schools" (c. 1969), folder: Opposition and Controversy, box 36, NCFRR.

86. David A. Noebel to "Concerned Americans," January 19, 1971, folder: Opposition and Controversy, box 36, NCFRR.

87. Highland Park Baptist Church (St. Paul, MN), newsletter, April 6, 1969, 2, folder: Opposition and Controversy, box 36, NCFRR.

88. Moran, *Teaching Sex*, 183.

89. Rose M. Somerville, "Family Life and Sex Education in the Turbulent Sixties," *Journal of Marriage and Family* 33, no. 1 (February 1971): 27.

90. Mehlman, "Sex Ed . . . and the Reds?," 230.

91. Doris Bloch and Mayhew Derryberry, "Effect of Political Controversy on Sex Education Research: A Case Study," *Family Coordinator* 20, no. 3 (July 1971): 259–64.

92. Janet S. Brown to Elizabeth S. Force, Report on Inter-Agency Conference on Current Opposition, March 25, 1969, folder: Opposition and Controversy, box 36, NCFRR. Twenty-seven national organizations were represented.

93. Richard K. Kerckhoff and panel, "Community Experiences with the 1969 Attack on Sex Education," *Family Coordinator* 19, no. 1 (January 1970): 104–5.

94. Luther G. Baker Jr., "The Rising Furor over Sex Education," *Family Coordinator* 18, no. 3 (July 1969): 214–15.

95. Roger W. Libby, "Parental Attitudes toward Content in High School Sex Education Programs: Liberalism-Traditionalism and Demographic Correlates," *Family Coordinator* 20, no. 2 (April 1971): 132.

96. Lord, *Condom Nation*, 132–34.

97. Gerald H. Wiechmann and Altis L. Ellis, "A Study of the Effects of 'Sex Education' on Premarital Petting and Coital Behavior," *Family Coordinator* 18, no. 3 (July 1969): 231–34.

98. William J. Brown, preface to *Teacher's Handbook on Venereal Disease Education*, by William F. Schwartz (Washington DC: American Association for Health, Physical Education, and Recreation—NEA, 1965), vi.

99. Lord, *Condom Nation*, 135–36.

100. Bloch and Derryberry, "Effect of Political Controversy on Sex Education Research," 263. Bloch would complete her research and publish in 1979; "Attitudes of Mothers Toward Sex Education," *American Journal of Public Health* 69, no. 9 (September 1979): 911.

101. Timothy Walch, *Parish School: American Catholic Parochial Education from Colonial Times to the Present* (New York: Crossroad Publishing, 1996), 161–68, 176.

CHAPTER THREE

1. Precis, c. 1973, cover and p. 8, Board of Education of the City of New York Grant 07300500, June 22, 1973–September 30, 1975, Ford Foundation Grants A–B, microfilm reel 1177, Ford Foundation Records, Rockefeller Archive Center, Sleepy Hollow, New York (hereafter cited as FFR).

2. Sylvia Hunter, memo to Jule M. Sugarman, "Student Proposal for Birth Control Information-and-Referral Services in Public High Schools," May 4, 1972, FFR; Maude Parker, memo on Publicity and the Family Living / Sex Education Peer Information Services 1973–1974, c. 1974, FFR.

3. Parker, memo on Publicity and the Family Living / Sex Education Peer Information Services 1973–1974, FFR.

4. Peter Scales, "Sex Education in the '70s and '80s: Accomplishments, Obstacles and Emerging Issues," *Family Relations* 30, no. 4 (October 1981): 559.

5. UPA, newsletter, 1972–73, FFR.

6. Hariette Surovell, "Most Girls Just Pray," *New York Times*, October 1, 1971.

7. C. Doubrovsky, "Sex Education," in *Report of Sex Bias in the Public Schools*, 4th ed., ed. A. J. Jawin (New York: Education Committee, National Organization for Women, New York Chapter, 1977), referenced in Kera Lovell, "Girls Are Equal Too: Education, Body Politics, and the Making of Teenage Feminism," *Gender Issues* 33, no. 2 (June 2016): 81.

8. Precis, 3, FFR.

9. Madeline Oberle, quoted in Georgia Dullea, "Teen-Agers Offer Information on Sex," *New York Times*, November 15, 1973.

10. Pat Hanson, Monthly Progress Report for Adlai Stevenson High School, May 1974, FFR.

11. Michael Carrera, memo to Susan Berresford, Adrienne Germaine, and Richard Lacey, "A Snapshot View," c. April 1974, FFR.

12. Irwin Tobin to Susan Berresford, August 13, 1974, FFR; M. Drexler, Monthly Report for Erasmus High School, December 1974, FFR; S. Gershowitz, Monthly Report for Thomas Jefferson High School, December 1974, FFR; Martha Drexler, Monthly Progress Report for Benjamin Franklin High School, October 1974, FFR; M. Drexler, Monthly Report for Cleveland High School, December 1974, FFR.

13. Jerry Cioffi, Monthly Progress Report for Flushing High School, December 1974, FFR; Pat Hanson, Monthly Progress Report for Flushing High School, May 1974, FFR.

14. Pat Hanson to Anne Welbourne, Monthly Progress Report for March and April 1974, FFR. I am super curious about those decorations.

15. "The Pregnant Schoolgirl," *Time*, April 7, 1961, 46, quoted in Bernard J. Oliver Jr., *Marriage and You: A Sociological and Psychological Study of American Marriage and Family Life* (New Haven, CT: College and University Press, 1964), 231.

16. Caroline Lund, "High School Women Take on Board of Ed," *Militant*, May 28, 1971.

17. Michael Carrera, memo to Susan Berresford, Adrienne Germaine, and Richard Lacey, February 20, 1974, FFR.

18. Irwin Tobin, memo to Susan Berresford, Adrianne Germaine, and Richard Lacey, May 8, 1974, FFR.

19. Dullea, "Teen-Agers Offer Information on Sex."

20. Ann Welbourne, Monthly Progress Report, April 1974, FFR; Adrienne Germaine, memo on 4/26/74 meeting, April 29, 1974, FFR.

21. Adrienne Germaine, memo on 4/26/74 meeting, FFR.

22. Pat Hanson, Monthly Progress Report for Martin Van Buren High School, May 1974, FFR; Pat Hanson to Anne Welbourne, Monthly Report for May 1974, FFR.

23. Irwin Tobin, memo to Susan Berresford, Adrianne Germaine, and Richard Lacey, May 8, 1974, FFR.

24. Michael A. Carrera, memo to Susan Berresford, June 19, 1974, FFR.

25. Michael A. Carrera to Susan Berresford and Adrienne Germaine, February Report, March 11, 1975, FFR.

26. Sharon Katz to Joan Dunlop, c. July 1974, FFR.

27. Ann Welbourne, Martha Drexler, Patrician Hanson, and Maude I. Parker, "A Family Living / Sex Information Peer Group Project," *Family Coordinator* 24, no. 1 (January 1975):

100–101. On "bogart," see the Urban Dictionary, https://www.urbandictionary.com/define.php?term=bogart.

28. Kim Phillips-Fein, *Fear City: New York's Fiscal Crisis and the Rise of Austerity Politics* (New York: Metropolitan Books, 2017), 221.

29. Maude I. Parker to Susan Berresford, April 25, 1975, FFR; Mel Warren to Irwin Tobin, March 24, 1975, FFR.

30. Maude I. Parker to Susan Berresford, June 12, 1975, FFR.

31. Alfred F. Moran, memo, November 19, 1975, FFR.

32. Maude Parker to Susan [Berresford], November 26, 1975, FFR.

33. William Van Til, "Reform of the High School in the Mid-1970s," *Phi Delta Kappan* 56, no. 7 (March 1975): 494.

34. Scales, "Sex Education in the '70s and '80s," 561–62.

35. Janice M. Irvine, *Talk about Sex: The Battles over Sex Education in the United States* (Berkeley: University of California Press, 2004), 9–10.

36. Marabel Morgan, *The Total Woman* (Old Tappan, NJ: Revell, 1973), 183.

37. David L. Kirp et al., *Learning by Heart: AIDS and Schoolchildren in America's Communities* (New Brunswick, NJ: Rutgers University Press, 1989), 34, 36.

38. D. Thompson Manning and Paul M. Balson, "Policy Issues Surrounding Children with AIDS in Schools," *Clearing House* 61, no. 3 (November 1987): 104.

39. Kirp et al., *Learning by Heart*, 63.

40. Kirp et al., 94–132, especially 129. The relationship between HIV and AIDS only crystalized in scientific literature after 1987, hence my word choices.

41. Kirp et al., 118, 95.

42. For both quotations and analysis, see Jennifer Brier, "'Save Our Kids, Keep AIDS Out': Anti-AIDS Activism and the Legacy of Community Control in Queens, New York," *Journal of Social History* 39, no. 4 (Summer 2006): 965–87.

43. New York probably had the nation's first AIDS Education program; Sally Reed, "AIDS in the Schools: A Special Report," *Phi Delta Kappan* 67, no. 7 (March 1986): 498; Ralph J. DiClemente et al., "Evaluation of School-Based AIDS Education Curricula in San Francisco," *Journal of Sex Research* 26, no. 2 (May 1989): 190.

44. See Gregg E. Newschwander, "Update on AIDS for Teachers and Policy-Makers," *Educational Horizons* 65, no. 3 (Spring 1987): 110–13; Edgar H. Bittle, "Private Rights v. Public Protection: AIDS in the Classroom," *Compleat Lawyer* 3, no. 3 (Summer 1986): 7–9; Manning and Balson, "Policy Issues Surrounding Children with AIDS in Schools," 101–4.

45. C. Everett Koop and the Centers for Disease Control, *Understanding AIDS* (Washington, DC: Government Printing Office, 1988).

46. Jennifer Brier, *Infectious Ideas: U.S. Political Responses to the AIDS Crisis* (Chapel Hill: University of North Carolina Press, 2009), 81, 88–91; Anthony M. Petro, *After the Wrath of God: AIDS, Sexuality, and American Religion* (New York: Oxford University Press, 2015), 69–86.

47. "Understanding AIDS: An Information Brochure Being Mailed to All U.S. Households," *Morbidity and Mortality Weekly Report* 37, no. 17 (May 6, 1988): 261.

48. Allan C. Ornstein, "AIDS: A Challenge to the Education Community," *Clearing House* 62, no. 3 (November 1988): 136.

49. W. James Popham, "Wanted: AIDS Education That Works," *Phi Delta Kappan* 74, no. 7 (March 1993): 559, 560. See also Jonathan Zimmerman, *Too Hot to Handle: A Global History of Sex Education* (Princeton, NJ: Princeton University Press, 2015), 138.

50. *New York Times*, September 4, 1988, clipping, folder 26: Committees, Youth Education Life Line (YELL), box 32, ACT UP New York Records, Manuscripts and Archives Division, New York Public Library, available at http://archives.nypl.org/mss/10#detailed (henceforth ACT UP NY).

51. Kate Barnhart, interview by Michael Thomas Ford, in *Voices of AIDS: Twelve Unforgettable People Talk about How AIDS Has Changed Their Lives* (New York: HarperCollins, 1995), 213.

52. YELL was initially identified as "Youth Brigade"; "The Very First ACT UP Youth Brigade Report," October 23, 1989, folder 26: Committees, Youth Education Life Line (YELL), box 32, ACT UP NY; "ACT-UP Testimony: Chancellor's Expense Budget," February 21, 1990, folder 26: Committees, Youth Education Life Line (YELL), box 32, ACT UP NY.

53. On ACT UP, see Tamar W. Carroll, *Mobilizing New York: AIDS, Antipoverty, and Feminist Activism* (Chapel Hill: University of North Carolina Press, 2015), chaps. 5–6.

54. "Testimony by Robert Rygor Before the Board of Education in Support of the Chancellor's AIDS Education Plan," January 16, 1991, folder 26: Committees, Youth Education Life Line (YELL), box 32, ACT UP NY.

55. Gilbert Elbaz, "Adolescent Activism for a Postmodern HIV/AIDS Education: A New Social Movement," *Urban Review* 29, no. 3 (1997): 150.

56. HAART refers to a multidrug combination therapy, one that transformed HIV/AIDS treatment after 1996.

57. On teens, see Victoria A. Harden, *AIDS at 30: A History* (Dulles, VA: Potomac Books, 2012), 138; Jonathan Engle, *The Epidemic: A Global History of AIDS* (Washington, DC: Smithsonian Books, 2006), 134.

58. "ACT-UP Testimony: Chancellor's Expense Budget," February 21, 1990, 1–4, folder 26: Committees, Youth Education Life Line (YELL), box 32, ACT UP NY.

59. Janie Victoria Ward and Jill McLean Taylor, "Sexuality Education for Immigrant and Minority Students: Developing a Culturally Appropriate Curriculum," in *Sexuality and the Curriculum*, ed. James Sears (New York: Teachers College Press, 1992), 191; Joseph Berger, "What Students Think about Condom Plan," *New York Times*, September 28, 1990.

60. On gay liberation and AIDS activism, see Brier, *Infectious Ideas*, 11–44.

61. In New York State, the Regents had made AIDS curriculum mandatory in 1987 but did so before the creation of an instructional guide. Thus, chaos ensued. See Cris Mayo, *Disputing the Subject of Sex: Sexuality and Public School Controversies* (New York: Rowman & Littlefield, 2004), 47.

62. Jeffrey Fennelly, interview by Sarah Schulman, January 4, 2010, ACT UP Oral History Project, 28. ACT UP Oral History Project transcripts can be viewed at http://www.actuporalhistory.org/.

63. Flyer, "We're Looking for New Members," folder 26: Committees, Youth Education Life Line (YELL), box 32, ACT UP NY; Kate Barnhart, interview by Sarah Schulman, March 21, 2004, ACT UP Oral History Project, 11.

64. Barnhart interview, ACT UP Oral History Project, 11, 12–13; Barnhart interview, *Voices of AIDS*, 203.

65. Barnhart interview, ACT UP Oral History Project, 14–15.

66. Barnhart interview, 12.

67. On the condom distribution program's enactment, see Joseph Berger's reporting, including "Desperation and Anger in Debate on Condoms," *New York Times*, February 7, 1991.

68. Lynnell Mancock and Jay Maeder, "Condom Plan Bars Parents," *Daily News* (New York), September 12, 1991, clipping, folder 26: Committees, Youth Education Life Line (YELL), box 32, ACT UP NY.

69. Joseph Berger, "Students' Demand for Condoms Seems Limited but Steady," *New York Times*, January 30, 1992.

70. Trudy S. Moore, "Should Schools Give Students Condoms without Parents' Consent?" *Jet* 81, no. 17 (February 17, 1992): 14–16.

71. Mayo, *Disputing the Subject of Sex*, 51.

72. National Guidelines Task Force, *Guidelines for Comprehensive Sexuality Education* (Washington, DC: SIECUS, 1992), 3.

73. "The Very First ACT UP Youth Brigade Report," October 23, 1989, folder 26: Committees, Youth Education Life Line (YELL), box 32, ACT UP NY; Fennelly interview, ACT UP Oral History Project, 31.

74. Affinity group Women's Caucus did encounter more resistance in an earlier attempt to distribute condoms; Carroll, *Mobilizing New York*, 151; Fennelly interview, ACT UP Oral History Project, 31.

75. Lei Chou, interview by Sarah Schulman, May 5, 2003, ACT UP Oral History Project, 23; Elbaz, "Adolescent Activism for Postmodern HIV/AIDS Education," 160. For disputing account, see Felicia R. Lee, "In Age of AIDS, Sex and Drugs Are Classroom Topics," *New York Times*, December 26, 1989.

76. *Journal of the Board of Education of the City of New York* 1 (New York: Board of Education, 1991): 1122.

77. Natalia Mehlman Petrzela, *Classroom Wars: Language, Sex, and the Making of Modern Political Culture* (New York: Oxford University Press, 2015), 216.

78. Ntanya Lee, Don Murphy, and Lisa North, "Sexuality, Multicultural Education, and the New York City Public Schools," *Radical Teacher* 45 (Winter 1994): 13.

79. Catherine A. Lugg, "The Religious Right and Public Education: The Paranoid Politics of Homophobia," in *Sexualities in Education: A Reader*, ed. Erica Meiners and Therese Quinn (New York: Peter Lang, 2012), 65–68. See also Petro, *After the Wrath of God*.

80. Steven Lee Myers, "Few Using Curriculum in Dispute," *New York Times*, December 6, 1992.

81. Irvine, *Talk about Sex*, xv.

82. This was Teri L. Lewis's persuasive assessment, expressed in a letter to Ramon C. Cortines, October 31, 1993, folder 12, box 13, AIDS and Adolescents Network of New York Records, Manuscripts and Archives Division, The New York Public Library (hereafter AANNYR).

83. University of the State of New York State Education Department, "A Compliance Review of HIV/AIDS Instruction in New York City Public Schools," July 1993, 3, folder 4, box 8, AANNYR.

84. Teri L. Lewis to Ramon Cortines, October 18, 1993, folder 12, box 13, AANNYR.

85. HIV/AIDS Advisory Council transcript, October 12, 1993, folder 4, box 8, AANNYR.

86. Andrea Schlesinger to Teri L. Lewis, December 27, 1993, folder 12, box 13, AANNYR; Carol A. Gresser to William Andrews, Memo on Student Members, April 28, 1994, folder 2, box 14, AANNYR.

87. Erica Zurer to Teri Lewis, March 18, 1994, folder 2, box 14, AANNYR; "Summary of BOE HIV/AIDS Council Actions," March 7, 1994, folder 2, box 14, AANNYR.

88. YELL, *'Zine #2* (1995): 6.

89. Jeffrey Fennelly, "Writing on the Wall of Plato's Cave: Education, Homophobia and AIDS," *Outweek*, June 27, 1990, 66.

90. Deborah Holtzman et al., "HIV Education and Health Education in the United States: A National Survey of Local School District Policies and Practices," *Journal of School Health* 62, no. 9 (November 1992): 421–27, quoted in Clark Robenstine, "HIV/AIDS Education for Adolescents: School Policy and Practice," *Clearing House* 67, no. 4 (March–April 1994): 230.

91. "OBSESSED!: Miss America Takes AIDS Education to Middle America," Playbill, https://www.youtube.com/watch?v=-GuLeT022Ag (accessed 6/5/2017).

92. Sarah Brabant, "Teaching about HIV Infection and AIDS in a Hostile Environment," *Teaching Sociology* 19, no. 4 (October 1991): 490.

93. "OBSESSED!: Miss America Takes AIDS Education to Middle America," Playbill. See also Jessica Fields, *Risky Lessons: Sex Education and Social Inequality* (New Brunswick, NJ: Rutgers University Press, 2008), 79.

94. José Esteban Muñoz, *Disidentifications: Queers of Color and the Performance of Politics* (Minneapolis: University of Minnesota Press, 1999), 152.

95. Christopher Pullen, *Pedro Zamora, Sexuality, and AIDS Education: The Autobiographical Self, Activism, and the* Real World (Amherst, NY: Cambria Press, 2016), xvi, 6.

96. Roger Hallas, *Reframing Bodies: AIDS, Bearing Witness, and the Queer Moving Image* (Durham, NC: Duke University Press, 2009), 115–16.

97. Brier, *Infectious Ideas*, 156–68.

98. Muñoz, *Disidentifications*, 146.

99. Harry A. Jessell, Lawrence B. Taishoff, and Ramona Flores, "Television and Radio: The Year in Review 1994," *Encyclopedia Britannica*, https://www.britannica.com/topic/television-and-radio-1573278 (accessed June 7, 2017). On the use of *The Real World* in AIDS curriculum in the humanities, see Douglas Bailey et al., "AIDS in American History: Four Perspectives on Experiential Learning," *Journal of American History* 86, no. 4 (March 2000): 1727.

100. Rocco Versaci, "How Comic Books Can Change the Way Our Students See Literature: One Teacher's Perspective," *English Journal* 91, no. 2 (November 2001): 63.

101. Kristy L. Slominski, *Teaching Moral Sex: A History of Religion and Sex Education in the United States* (New York: Oxford University Press, 2021), 250.

102. Rebecca Ruiz, "The Trump Administration Has Been Steadily Sabotaging Sex Ed. Here's How," Mashable.com, October 29, 2018, https://mashable.com/article/trump-sex-education/.

CHAPTER FOUR

1. I recognize that the norms of reason and truth are themselves shaped by power dynamics and take certain privileges for granted, as feminist, post-structuralist, and anti-colonial scholars (among others) have pointed out. These critiques are important cautions against liberal absolutism, but we reject the "post-truth" attitude that public reality is unconfirmable or irrelevant.

2. Janice M. Irvine, *Talk about Sex: The Battles over Sex Education in the United States* (Berkeley: University of California Press, 2004); Kristin Luker, *When Sex Goes to School: Warring Views on Sex—and Sex Education—since the Sixties* (New York: W. W. Norton, 2007); Nancy Kendall, *The Sex Education Debates* (Chicago: University of Chicago Press, 2013).

3. Nicholas Hune-Brown, "The Sex Ed Revolution: A Portrait of the Powerful Political Bloc That's Waging War on Queen's Park," *Toronto Life*, September 3, 2015, http://torontolife.com/city/ontario-sex-ed-revolution/; PHD Media, "Behind the Scenes of Yasmin's 'Sex-Ed Revolution' Campaign by PHD," July 25, 2017, https://www.phdmedia.com/china/behind-scenes-yasmins-sex-ed-revolution-campaign-phd-chinas-media-agency-win-lion-cannes-2017/; M. B. Warnke, "These Women Are Leading the Sex Ed Revolution Online," Girlboss, May 1, 2018, https://www.girlboss.com/life/online-sex-education.

4. Helen Lenskyj, "Beyond Plumbing and Prevention: Feminist Approaches to Sex Education," *Gender and Education* 2, no. 2 (1990): 217–30.

5. Liliana Mason, *Uncivil Agreement: How Politics Became Our Identity* (Chicago: University of Chicago Press, 2018).

6. Irvine, *Talk about Sex*; Kendall, *Sex Education Debates.*

7. Jonathan Zimmerman, *Too Hot to Handle: A Global History of Sex Education* (Princeton, NJ: Princeton University Press, 2015), 115–43.

8. Irvine, *Talk about Sex*. The irony (some might say cruelty) of denying unmarried people access to sex education and contraception, and then denouncing abortion in the most judgmental terms, should not go unnoticed.

9. Cris Mayo, *Disputing the Subject of Sex: Sexuality and Public School Controversies* (New York: Rowman & Littlefield, 2004), 65–94.

10. You can look them up, but here's a taste: "Sexual activity outside the context of marriage is likely to have harmful psychological and physical effects." "Abstinence-Only Sex Education Description," K12 Academics, https://www.k12academics.com/sex-education/abstinence-only-sex-education/description.

11. California, Maine, and New Jersey were early refuseniks.

12. SIECUS, "A History of Federal Funding for AOUM," 2018, 1, https://siecus.org/wp-content/uploads/2018/08/A-History-of-AOUM-Funding-Final-Draft.pdf.

13. For a description of the gradations of AOUME and CSE, see Kendall, *Sex Education Debates*, 4–8.

14. Mary Lou Rasmussen, *Progressive Sexuality Education: The Conceits of Secularism* (New York: Routledge, 2016).

15. Sharon Lamb, "Just the Facts? The Separation of Sex Education from Moral Education," *Educational Theory* 63, no. 5 (2013): 443–60.

16. There are exceptions. Increasingly, a culturally sensitive and context-specific approach to sex education requires that adolescent pregnancy and parenthood not be cast as automatic failures, since community values vary.

17. Centers for Disease Control and Prevention (CDC), "16 Critical Sexual Education Topics" (National Center for HIV/AIDS, Viral Hepatitis, and STD, and TB Prevention, 2014), 1, www.cdc.gov/healthyyouth.

18. Planned Parenthood, "What Are the Goals of Sex Education for Youth?," https://www

.plannedparenthood.org/learn/for-educators/what-are-goals-sex-education-youth; Planned Parenthood, "What Are the Benefits and Disadvantages of Abstinence and Outercourse?," https://www.plannedparenthood.org/learn/birth-control/abstinence-and-outercourse/what-are-benefits-and-disadvantages-abstinence-and-outercourse. Amusingly, the benefits of abstinence are listed alongside those of "outercourse." Planned Parenthood is nothing if not realistic.

19. Planned Parenthood Federation of America, "Planned Parenthood's *Get Real* Program Works; It Changes Sexual Behavior among Middle Schools Students," October 20, 2014, https://www.plannedparenthood.org/about-us/newsroom/press-releases/planned-parenthoods-get-real-program-works-it-changes-sexual-behavior-among-middle-school-students.

20. Quoted in Hune-Brown, "Sex Ed Revolution."

21. Government of Ontario, *Ontario Health and Physical Education Curriculum: Grades 1–8* (Toronto, ON: 2015), 204.

22. Government of Ontario, 195; emphasis added.

23. Lawrence Finer, "Trends in Premarital Sex in the United States, 1954–2003," *Public Health Reports* 122, no. 1 (2007): 73–78. No significant follow-up study has been conducted since this widely cited article, but a study published in 2019 found that 93% of Americans had had sex by age twenty-five. (Guttmacher Institute, *Adolescent Sexual and Reproductive Health in the United States*, 2019, https://www.guttmacher.org/sites/default/files/factsheet/adolescent-sexual-and-reproductive-health-in-united-states.pdf). Even more revealing is that Finer was only counting vaginal intercourse as "sex." About 45% of fifteen- to nineteen-year-olds have had oral sex with an opposite-sex partner and 9% have had anal sex with an opposite-sex partner (Guttmacher, *Adolescent*).

24. Guttmacher Institute, *Teen Pregnancy Rates Declined in Many Countries between Mid-1990s and 2011*, 2015, https://www.guttmacher.org/news-release/2015/teen-pregnancy-rates-declined-many-countries-between-mid-1990s-and-2011. In Switzerland, "long-established sex education programs, free family planning services and low-cost emergency contraception are widely available, and sexually active teens are expected to use contraceptives."

25. A sample of studies includes Pamela Kohler, Lisa Manhart, and William Lafferty, "Abstinence-Only and Comprehensive Sex Education and the Initiation of Sexual Activity and Teen Pregnancy," *Journal of Adolescent Health* 42, no. 4 (2008): 344–51; John Santelli et al., "Abstinence-Only-Until-Marriage: An Updated Review of US Policies and Programs and Their Impact," *Journal of Adolescent Health* 61, no. 3 (2017): 273–80; Douglas Kirby, "The Impact of Abstinence and Comprehensive Sex and STD/HIV Education Programs on Adolescent Sexual Behavior," *Sexuality Research & Social Policy* 5, no. 3 (2008): 18–27; Debra Hauser, *Five Years of Abstinence-Only-Until-Marriage Education* (Washington, DC: Advocates for Youth, 2004); Jillian Carr and Analisa Packham, "The Effects of State-Mandated Abstinence-Based Sex Education on Teen Health Outcomes," *Health Economics* 26, no. 4 (2017): 403–20; Christopher Trenholm, Barbara Devany, Kenneth Fortson, Melissa Clark, Lisa Quay, and Justin Wheeler, "Impacts of Abstinence Education on Teen Sexual Activity, Risk of Pregnancy, and Risk of Sexually Transmitted Diseases," *Journal of Policy Analysis and Management* 27, no. 2 (2008): 255–76.

26. United Nations Educational, Scientific and Cultural Organization (UNESCO), *International Technical Guidance on Sexuality Education: An Evidence-Informed Approach*, rev. ed.

(Paris: United Nations, 2018), http://www.unaids.org/sites/default/files/media_asset/ITGSE_en.pdf, 29. Perhaps most tragically, the United States has been the primary funder of AOUME in parts of the developing world, where programs' inefficacy can be correlated more directly to HIV infection and poverty. The President's Emergency Plan for AIDS Relief (PEPFAR), for example, "has been the largest funder of abstinence and faithfulness programming in sub-Saharan Africa, with a cumulative investment of over US $1.4 billion in the period 2004–13." (Nathan Lo, Anita Lowe, and Eran Bendavid, "Abstinence Funding Was Not Associated with Reductions in HIV Risk Behavior in Sub-Saharan Africa," *Health Affairs* 35, no. 5 [2016]: 856.) A systematic review of this initiative found no significant positive impacts of these programs on any of the targeted sexual behaviors in any of the twenty-two countries examined.

27. Jennifer Grossman, Allison Tracy, Linda Charmaraman, Ineke Ceder, and Sumru Erkut, "Protective Effects of Middle School Comprehensive Sex Education with Family Involvement," *Journal of School Health* 84, no. 11 (2014): 739–47; Douglas Kirby, B. A. Laris, and Lori Rolleri, "Sex and HIV Education Programs: Their Impact on Sexual Behaviors of Young People throughout the World," *Journal of Adolescent Health* 40, no. 3 (2007): 206–17.

28. David Hargreaves, "Teaching as a Research-Based Profession: Possibilities and Prospects," *The Teacher Training Agency Annual Lecture* (1996), 1–12.

29. David Bridges, "Reasoning from Educational Research to Policy," in *Educational Research: Proofs, Arguments, and Other Reasonings*, ed. P. Smeyers and M. Depaepe (New York: Springer, 2009), 182–83.

30. Bridges, 185.

31. Harry Brighouse, Helen Ladd, Susanna Loeb, and Adam Swift, *Educational Goods: Values, Evidence, and Decision-Making* (Chicago: University of Chicago Press, 2018), 75–85.

32. CDC, "16 Critical Sexual Education Topics"; Future of Sex Education Initiative (FoSE), *National Sexuality Education Standards: Core Content and Skills, K–12* (United States, 2012), http://www.futureofsexeducation.org/documents/josh-fose-standards-web.pdf; Sexual Information and Education Council of Canada (SIECCAN), *Canadian Guidelines for Sexual Health Education* (Toronto, 2019); World Health Organization (WHO) Regional Office for Europe and BZgA, *Standards for Sexuality Education in Europe: A Framework for Policy Makers, Educational and Health Authorities and Specialists* (Cologne, Germany: World Health Organization, 2010), https://www.bzga-whocc.de/fileadmin/user_upload/WHO_BZgA_Standards_English.pdf; UNESCO, *International Technical Guidance on Sexuality Education*.

33. Joshua Blank and Daron Shaw, "Does Partisanship Shape Attitudes toward Science and Public Policy? The Case for Ideology and Religion," *Annals of the American Academy of Political and Social Science* 658, no. 1 (2015): 18–35.

34. Blank and Shaw, "Does Partisanship Shape Attitudes?," 20.

35. Patrick Kraft, Milton Lodge, and Charles Taber, "Why People 'Don't Trust the Evidence': Motivated Reasoning and Scientific Beliefs," *Annals of the American Academy of Political and Social Science* 658, no. 1 (2015): 122.

36. Blank and Shaw, "Does Partisanship Shape Attitudes?"

37. Political scientist Elizabeth Suhay, quoted in Jeffrey Mervis, "Politics, Science, and Public Attitudes: What We're Learning, and Why It Matters," *Science*, February 25, 2015,

https://www.sciencemag.org/news/2015/02/politics-science-and-public-attitudes-what-we-re-learning-and-why-it-matters.

38. Christine Kim and Robert Rector, "Evidence on the Effectiveness of Abstinence Education: An Update," Heritage Foundation, February 19, 2010, https://www.heritage.org/education/report/evidence-the-effectiveness-abstinence-education-update.

39. See Jessica Valenti, *The Purity Myth: How America's Obsession with Virginity Is Hurting Young Women* (New York: Basic Books, 2009).

40. Michael Resnick et al., "Protecting Adolescents from Harm: Findings from the National Longitudinal Study on Adolescent Health," *Journal of the American Medical Association* 278, no. 10 (1997): 823–32; Peter Bearman and Hannah Brückner, "Promising the Future: Virginity Pledges and First Intercourse," *American Journal of Sociology* 106, no. 4 (2001): 852–912. On the limits of these data, see Janet Rosenbaum, "Reborn a Virgin: Adolescents' Retracting of Virginity Pledges and Sexual Histories," *American Journal of Public Health* 96, no. 6 (2006): 1098–103.

41. Resnick et al., "Protecting Adolescents from Harm," 830.

42. Beth Kotchick, Ann Shaffer, Kim Miller, and Rex Forehand, "Adolescent Sexual Risk Behavior: A Multi-System Perspective," *Clinical Psychology Review* 21, no. 4 (2001): 493–519.

43. John Jemmott, Loretta Jemmott, and Geoffrey Fong, "Abstinence and Safer Sex HIV Risk-Reduction Interventions for African American Adolescents: A Randomized Controlled Trial," *Journal of the American Medical Association* 279, no. 19 (1998): 1529–36. The researchers followed 659 African American urban middle-school students whose mean age was 11.8 years. If you would guess that abstinence is an easier sell for a three-month period among eleven-year-olds than for an indefinite period among older teenagers, you would probably be right. The study's authors do not even advocate exclusive abstinence education in light of their own findings.

44. Kirby, "The Impact of Abstinence and Comprehensive Sex and STD/HIV Education Programs."

45. Hannah Brückner and Peter Bearman, "After the Promise: The STD Consequences of Adolescent Virginity Pledges," *Journal of Adolescent Health* 36, no. 4 (April 2005): 271–78.

46. Lawrence Altman, "Study Finds That Teenage Virginity Pledges Are Rarely Kept," *New York Times*, March 10, 2004, https://www.nytimes.com/2004/03/10/us/study-finds-that-teenage-virginity-pledges-are-rarely-kept.html.

47. Sexual Information and Education Council of the United States (SIECUS), "On Our Side: Public Support for Sex Education," 2018, https://siecus.org/resources/public-support-sex-education/.

48. SIECUS, "On Our Side." Other large-scale polls have found similar numbers. See Planned Parenthood and New York University's Center for Latino Adolescent and Family Health, "Parents and Teens Talk about Sexuality: A National Survey," 2014, https://www.plannedparenthood.org/uploads/filer_public/ac/50/ac50c2f7-cbc9-46b7-8531-ad3e92712016/nationalpoll_09-14_v2_1.pdf.

49. Leslie Kantor and Nicole Levitz, "Parents' Views on Sex Education in Schools: How Much Do Democrats and Republicans Agree?" *PLoS ONE* 12, no. 7 (2017): e0180250.

50. Alexander McKay, Sandra Byers, Susan Voyer, Terry Humphreys, and Chris Markham, "Ontario Parents' Opinions and Attitudes towards Sexual Health Education in the Schools," *Canadian Journal of Human Sexuality* 23, no. 3 (2014): 159–66.

51. Nick Westoll, "Ontario Parents Divided over Repeal of Sex-Ed Curriculum, yet Majority Approve of Content: Ipsos Poll," *Global News*, September 4, 2018, https://globalnews.ca/news/4424744/ontario-sex-ed-curriculum-ipsos-poll/.

52. Jacqueline Cohen, Sandra Byers, and Heather Sears, "Factors Affecting Canadian Teachers' Willingness to Teach Sexual Health Education," *Sex Education* 12, no. 3 (2012): 299–316; Debbie Ollis, "'I Haven't Changed Bigots but . . .': Reflections on the Impact of Teacher Professional Learning in Sexuality Education," *Sex Education* 10, no. 2 (2010): 217–30.

53. Meira Levinson, *The Demands of Liberal Education* (Oxford: Oxford University Press, 1999); Harry Brighouse, "Channel One, the Anti-Commercial Principle, and the Discontinuous Ethos," *Educational Policy* 19, no. 3 (2005): 528–49.

54. This thinking likely explains why the same religious conservatives who oppose sex education also oppose abortion rights and parenthood out of wedlock. Logically, and empirically, reducing teenage pregnancy and abortion requires CSE and easy access to contraception; and reducing childbirth out of wedlock requires access to safe abortion. But for those who believe that these things are sinful in themselves, it is preferable to counsel adolescents to remain abstinent than to express approval for the more successful, but (in their view) fundamentally immoral, strategies. It's moral absolutism instead of means-ends reasoning.

55. We will discuss media culture in chapter 6.

56. Focus on the Family, *Talking about Sex and Puberty*, 2011, https://www.focusonthefamily.com/parenting/sexuality/talking-about-sex/talking-about-sex-and-puberty. In spite of these similarities, this point shouldn't be overstated. While Focus on the Family endorses some of the same messages and pedagogical strategies in sex education as its nemeses do, Focus on the Family is directing this guidance to *parents*, whom it takes to be the appropriate sex educators of their children. A conservative organization can therefore champion some forms of sex education that are characteristic of CSE in the home while objecting to school-based education of the same type.

57. Focus on the Family, *Talking about Sex and Puberty*.

58. Kendall, *Sex Education Debates*, 151–78, 209–23.

59. Kendall, 162–63.

60. See, for example, Valenti, *The Purity Myth*.

61. True Tolerance, https://www.truetolerance.org.

62. AOUME advocates, for example, coordinate with such organizations as PFOX (Parents and Friends of Ex-Gays) and NARTH (National Association for Research and Therapy of Homosexuality) (Kendall, *Sex Education Debates*, 200) and other anti-gay groups (Irvine, *Talk about Sex*, 165–86).

63. Kendall, *Sex Education Debates*, 204.

64. Zimmerman, *Too Hot to Handle*, 134; Mayo, *Disputing the Subject of Sex*, 98–102; Irvine, *Talk about Sex*, 162.

65. Michael Halstead and Michael Reiss, *Values in Sex Education: From Principles to Practice* (London: Routledge Falmer, 2003), 160. See also Michael Reiss, "Teaching about Homosexuality and Heterosexuality," *Journal of Moral Education* 26, no. 2 (1997): 343–52.

66. Halstead and Reiss, *Values in Sex Education*, 161.

67. David Archard, "Sex Education," *Impact* (Philosophy of Education Society of Great Britain) 7 (2000): 41–42.

68. Cris Mayo, *LGBTQ Youth and Education: Policies and Practices* (New York: Teachers College Press, 2014); Tara Goldstein, *Teaching Gender and Sexuality at School: Letters to Teachers* (New York: Routledge, 2019).

69. Joseph Kosciw, Caitlin Clark, Nhan Truong, and Adrian Zongrone, *The 2019 National School Climate Survey: The Experiences of Lesbian, Gay, Bisexual, Transgender, and Queer Youth in Our Nation's Schools* (New York: GLSEN, 2020). Unfortunately, rather than attributing the depression and suicidal ideation to the fact of being LGBTQ+ in a homophobic world, as social scientists do, some conservatives invert the cause and effect, arguing that the wrongness of being gay is the source of the discomfort. This is another dangerous example of misinterpreting evidence (see Kendall, *Sex Education Debates*, 202). It can be easily disproven by pointing out how the mental health risks dissipate when LGBTQ+ youths are affirmed and supported.

70. Kosciw, Clark, Truong, and Zongrone, *The 2019 National School Climate Survey*, xviii–xix.

71. Jonathan Zimmerman and Emily Robertson, *The Case for Contention* (Chicago: University of Chicago Press, 2017), 45.

72. Michael Hand also argues that homosexuality should not be taught as a controversial issue, but his argument proceeds from a "epistemic" criterion that says all the moral arguments against homosexuality are indefensible. (Michael Hand, "Should We Teach Homosexuality as a Controversial Issue?" *Theory and Research in Education* 5, no. 1 [2007]: 69–86). I worry about resting the case for inclusive education on this foundation. We do not need to convince everyone to adopt the same moral attitudes in order to prove that homophobia is both politically indefensible and materially harmful.

73. "Neoliberalism" refers to a late capitalist strand of conservatism that favors deregulation, privatization, and minimal social services. It has been widely critiqued in educational scholarship for overburdening schools and exacerbating inequities. See Michael W. Apple, *Educating the "Right" Way: Markets, Standards, God, and Inequality*, 2nd ed. (New York: Routledge, 2006).

74. James Laming, "In Search of Effective Character Education," *Educational Leadership* 51, no. 3 (1993): 63–71; Sue Winton, "The Appeal(s) of Character Education in Threatening Times: Caring and Critical Democratic Responses," *Comparative Education* 44, no. 3 (2008): 305–16; Nel Noddings, *Educating Moral People: A Caring Alternative to Character Education* (New York: Teachers College Press, 2002).

75. Randall Curren, "Why Character Education?" *Impact* (Philosophy of Education Society of Great Britain) 24 (2017): 25–29.

76. Michael Hand, *A Theory of Moral Education* (London: Routledge, 2018).

77. All education involves telling children what is right and wrong, and how they ought to behave; but many programs of moral education go further and seek to institutionalize a single set of beliefs, values, and customs, without room for critique or diversity.

78. Alison MacKenzie, Penny Enslin, and Nicki Hedge offer the term "moral literacy" to mean roughly what I mean by "ethics" in the context of sex education, in "Sex Education: Challenges and Choices," *British Journal of Educational Studies* 65, no. 1 (2017): 35.

79. Robert Fullinwider, "Moral Conventions and Moral Lessons," in *Philosophy of Education: An Anthology*, ed. Randall Curren (Malden, MA: Blackwell, 2007), 498–506.

80. See https://www.sexualethics.org/. Another example of an ethics-based sex education program, designed by Moira Carmody, is used primarily in Australia and New Zealand. See Carmody, *Sex, Ethics, and Young People* (New York: Palgrave Macmillan, 2015).

81. Sharon Lamb, "Toward a Sexual Ethics Curriculum: Bringing Philosophy and Society to Bear on Individual Development," *Harvard Educational Review* 80, no. 1 (2010): 82. For a discussion of the difficulties involved in implementing this approach, see Sharon Lamb and Renee Randazzo, "Obstacles to Teaching Ethics in Sex Education," in *Evidence-Based Approaches to Sexuality Education*, ed. James Ponzetti (New York: Routledge, 2016), 113–27.

82. Paula McAvoy, "The Aims of Sex Education: Demoting Autonomy and Promoting Mutuality," *Educational Theory* 63, no. 5 (2013): 483–96; Sharon Lamb, "Sex Education as Moral Education: Teaching for Pleasure, about Fantasy, and against Abuse," *Journal of Moral Education* 26, no. 3 (1997): 301–15.

83. Sharon Lamb and Renee Randazzo, "From I to We: Sex Education as a Form of Civics Education in a Neoliberal Context," *Curriculum Inquiry* 46, no. 2 (2016): 148–67.

84. Nel Noddings, *The Challenge to Care in Schools: An Alternative Approach to Education*, 2nd ed. (New York: Teachers College Press, 2005). Disclaimers are in order here, including Lamb's warning: "The risk of including lessons about caring and love in sex curricula is that girls in particular will fall into heterosexual romance narratives that have worked against their sexual agency and self-protection" (Lamb, "Toward a Sexual Ethics," 94).

CHAPTER FIVE

1. For discussions of common schooling, see Eamonn Callan, "Common Schools for Common Education," *Canadian Journal of Education* 20, no. 3 (1995): 251–71.

2. Eamonn Callan, *Autonomy and Schooling* (Kingston, ON: McGill-Queen's University Press, 1988), 128.

3. Meira Levinson, *The Demands of Liberal Education* (Oxford: Oxford University Press, 1999), 47. There are also questions about when and how paternalism ends, but the first hurdle is to show that some measure of paternalism is unavoidable.

4. Emily Brown, "When Insiders Become Outsiders: Parental Objections to Public School Sex Education Programs," *Duke Law Journal* 59, no. 1 (2009): 136; Melissa Murray, "Sex and the Schoolhouse," *Harvard Law Review* 132 (2019): 1473.

5. Amy Gutmann, *Democratic Education* (Princeton, NJ: Princeton University Press, 1987), 23. Gutmann calls this idea the "Family State."

6. E.g., John Stuart Mill, *On Liberty* (1859).

7. William Galston, "Two Concepts of Liberalism," *Ethics* 105 (1995): 516–34.

8. The Truth and Reconciliation Commission of Canada, *Honouring the Truth, Reconciling for the Future: Summary of the Final Report of the Truth and Reconciliation Commission of Canada* (Ottawa, 2015). Similarly, compulsory assimilationist "Indian boarding schools" existed throughout the United States until they began to be dismantled or handed over to tribes in the 1970s to 1990s.

9. Niigaanwewidam James Sinclair and Sharon Dainard, "Sixties Scoop," *The Canadian Encyclopedia* (Historica Canada, 2016), https://thecanadianencyclopedia.ca/en/article/sixties-scoop.

10. Levinson, *Demands of Liberal Education*; Harry Brighouse, "Channel One, the Anti-Commercial Principle, and the Discontinuous Ethos," *Educational Policy* 19, no. 3 (2005): 528–49; Eamonn Callan, *Creating Citizens: Political Education and Liberal Democracy* (Oxford: Clarendon, 1997).

11. *Mozert v. Hawkins County Board of Education*, 827 F.2d 1058 (6th Cir. 1987).

12. *Chamberlain v. Surrey School District No. 36* (Supreme Court of Canada, 2002), https://scc-csc.lexum.com/scc-csc/scc-csc/en/item/2030/index.do.

13. *Chamberlain*, paras. 65–66.

14. This is also affirmed in the UN Declaration of Human Rights (1948, article 26).

15. *Meyer v. Nebraska, 262 U.S. 390* (1923); *Pierce v. Society of Sisters, 268* U.S. 510 (1925); Brown, "When Insiders Become Outsiders."

16. Levinson, *Demands of Liberal Education*, 65.

17. Roger Marples, "Parents' Rights and Educational Provision," *Studies in Philosophy of Education* 33, no. 1 (2014): 23–39.

18. Quoted in Nancy Kendall, *The Sex Education Debates* (Chicago: University of Chicago Press, 2013), 47.

19. Gutmann, *Democratic Education*, 111; Kenneth Strike, *Liberty and Learning* (Oxford: Oxford University Press, 1982), 58–60.

20. John Santelli et al., "Abstinence-Only-Until-Marriage: An Updated Review of US Policies and Programs and Their Impact," *Journal of Adolescent Health* 61, no. 3 (2017): 273–80.

21. Kendall, *The Sex Education Debates*, 27. The coordination between levels of government may have been facilitated by the fact that Jeb Bush was the governor of Florida and his brother George W. Bush was the president at the time.

22. Kendall, 27.

23. The website is still available: http://www.greattowait.com/.

24. Kendall, *The Sex Education Debates*, 51.

25. Kendall also describes how "state actors . . . talked about sex education as a market. Instead of passing new laws or directly providing AOUME training or curricula to schools, the state adopted a marketizing managerialist role designed to increase public schools' demand for AOUME and the supply of AOUME educators" (33). There is surely a dissertation to be written here about the description of sex education as a "market," but that's beyond our scope for now.

26. American Civil Liberties Union (ACLU) Northern California, "Historic Ruling in ACLU Lawsuit: Abstinence-Only Sex Ed Violated State Law," May 11, 2015, https://www.aclunc.org/news/historic-ruling-aclu-lawsuit-abstinence-only-sex-ed-violated-state-law. The plaintiffs, led by the American Academy of Pediatrics, complained that it "included a video that compared a woman who was not a virgin to a dirty shoe."

27. California Senate Bill 71, 2003, article 2, http://leginfo.legislature.ca.gov/faces/billNavClient.xhtml?bill_id=200320040SB71.

28. Gutmann, *Democratic Education*, 45.

29. John Locke, *Some Thoughts Concerning Education* (1693).

30. Gutmann, *Democratic Education*, 28.

31. E.g., Amy Gutmann, "Children, Paternalism and Education: A Liberal Argument," *Philosophy & Public Affairs* 9, no. 4 (1980): 338–58. None of this is to say that other authorities don't have complementary roles to play; it is just a *prima facie* argument for starting with parental authority.

32. David Bridges, "Non-Paternalistic Arguments in Support of Parents' Rights," *Journal of Philosophy of Education* 18, no. 1 (1984): 55–61.

33. Callan, *Creating Citizens*, 157; Colin MacLeod, "Conceptions of Parental Autonomy," *Politics and Society* 25, no. 1 (1997): 121–22; Bryan Warnick, "Parental Authority over Education and the Right to Invite," *Harvard Educational Review* 84, no. 1 (2014): 56–58. There are also other, mostly bad, non-paternalistic arguments for parents' rights, such as the idea that children are parents' "property." We need not be detained by such views.

34. Harry Brighouse and Adam Swift, *Family Values* (Princeton, NJ: Princeton University Press, 2014).

35. Sarah Hannan and Richard Vernon call this "the Plato worry" in "Parental Rights: A Role-Based Approach," *Theory and Research in Education* 6, no. 2 (2008): 173.

36. Charles Fried, *Right and Wrong* (Cambridge, MA: Harvard University Press, 1978); Ferdinand Schoeman, "Rights of Children, Rights of Parents, and the Moral Basis of the Family," *Ethics* 91, no. 1 (1980): 6–19; Edgar Page, "Parental Rights," *Journal of Applied Philosophy* 1, no. 2 (1984): 187–203.

37. Joel Feinberg, "The Child's Right to an Open Future," in *Whose Child? Children's Rights, Parental Authority, and State Power*, ed. William Aiken and Hugh LaFollette (Totowa, NJ: Rowman and Littlefield, 1980), 124–15; David Archard, *Children: Rights and Childhood* (New York: Routledge, 2015).

38. Brighouse and Swift, *Family Values*, 121. This doesn't mean that parents can't also have non-parenting rights and interests that are not defined with respect to their children.

39. "language of 'rights'": e.g., Philip Montague, "The Myth of Parental Rights," *Social Theory and Practice* 26, no. 1 (2000): 47–68; "privileges": Levinson, *Demands of Liberal Education*, 50; "interests": Hannan and Vernon, "Parental Rights," and Marples, "Parents' Rights"; "children's rights": James Dwyer, *The Relationship Rights of Children* (Cambridge: Cambridge University Press, 2006). We will come back to children's rights in the next section.

40. See, e.g., *United Nations Convention on the Rights of the Child* (Geneva: United Nations, 1989), Article 9, http://www.ohchr.org/en/professionalinterest/pages/crc.aspx.

41. Lawrence Finer, "Trends in Premarital Sex in the United States, 1954–2003," *Public Health Reports* 122, no. 1 (2007): 73–78.

42. An Australian study showed that "parents found it hard to believe that their own children might have experienced intercourse even though they recognized that similarly aged teenagers were often sexually active." Meredith Temple-Smith, Susan Moore, and Doreen Rosenthal, *Sexuality in Adolescence: The Digital Generation* (East Sussex: Routledge, 2016), 70.

43. Recall the means-ends discussion from chapter 4. How dogmatically can we insist on particular means when they repeatedly fail to achieve their stated aim?

44. Jochen Peter and Patti Valkenburg, "Adolescents and Pornography: A Review of 20 Years of Research," *Journal of Sex Research* 53, nos. 4–5 (2016): 509–31. A related topic, to which all

the same arguments apply, is kids' circulation of their own sexual images (i.e., "sexting"). See Hanna Rosin, "Why Kids Sext," *Atlantic*, November 2014, https://www.theatlantic.com/magazine/archive/2014/11/why-kids-sext/380798/. These phenomena are discussed in more detail in chapter 6 and the conclusion.

45. Maggie Jones, "What Teenagers Are Learning from Online Porn," *New York Times Magazine*, February 7, 2018, https://nyti.ms/2BfErWv.

46. Don't rely on parent "internet filters" either: research shows they are ineffective at controlling children's exposure to explicit material. Andrew Przybylski and Victoria Nash, "Internet Filtering and Adolescent Exposure to Online Sexual Material," *Cyberpsychology, Behavior, and Social Networking* 21, no. 7 (2018): 405–10.

47. See also the discussion of sexual diversity in chapter 4. One of the most common ways that parents' beliefs about sexuality harm their children is when LGBTQ+ kids are raised in anti-LGBTQ+ households. These parents often sincerely believe that they have their children's best interests at heart. But the mismatch can result in tremendous suffering and danger for the children.

48. In the United States, the "Free Exercise" clause does most of the heavy lifting, but similar freedoms are enshrined in other constitutions as well as in the Universal Declaration of Human Rights (Geneva: United Nations, 1948).

49. See Eli Reiter, "The Late Bloomer: Learning about the Birds and Bees in College," *New York Times*, June 25, 2019, https://www.nytimes.com/2019/06/25/well/family/the-late-bloomer-learning-about-the-birds-and-bees-in-college.html?searchResultPosition=1; Claire Renzetti and Sandra Yocum, eds., *Clergy Sexual Abuse: Social Science Perspectives* (Boston: Northeastern, 2013); Wayne Besen, *Ex-Gay and the Law* (New York: Truth Wins Out and Lambda Legal, 2008); Alex Hannaford, "The Woman Who Escaped a Polygamous Cult—and Turned Its HQ into a Refuge," *Guardian*, October 13, 2018, https://www.theguardian.com/world/2018/oct/13/woman-escaped-cult-hq-flds-refuge; and Sharon Otterman, "When Living Your Truth Can Mean Losing Your Children," *New York Times*, May 25, 2018, https://www.nytimes.com/2018/05/25/nyregion/orthodox-jewish-divorce-custody-ny.html.

50. Brown, "When Insiders Become Outsiders."

51. For discussion of religious schooling, see Benjamin Justice and Colin MacLeod, *Have a Little Faith: Religion, Democracy, and the American Public School* (Chicago: University of Chicago Press, 2016). For discussion of homeschooling, see James Dwyer and Shawn Peters, *Homeschooling: The History and Philosophy of a Controversial Practice* (Chicago: University of Chicago Press, 2019).

52. Lauren Bialystok and Jessica Wright, "'Just Say No': Public Dissent over Sexuality Education and the Canadian National Imaginary," *Discourse: Studies in the Cultural Politics of Education* 40, no. 4 (2019): 343–57.

53. See Mary Lou Rasmussen, *Progressive Sexuality Education: The Conceits of Secularism* (New York: Routledge, 2016).

54. For example, Planned Parenthood has a Clergy Advocacy Board: https://www.plannedparenthoodaction.org/communities/clergy-advocacy-board/what-we-do/sex-education.

55. Gutmann, *Democratic Education*, 34. Gutmann describes a society that tries to give children a neutral education as a "State of Individuals."

56. Jo Westwood and Barbara Mullan, "Knowledge and Attitudes of Secondary School Teachers Regarding Sexual Health Education in England," *Sex Education* 7, no. 2 (2007): 154.

57. Jacqueline Cohen, Sandra Byers, and Heather Sears, "Factors Affecting Canadian Teachers' Willingness to Teach Sexual Health Education," *Sex Education* 12, no. 3 (2012): 299–316; Debbie Ollis, "'I Haven't Changed Bigots but . . .': Reflections on the Impact of Teacher Professional Learning in Sexuality Education," *Sex Education* 10, no. 2 (2010): 217–30.

58. Marianne Whatley, "Whose Sexuality Is It Anyway?," in *Sexuality and the Curriculum*, ed. James Sears (New York: Teachers College Press, 1992), 78.

59. Life Choices: https://lifechoices.org/about/. See Becca Andrews, "As a Girl, I Went Through Abstinence Ed. As a Woman, I'm Trying to Understand the Damage Done," *Mother Jones*, March/April 2016, https://www.motherjones.com/politics/2016/03/abstinence-education-tennessee-sex-ed-virginity-pledge/.

60. Another type of expert is the "identity expert," such as a person living with HIV or a teen mother (Kendall, *The Sex Education Debates*, 100). Assuming they are appropriately trained and vetted, these individuals can teach students something beyond what well-prepared teachers can. However, as Kendall also observed, using "identity" as a category of expertise allows very conservative schoolboards to smuggle religious representatives into sex education without getting caught in an Establishment Clause problem (Kendall, 44).

61. Kendall, 102.

62. Even more excluded from formal education but still experts in their own right are community-based sex educators, professionals who work with sex offenders and their victims, consent workshop facilitators, kink and pornography educators, sex workers, reproductive rights activists, and a growing cadre of YouTubers and bloggers.

63. As noted earlier, people occupy many roles simultaneously; one's judgment as a high school teacher may no doubt differ from one's judgment as a parent in the same situation.

64. By "children" we refer to anyone up to the age of eighteen, although, as will become clear, many bad arguments about sex education proceed from the conflation of different age brackets in this group.

65. E.g., Archard, *Children*; Howard Cohen, *Equal Rights for Children* (Totowa, NJ: Rowman and Littlefield, 1980); Gutmann, "Children, Paternalism and Education"; Dwyer, *Relationship Rights of Children*.

66. United Nations, *Rights of the Child*.

67. UNESCO, *International Technical Guidance on Sexuality Education: An Evidence-Informed Approach*, rev. ed. (Paris: United Nations, 2018), http://www.unaids.org/sites/default/files/media_asset/ITGSE_en.pdf, 29; World Health Organization (WHO) Regional Office for Europe and BZgA, *Standards for Sexuality Education in Europe: A Framework for Policy Makers, Educational and Health Authorities and Specialists* (Cologne, Germany: World Health Organization, 2010), https://www.bzga-whocc.de/fileadmin/user_upload/WHO_BZgA_Standards_English.pdf; Patrick Malone and Monica Rodriguez, "Comprehensive Sex Education vs. Abstinence-Only-Until-Marriage Programs," *American Bar Association*, 2011, https://www.americanbar.org/groups/crsj/publications/human_rights_magazine_home/human_rights_vol38_2011/human_rights_spring2011/comprehensive_sex_education_vs_abstinence_only_until_marriage_programs/.

68. Michael Halstead and Michael Reiss, *Values in Sex Education: From Principles to Practice* (London: Routledge Falmer, 2003), 31. See also Louisa Allen, *Young People and Sexuality Education: Rethinking Key Debates* (Houndmills, UK: Palgrave Macmillan, 2011).

69. Allen Buchanan and Dan Brock, *Deciding for Others: The Ethics of Surrogate Decision Making* (Cambridge: Cambridge University Press, 1989), 216–46.

70. Cohen, *Equal Rights for Children*, 11.

71. I think this qualifies as gaslighting.

72. Callan, *Autonomy and Schooling*, 124.

73. On the distinction between the "best interest standard" and the "substituted judgment standard," see Buchanan and Brock, *Deciding for Others*, 94–98.

74. Pandora Pound, Rebecca Langford, and Rona Campbell, "What Do Young People Think about Their School-Based Sex and Relationship Education? A Qualitative Synthesis of Young People's Views and Experiences," *British Medical Journal* 6, no. 9 (2016): 1–14.

75. Emma Paling, "Toronto Students Fight Doug Ford's Cuts with Modern Sex Ed Conference 'Mic Drop,'" *Huffington Post*, January 12, 2019, https://www.huffingtonpost.ca/2019/01/11/toronto-students-fight-doug-fords-cuts-with-modern-sex-ed-conference-mic-drop_a_23640715/.

76. Indeed, children younger than these activists are already consulted in legal matters concerning their own interests, such as in custody battles.

77. Ralph DiClemente, Cheri Pies, Elizabeth Stoller, Christie Straits, Geraldine Olivia, Joan Haskin, and George Rutherford, "Evaluation of School-Based AIDS Education Curricula in San Francisco," *Journal of Sex Research* 26, no. 2 (1989): 188–98.

78. Roger Holdsworth, "Schools That Create Real Roles of Value for Young People," *UNESCO International Prospect* 3 (2000): 349–62.

79. A. S. Neill, *Summerhill* (New York: Hart, 1960), 86.

80. To be sure, some adults wish that they had made different sexual choices in their youth, or that they had received *different* sex education. But neither of these regrets amounts to wishing for more ignorance.

81. After ruling out the Family State, the State of Families, and the State of Individuals, Gutmann comes to the same conclusion. In her democratic conception, "educational authority must be shared among parents, citizens, and professional educators" (Gutmann, *Democratic Education*, 42).

82. See discussion in chapter 4.

83. Jo Frankham, "Sexual Antimonies and Parent/Child Sex Education: Learning from Foreclosure," *Sexualities* 9, no. 2 (2006): 236–54; Mona Malacane and Jonathon Beckmeyer, "A Review of Parent-Based Barriers to Parent-Adolescent Communication about Sex and Sexuality: Implications for Sex and Family Educators," *American Journal of Sexuality Education* 11, no. 1 (2016): 27–40; Joy Walker, "A Qualitative Study of Parents' Experiences of Providing Sex Education for Their Children: The Implications for Health Education," *Health Education Journal* 60, no. 2 (2001): 132–46.

84. Marla Eisenberg, Linda Bearinger, Renee Sieving, Carolyne Swain, and Michael Resnick, "Parents' Beliefs about Condoms and Oral Contraceptives: Are They Medically Accurate?" *Perspectives on Sexual and Reproductive Health* 36, no. 2 (2004): 50–57; Sahara

Byrne, Sherri Katz, Theodore Lee, Daniel Linz, and Mary McIlrath, "Peers, Predators, and Porn: Predicting Parental Underestimation of Children's Risky Online Experiences," *Journal of Computer-Mediated Communication* 19, no. 2 (2014): 215–31; Malacane and Beckmeyer, "A Review of Parent-Based Barriers."

85. Ronny Shtarkshall, John Santelli, and Jennifer Hirsch, "Sex Education and Sexual Socialization: Roles for Educators and Parents," *Perspectives on Sexual and Reproductive Health* 39, no. 2 (2007): 116–19; Triece Turnbull, Anna van Wersch, and Paul van Schaika, "A Review of Parental Involvement in Sex Education: The Role for Effective Communication in British Families," *Health Education Journal* 67, no. 3 (2008): 182–95; Pam Alldred, Nick Fox, and Robert Kulpa, "Engaging Parents with Sex and Relationship Education: A UK Primary School Case Study," *Health Education Journal* 75, no. 7 (2016): 855–68; Simon Blake and Peter Aggleton, "Young People, Sexuality and Diversity: What Does a Needs-Led and Rights-Based Approach Look Like?" *Sex Education* 17, no. 3 (2017): 363–69.

86. For those parents who *are* well informed and comfortable teaching their children about sexuality, of course, there is no reason that they should not also be providers. Their role does not obviate the need for school-based education, however, since children need to learn the same things *together* for some of the goals of sex education to be met (e.g., about the meaning of consent).

87. As discussed in the previous chapter, the path from evidence to policy is complex, but evidence has to be the starting point.

88. Murray, "Sex and the Schoolhouse"; Brown, "When Insiders Become Outsiders."

89. Melody Alemansour et al., "Sex Education in Schools," *Georgetown Journal of Gender and Law* 20 (2019): 484.

90. Brown, "When Insiders Become Outsiders," 140; see also Gutmann, *Democratic Education*, 110.

91. This argument is developed in Lauren Bialystok, "My Child, My Choice? Mandatory Curriculum, Sex, and the Conscience of Parents," *Educational Theory* 68, no. 1 (2018): 11–29.

CHAPTER SIX

1. Jen Gilbert, *Sexuality in School: The Limits of Education* (Minneapolis: University of Minnesota Press, 2014).

2. Michel Foucault, *A History of Sexuality*, vol. 1, trans. Robert Hurley (New York: Vintage, 1976).

3. Foucault, 57.

4. Foucault, 57.

5. Brian Schultz, "Informal Curriculum," in *Encyclopedia of Curriculum Studies*, ed. Craig Kridel (Thousand Oaks, CA: Sage, 2010), 476; Robert Boostrom, "Hidden Curriculum," in *Encyclopedia of Curriculum Studies*, ed. Kridel, 440.

6. Jessica Fields, Jen Gilbert, and Michelle Miller, "Sexuality and Education: Toward the Promise of Ambiguity," in *Handbook of the Sociology of Sexualities*, ed. John DeLamater and Rebecca Plante (New York: Springer International, 2015), 371–87.

7. Nancy Lesko, "Feeling Abstinent? Feeling Comprehensive? Touching the Affects of Sexuality Curricula," *Sex Education* 10, no. 3 (2010): 281–97.

8. Michelle Fine, "Sexuality, Schooling, and Adolescent Females: The Missing Discourse of Desire," *Harvard Educational Review* 58, no. 1 (1988): 29–53; Louisa Allen, "Beyond the Birds and the Bees: Constituting a Discourse of Erotics in Sexuality Education," *Gender and Education* 16, no. 2 (2004): 151–67; Michelle Fine and Sarah McClelland, "Sexuality Education and Desire: Still Missing after All These Years," *Harvard Educational Review* 76, no. 3 (2006): 297–338.

9. Marijke Naezer, Els Rommes, and Willy Jansen, "Empowerment through Sex Education? Rethinking Paradoxical Policies," *Sex Education* 17, no. 6 (2017): 712–28.

10. Louisa Allen, *Young People and Sexuality Education: Rethinking Key Debates* (Houndmills, UK: Palgrave Macmillan, 2011), 42–43.

11. Jessica Fields, *Risky Lessons: Sex Education and Social Inequality* (New Brunswick, NJ: Rutgers University Press, 2008); Lorena Garcia, "Now Why Do You Want to Know about That? Heteronormativity, Sexism, and Racism in the Sexual (Mis)education of Latina Youth," *Gender & Society* 23, no. 4 (2009): 520–41; Jessica Yee, "Introduction: Sex Ed and Youth: Colonization, Sexuality and Communities of Colour," *Canadian Centre for Policy Alternatives* 18, no. 94 (2009): 1–6; Stephen Hobaica and Paul Kwon, "'This Is How You Hetero': Sexual Minorities in Heteronormative Sex Education," *American Journal of Sexuality Education* 12, no. 4 (2017): 423–50; L. Kris Gowen and Nichole Winges-Yanez, "Lesbian, Gay, Bisexual, Transgender, Queer, and Questioning Youths' Perspectives of Inclusive School-Based Sexuality Education," *Journal of Sex Research* 51, no. 7 (2014): 788–800; Charmaine Ferrante and Eileen Oak, "'No Sex Please!' We Have Been Labelled Intellectually Disabled," *Sex Education* 20, no. 4 (2020): 383–97.

12. Many Indigenous people continue to be sexually victimized by other state institutions that claim to be dedicated to their well-being, including the foster care system and juvenile corrections (Dustin Louie, "Sexual Exploitation Prevention Education for Indigenous Girls," *Canadian Journal of Education* 41, no. 2 [2018]: 633–63). These realities make a farce of the typical school-based sex education curriculum, with its template of the abstinent child who needs to be educated in anticipation of some future consensual sexual behavior.

13. The aims of schooling may not be identical to the aims of education: this is because, first, schools are not the only sites of education and may not be able to achieve all its aims; and second, schools may have legitimate aims in addition to education. Here I discuss only the aims that could pertain to schools.

14. Danielle Allen, *Education and Equality* (Chicago: University of Chicago Press, 2016).

15. The seminal statement is John Dewey's *Democracy and Education* (New York: Macmillan, 1916).

16. Amy Gutmann, *Democratic Education* (Princeton, NJ: Princeton University Press, 1987).

17. Sharon Lamb and Renee Randazzo argue that sex education itself should be treated as a form of civics education. "Obstacles to Teaching Ethics in Sex Education," in *Evidence-Based Approaches to Sexuality Education*, ed. James Ponzetti (New York: Routledge, 2016), 113–27.

18. Eamonn Callan, *Creating Citizens: Political Education and Liberal Democracy* (Oxford: Clarendon, 1997); Meira Levinson, *The Demands of Liberal Education* (Oxford: Oxford University Press, 1999); Kevin McDonough and Walter Feinberg, eds., *Education and Citizenship in Liberal-Democratic Societies: Teaching for Cosmopolitan Values and Collective Identities* (Oxford: Oxford University Press, 2003).

19. Democratic education (as formulated by Dewey) was originally associated with "child-centered" and "progressive" education, not what came to be known as "liberal education." See Paul Standish, "Education without Aims," in *The Aims of Education*, ed. Roger Marples (New York: Routledge, 1999).

20. Some use the notion of "sexual citizenship" to blend the demands of citizenship with our sexual identities, but this term has been critiqued. See David Bell and John Binnie, *The Sexual Citizen: Queer Politics and Beyond* (Cambridge: Polity Press, 2000); and Diane Richardson, "Rethinking Sexual Citizenship," *Sociology* 51, no. 2 (2017): 208–24.

21. Alexander McKay, *Sexual Ideology and Schooling: Towards Democratic Sexuality Education* (London: Althouse, 1998); Josh Corngold, "Moral Pluralism and Sex Education," *Educational Theory* 63, no. 5 (2013): 461–82.

22. "self-fulfillment": R. S. Peters, "Democratic Values and Educational Aims," in *Education and Values*, ed. Douglas Sloan (New York: Teachers College Press, 1979), 83; "human life": Richard Pring, "Neglected Educational Aims: Moral Seriousness and Social Commitment," in *The Aims of Education*, ed. Roger Marples (New York: Routledge, 1999), 162; "opening visions": Douglas Stewart, "Schooling as a Journey in Humanization," *Paideusis* 13, no. 2 (2000): 17; "flourishing": Allen, *Education and Equality*.

23. Pring, "Neglected Educational Aims," 164.

24. John Miller, *Whole Child Education* (Toronto: University of Toronto Press, 2010).

25. As it happens, many philosophers believe that these things are good both intrinsically *and* instrumentally. Allen, *Education and Equality*; Peters, "Democratic Values."

26. Alasdair MacIntyre, "Against Utilitarianism," in *Aims in Education: The Philosophic Approach*, ed. T. Hollins (Manchester: Manchester University Press, 1964), 19.

27. Allen, *Education and Equality*, 14. She refers to this condition as "the humanistic baseline."

28. Michael W. Apple, *Educating the "Right" Way: Markets, Standards, God, and Inequality*, 2nd ed. (New York: Routledge, 2006); Allen, *Education and Equality*, 7.

29. R. S. Peters, *Ethics and Education* (London: George Allen and Unwin, 1966).

30. Sinikka Elliott, "'Who's to Blame?' Constructing the Responsible Sexual Agent in Neoliberal Sex Education," *Sexuality Research and Social Policy* 11, no. 3 (2014): 211–24.

31. Lauren Clark and Sarah Stitzlein, "Neoliberal Narratives and the Logic of Abstinence Only Education: Why Are We Still Having This Conversation?" *Gender and Education* 30, no. 3 (2018): 322–40.

32. Laina Bay-Cheng, "The Agency Line: A Neoliberal Metric for Appraising Young Women's Sexuality," *Sex Roles* 73, nos. 7–8 (2015): 279–91; Elliott, "'Who's to Blame?'"

33. Pierre Bourdieu and Jean-Claude Passeron, *Reproduction in Education, Society and Culture*, trans. Richard Nice (London: Sage, 1977).

34. Standish, "Education without Aims," 35.

35. Louis Althusser, "Ideology and Ideological State Apparatuses," in *Lenin and Philosophy and Other Essays*, trans. Ben Brewster (New York: New York University Press), 85–126.

36. Valerie Straus, "Texas GOP Rejects 'Critical Thinking' Skills. Really," *Washington Post*, July 9, 2012, https://www.washingtonpost.com/blogs/answer-sheet/post/texas-gop-rejects-critical-thinking-skills-really/2012/07/08/gJQAHNpFXW_blog.html. The original platform document has since been removed from the Internet.

37. Marcelo Suarez-Orozco, "Comment," in *Education and Equality*, by Danielle Allen (Chicago: University of Chicago Press, 2016).

38. Lauren Bialystok, "Politics without 'Brainwashing': A Philosophical Defense of Social Justice Education," *Curriculum Inquiry* 44, no. 3 (2014): 413–40.

39. Kathy Hytten and Silvia Bettez, "Understanding Education for Social Justice," *Educational Foundations* 25, nos. 1–2 (2011): 7–24.

40. As one prominent scholar argues, "Sexuality is not simply a biological product of innate and immutable quality, but the consequence of social practices which are infused by power and mutable." Louisa Allen, *Sexual Subjects: Young People, Sexuality and Education* (Houndmills, UK: Palgrave Macmillan, 2005), 8.

41. CDC, *Sexually Transmitted Disease Surveillance 2018* (Atlanta: US Department of Health and Human Services, 2019), DOI: 10.15620/cdc.79370.

42. James Sears, ed., *Sexuality and the Curriculum: The Politics and Practices of Sexuality Education* (New York: Teachers College Press, 1992), 15.

43. Not to worry: the newfound protection against genital warts has not been correlated with any increase in adolescent sexual activity. Erin Cook, Atheendar Venkataramani, Jane Kim, Rulla Tamimi, and Michelle Holmes, "Legislation to Increase Uptake of HPV Vaccination and Adolescent Sexual Behaviors," *Pediatrics* 142, no. 3 (2018), e20180458.

44. Pam Alldred and Miriam David, *Get Real about Sex: The Politics and Practice of Sex Education* (Maidenhead, UK: Open University Press, 2007), 108–9.

45. Tiffany Bartz, "Sex Education in Multicultural Norway," *Sex Education* 7, no. 1 (2007): 17–33.

46. Foucault, *History*, 36–37.

47. Harry Brighouse et al., *Educational Goods: Values, Evidence, and Decision-Making* (Chicago: University of Chicago Press, 2018); Allen, *Education and Equality*.

48. Clarissa Smith, "Pornographication: A Discourse for All Seasons," *International Journal of Media and Cultural Politics* 6, no. 1 (2010): 103–8.

49. Danielle Egan, *Becoming Sexual: A Critical Appraisal of the Sexualization of Girls* (Cambridge, MA: Polity, 2013).

50. Jean Twenge, Jonathan Haidt, Thomas Joiner, and Keith Campbell, "Underestimating Digital Media Harm," *Nature Human Behavior* 4, no. 4 (2020): 346–48.

51. Kaitlyn Goldsmith, Cara Dunkley, Silvain Dang, and Boris Gorzalka, "Pornography Consumption and Its Association with Sexual Concerns and Expectations among Young Men and Women," *Canadian Journal of Human Sexuality* 26, no. 2 (2017): 151–62. Committee on Adolescent Health Care, "Committee Opinion No. 686: Breast and Labial Surgery in Adolescents," *Obstetrics & Gynecology* 129, no. 1 (2017): e17–e19. Labiaplasty is the surgical reduction of the labia minora for cosmetic reasons. Critics have likened it to female genital mutilation.

52. Miranda Horvath, Llian Alys, Kristina Massey, Afroditi Pina, Mia Scally, and Joanna Adler, *Basically . . . Porn Is Everywhere: A Rapid Evidence Assessment on the Effects that Access and Exposure to Pornography Has on Children and Young People* (London: Office of the Children's Commissioner for England, 2013).

53. Matthew Ezzell, "Men's Use of Pornography," in *The Routledge Companion to Media and Gender*, ed. Cynthia Carter, Linda Steiner, and Lisa McLaughlin (New York: Routledge, 2013),

473–82; Michael Flood, "The Harms of Pornography Exposure among Children and Young People," *Child Abuse Review* 18, no. 6 (2009): 384–400.

54. Ana Bridges, Robert Wosnitzer, Erica Scharrer, Chyng Sun, and Rachael Liberman, "Aggression and Sexual Behavior in Best-Selling Pornography Videos: A Content Analysis Update," *Violence Against Women* 16, no. 10 (2010): 1077.

55. Cicely Marston and Ruth Lewis, "Anal Heterosex among Young People and Implications for Health Promotion: A Qualitative Study in the UK," *British Medical Journal* 4, no. 8 (2014): e004996–e004996. Research has found a correlation between young people's exposure to pornography and the likelihood that they have had anal heterosex, which is significant because a majority of young women describe anal sex as a negative experience (Christina Rogala and Tanja Tyden, "Does Pornography Influence Young Women's Sexual Behavior?" *Women's Health Issues* 13, no. 1 [2003]: 39–43), whereas their male heterosexual counterparts describe it positively (Tanja Tyden and Christina Rogala, "Sexual Behaviour among Young Men in Sweden and the Impact of Pornography," *International Journal of STD & AIDS* 15, no. 9 [2004]: 590–93). It is important not to conclude that anal sex is always bad for women, or that sex education should denounce it. Rather, this is exactly why young people need to be able to critically analyze pornography and talk about consent and pleasure in sexual relationships.

56. Sex education cannot and need not take a hard stance on the complicated pornography debates and long-standing feminist sex wars to make a contribution here. There is sufficient evidence that mainstream pornography is potentially very harmful, especially to girls, and that young people need a critical perspective on what they are encountering. For a primer on how to start talking to children about pornography, see Natasha Singh, "Talk to Your Kids about Porn," *Atlantic*, August 29, 2018, https://www.theatlantic.com/ideas/archive/2018/08/talking-to-kids-about-porn/568744/.

57. Peggy Orenstein, *Girls & Sex: Navigating the Complicated New Landscape* (New York: HarperCollins, 2016); Maggie Jones, "What Teenagers Are Learning from Online Porn," *New York Times Magazine*, February 7, 2018, https://nyti.ms/2BfErWv.

58. Mary Anne Layden, "Pornography and Violence: A New Look at the Research," in *The Social Costs of Pornography: A Collection of Papers*, ed. James Stoner and Donna Hughes (Princeton, NJ: Witherspoon Institute, 2010), 57.

59. Crazy/Genius Podcast, "What Is Pornography Doing to Our Sex Lives?" *Atlantic*, May 16, 2019, https://www.theatlantic.com/ideas/archive/2019/05/what-is-pornography-doing-to-our-sex-lives/589576/.

60. There are good reasons to believe that the examples described in this paragraph comprise a particularly American phenomenon, which may not impact young people in other Western countries to the same extent or in the same way.

61. It is girls whose purity or sexual experience is most scrutinized in both cultures, and many girls are subjected to the old "virgin/whore" double bind. Girls often find that their sexual past is held against them no matter what it is, while boys are more rewarded for experience.

62. Nancy Kendall, *The Sex Education Debates* (Chicago: University of Chicago Press, 2013).

63. Katelyn Burns, "Sex Education Rally Reminds Teens 'You Are Not Chewed Gum,'" *Teen Vogue*, October 31, 2019, https://www.teenvogue.com/story/sex-education-rally-reminds-teens-you-are-not-chewed-gum; Becca Andrews, "As a Girl I Went Through Abstinence

Ed. As a Woman, I'm Trying to Understand the Damage Done," *Mother Jones*, March/April 2016, https://www.motherjones.com/politics/2016/03/abstinence-education-tennessee-sex-ed-virginity-pledge/; American Civil Liberties Union (ACLU) Northern California, "Historic Ruling in ACLU Lawsuit: Abstinence-Only Sex Ed Violated State Law," May 11, 2015, https://www.aclunc.org/news/historic-ruling-aclu-lawsuit-abstinence-only-sex-ed-violated-state-law.

64. Jessica Valenti, *The Purity Myth: How America's Obsession with Virginity Is Hurting Young Women* (New York: Basic Books, 2009). For a discussion of the evidence on the effectiveness of abstinence-only education and virginity pledges, see chapter 4.

65. Fields, *Risky Lessons*; Egan, *Becoming Sexual*.

66. Linda Kay Klein, *Pure* (New York: Simon and Shuster, 2018). Other traditional or fundamentalist religious groups also enforce purity and chastity requirements, particularly on girls.

67. Susan Faludi, *Backlash: The Undeclared War against American Women* (New York: Crown, 1991).

68. Jessica Ringrose, *Postfeminist Education? Girls and the Sexual Politics of Schooling* (London: Routledge, 2013).

69. "Incel" is short for "involuntary celibate."

70. Ringrose, *Postfeminist Education?*, 2013.

71. Shauna Pomerantz, Rebecca Raby, and Andrea Stefanik, "Girls Run the World? Caught between Sexism and Postfeminism in School," *Gender & Society* 27, no. 2 (2013): 185–207.

72. Lamb and Randazzo, "Obstacles to Teaching Ethics."

73. Orenstein, *Girls & Sex*.

74. Rosalind Gill, "Postfeminist Sexual Culture," in *The Routledge Companion to Media and Gender*, ed. Cynthia Carter, Linda Steiner, and Lisa McLaughlin (New York: Routledge, 2013), 589–599; Nicola Gavey, "Beyond 'Empowerment'? Sexuality in a Sexist World," *Sex Roles* 66, nos. 11–12 (2012): 718–24; Hanna Rosin, "Why Kids Sext," *Atlantic*, November 2014, https://www.theatlantic.com/magazine/archive/2014/11/why-kids-sext/380798/.

75. Egan, *Becoming Sexual*.

76. Gabriel Dance and M. K. Keller, "An Explosion in Online Child Sex Abuse: What You Need to Know," *New York Times*, September 29, 2019, https://www.nytimes.com/2019/09/29/us/takeaways-child-sex-abuse.html.

77. Lauren McKeown, "The Sweetened Life," *Toronto Life*, March 20, 2013, https://torontolife.com/city/the-sweetened-life/; Caitlin Flanagan, "A High-School Porn Star's Cry for Help," *Atlantic*, June 5, 2019, https://www.theatlantic.com/ideas/archive/2019/06/high-school-porn-stars-cry-help/590986.

78. Melissa Burkett and Karine Hamilton, "Postfeminist Sexual Agency: Young Women's Negotiations of Sexual Consent," *Sexualities* 15, no. 7 (2012): 815–33. Sadly, these girls tend to blame themselves and other girls for ending up in situations where sexual assault may happen.

79. Richard Whitmire, *Why Boys Fail: Saving Our Sons from an Educational System That's Leaving Them Behind* (New York: American Management Association, 2010).

80. Richard Whitmire and Susan McGee, "Gender Gap: Are Boys Being Shortchanged in K–12 Schooling?" *Education Next* 10, no. 2 (2010): 52–61; Debbie Epstein, Jannette Elwood, Valeria Hey, and Janet Maw, eds., *Failing Boys? Issues in Gender and Achievement* (Buckingham, UK: Open University Press, 1998).

81. Susan Jones and Debra Myhill, "'Troublesome Boys' and 'Compliant Girls': Gender Identity and Perceptions of Achievement and Underachievement," *British Journal of Sociology of Education* 25, no. 5 (2004): 547–61; Angela Duckworth and Martin Seligman, "Self-Discipline Gives Girls the Edge: Gender in Self-Discipline, Grades, and Achievement Test Scores," *Journal of Educational Psychology* 98, no. 1 (2006): 198–208.

82. Wayne Martino, "'Cool Boys,' 'Party Animals,' 'Squids' and 'Poofters': Interrogating the Dynamics and Politics of Adolescent Masculinities in School," *British Journal of Sociology of Education* 20, no. 2 (1999): 239–63.

83. C. J. Pascoe, *Dude, You're a Fag: Masculinity and Sexuality in High School* (Berkeley: University of California Press, 2007); Michael Kimmel, *Guyland: The Perilous World Where Boys Become Men* (New York: Harper, 2008).

84. Peggy Orenstein, *Boys & Sex: Young Men on Hookups, Love, Porn, Consent, and Navigating the New Masculinity* (New York: HarperCollins, 2020); Kimmel, *Guyland.*

85. Kimmel, *Guyland*, 47.

86. Jennifer Siebel Newsom, dir., *The Mask You Live In* (The Representation Project, 2015).

87. Orenstein, *Boys & Sex*, 108.

88. Andrew Smiler, *Is Masculinity Toxic? A Primer for the 21st Century* (London: Penguin Random House, 2019).

89. Orenstein, *Boys & Sex.*

90. Vicky Rideout, *Common Sense Census: Media Use by Tweens and Teens, 2019* (San Francisco: Common Sense Media, 2019), https://www.commonsensemedia.org/sites/default/files/uploads/research/census_researchreport.pdf.

91. Kate Smith, "Need Birth Control? Planned Parenthood Says There's an App for That," *CBS News*, September 4, 2019, https://www.cbsnews.com/news/new-planned-parenthood-app-need-birth-control-planned-parenthood-says-theres-an-app-for-that-2019-09-04/.

92. The storylines also show how they intersect with other real pressures in young people's lives, including parental divorce, depression, poverty, and academic expectations.

93. Meredith Temple-Smith, Susan Moore, and Doreen Rosenthal, *Sexuality in Adolescence: The Digital Generation* (East Sussex: Routledge, 2016), 134.

94. Temple-Smith, Moore, and Rosenthal, 122.

95. Marijke Naezer, "From Risky Behaviour to Sexy Adventures: Reconceptualising Young People's Online Sexual Activities," *Culture, Health & Sexuality* 20, no. 6 (2018): 715–29.

96. "Social reproduction" may be an inaccurate description insofar as the sexual regime they seek to retain never actually existed, at least not across the board (see chapters 1–3). But it is fair to generalize that this group longs for old-fashioned sexual values to be transmitted, while progressives long for change.

97. This is how the physical education teacher covers sex education in the 2004 film *Mean Girls*.

98. Conservatives may insist that if abstinence is the right goal, then we ought to preach it because it is right, not because it is popular. I think it is the wrong goal, but the argument can be more easily refuted on practical grounds.

99. The qualifier "truly" here is meant to exclude instruction that tacks contraception on to AOUME (see chapter 4).

100. Bialystok, "Politics without 'Brainwashing.'"

101. UNESCO, *International Technical Guidance on Sexuality Education*; Sharon Lamb, "Toward a Sexual Ethics Curriculum: Bringing Philosophy and Society to Bear on Individual Development," *Harvard Educational Review* 80, no. 1 (2010); Future of Sex Education Initiative (FoSE), *National Sexuality Education Standards: Core Content and Skills, K–12* (United States, 2012), http://www.futureofsexeducation.org/documents/josh-fose-standards-web.pdf; Allen, *Young People and Sexuality Education*; World Health Organization (WHO) Regional Office for Europe and BZgA, *Standards for Sexuality Education in Europe: A Framework for Policy Makers, Educational and Health Authorities and Specialists* (Cologne, Germany: World Health Organization, 2010), https://www.bzga-whocc.de/fileadmin/user_upload/WHO_BZgA_Standards_English.pdf. Importantly, the comprehensive topics must be more than a set of facts to master. "Comprehensiveness" refers to opening up topics, rather than always telling students the "right" answer.

102. Natalia Mehlman Petrzela, "Make Every Class Sex Ed Class," *Huffington Post*, March 14, 2018, https://www.huffpost.com/entry/opinion-petrzela-sex-education_n_5aa8304fe4b001c8bf149605.

103. This well-meaning approach in Quebec has also been criticized for being easily evaded in the neoliberal professional climate. Dan Parker and Robert McGray, "Tensions between Teaching Sexuality Education and Neoliberal Policy Reform in Quebec's Professional Competencies for Beginning Teachers," *McGill Journal of Education* 50, no. 1 (2015): 1–15; Norway: Temple-Smith, Moore, and Rosenthal, *Sexuality in Adolescence*, 102.

104. Deborah Rogow and Nicole Haberland, "Sexuality and Relationships Education: Toward a Social Studies Approach," *Sex Education* 5, no. 4 (2005): 333–44; Jen Gilbert, "Literature as Sex Education," *Changing English* 11, no. 2 (2004): 233–41. Many sex education scholars, especially those inclined to democratic or ethics-based approaches, have also advocated for cross-curricular sex education, e.g., Sharon Lamb, "Sex Education as Moral Education: Teaching for Pleasure, about Fantasy, and against Abuse," *Journal of Moral Education* 26, no. 3 (1997): 301–15; Kendall, *The Sex Education Debates*; and Paula McAvoy, "The Aims of Sex Education: Demoting Autonomy and Promoting Mutuality," *Educational Theory* 63, no. 5 (2013): 483–96.

105. Formative assessment—ascertaining what students have learned in order to improve teaching and learning—is not included in this discussion.

106. For more discussion, see Lisa Andersen and Lauren Bialystok, "Assessing a Touchy Subject," *Journal of Philosophy of Education* (forthcoming).

107. SIECUS, "National Teacher Preparation Standards for Sexuality Education," https://siecus.org/resources/national-teacher-preparation-standards-for-sexuality-education/. Emphasis added.

108. As discussed in chapter 5, institutional constraints and fear of reprisal also inhibit sex educators' work, even when they have appropriate technical preparation.

109. Elissa Barr, Eva Goldfarb, Susan Russell, Denise Seabert, Michele Wallen, and Kelly Wilson, "Improving Sexuality Education: The Development of Teacher-Preparation Standards," *Journal of School Health* 84, no. 6 (2014): 397.

110. Sex Education Collaborative (SEC), *Professional Learning Standards for Sex Education*, 2019, https://www.etr.org/default/assets/File/PLSSE.pdf.

111. E.g., Sharyn Burns and Jacqueline Hendriks, "Sexuality and Relationship Education Training to Primary and Secondary School Teachers: An Evaluation of Provision in Western Australia," *Sex Education* 18, no. 6 (2018): 672–88.

112. Mario Vargas Llosa, "The Disappearance of Eroticism," in *Notes on the Death of Culture*, trans. John King (New York: Farrar, Straus and Giroux, 2015), 98.

113. Foucault, *History*, 57.

CONCLUSION

1. Nina Burleigh, "Sexting, Shame and Suicide: A Shocking Tale of Sexual Assault in the Digital Age," *Rolling Stone*, September 13, 2017, https://www.rollingstone.com/culture/culture-news/sexting-shame-and-suicide-72148/.

2. Alyssa Newcomb, "Classmates Who Saw Photo of Alleged Sexual Assault to Come Forward," ABC News, April 15, 2013, https://abcnews.go.com/US/audrie-potts-parents-classmates-photo-alleged-sexual-assault/story?id=18956803.

3. "Suicide of Amanda Todd," Wikipedia, February 13, 2021, https://en.wikipedia.org/wiki/Suicide_of_Amanda_Todd#Mainstream_media.

4. CBC News, "Rape, Bullying Led to N.S. Teen's Death, Says Mom," April 9, 2013, https://www.cbc.ca/news/canada/nova-scotia/rape-bullying-led-to-n-s-teen-s-death-says-mom-1.1370780. The prior assault was never proven in court.

5. Hanna Rosin, "Why Kids Sext," *Atlantic*, November 2014, https://www.theatlantic.com/magazine/archive/2014/11/why-kids-sext/380798/. The term "revenge porn" has been aptly criticized for being neither "porn" (which is created for others' pleasure) nor "revenge" (which implies the victim had done something wrong).

6. Sophia Ankel, "Many Revenge Porn Victims Consider Suicide. Why Aren't Schools Doing More to Stop It?" *Guardian*, May 7, 2018, https://www.theguardian.com/lifeandstyle/2018/may/07/many-revenge-porn-victims-consider-suicide-why-arent-schools-doing-more-to-stop-it.

7. Rosie DiManno, "Prestigious Toronto School Sinks Deeper into Hellish Sex Assault Scandal," *Toronto Star*, November 20, 2018, https://www.thestar.com/opinion/star-columnists/2018/11/20/prestigious-toronto-school-sinks-deeper-into-hellish-sex-assault-scandal.html.

8. Jon Cardin, "Curbing Online Harassment in Md. through Legislation, Kindness," *Baltimore Sun*, September 30, 2019, https://www.baltimoresun.com/opinion/op-ed/bs-ed-op-0930-grace-law-20190930-fqon5y4fm5ayjnreptc72pxg2a-story.html; Megan Meier Foundation, https://meganmeierfoundation.org/what-we-do; Stop Cyberbullying Day, https://stopcyberbullyingday.org/.

9. In at least some cases, social media provides the missing lifeline to a victim of bullying. Alyssa Rosenberg, "'Audrie & Daisy' Challenges Our Knee-Jerk Ideas about Social Media and Bullying," *Washington Post*, September 26, 2016, https://www.washingtonpost.com/news/act-four/wp/2016/09/26/audrie-daisy-challenges-our-knee-jerk-ideas-about-social-media-and-bullying/.

10. Cris Mayo, *Disputing the Subject of Sex: Sexuality and Public School Controversies* (New York: Rowman & Littlefield, 2004).

11. Centers for Disease Control and Prevention (CDC), "10 Ways STDs Impact Women Differently from Men," April 2011, https://www.cdc.gov/STD/health-disparities/stds-Women-042011.pdf.

12. Joseph Kosciw, Caitlin Clark, Nhan Truong, and Adrian Zongrone, *The 2019 National School Climate Survey: The Experiences of Lesbian, Gay, Bisexual, Transgender, and Queer Youth in Our Nation's Schools* (New York: GLSEN, 2020).

13. Kristin Luker, *When Sex Goes to School: Warring Views on Sex—and Sex Education—since the Sixties* (New York: W. W. Norton, 2007).

14. Mary Lou Rasmussen, *Progressive Sexuality Education: The Conceits of Secularism* (New York: Routledge, 2016); Stine Bang Svendsen, "The Cultural Politics of Sex Education in the Nordics," in *The Palgrave Handbook of Sex Education*, ed. Mary Lou Rasmussen and Louisa Allen (London: Palgrave Macmillan, 2017), 137–55.

15. Alice Kessler-Harris, "In the Nation's Image: The Gendered Nature of Social Citizenship in the Depression Era," *Journal of American History* 86, no. 3 (December 1999): 1251–79; Daniel T. Rodgers, *Atlantic Crossings: Social Politics in a Progressive Age* (Cambridge, MA: Harvard University Press, 1998).

16. There are analogs to our conception in some of the guidelines put out by expert organizations, but none that have been spelled out via a similar historical-philosophical analysis. Moreover, they serve different purposes. The Future of Sex Education Initiative (FoSE), *National Sexuality Education Standards: Core Content and Skills, K–12* (United States, 2012) seeks to articulate a set of concrete standards for sex education by grade level in the United States, which conform with the National Health Education Standards (FoSE, *National Sexuality Education Standards: Core Content and Skills, K–12* [United States, 2012]). They are at once very general (as they are intended to serve all students in the country) and not easily transferable (since they are specific to the United States and based on particular realities at the time of publication). UNESCO's *International Technical Guidance on Sexuality Education* covers gender, culture, and ethical relationships, among other important topics, but in its global purview it also addresses itself to states where such practices as forced marriage and female genital mutilation may still be legal (UNESCO, *International Technical Guidance on Sexuality Education: An Evidence-Informed Approach*, rev. ed. [Paris: United Nations, 2018], http://www.unaids.org/sites/default/files/media_asset/ITGSE_en.pdf.)

17. Jonathan Zimmerman, *Too Hot to Handle: A Global History of Sex Education* (Princeton, NJ: Princeton University Press, 2015), 123–26.

18. Peggy Orenstein, "Worried about Your Teenage Daughter? Move to the Netherlands," *Los Angeles Times*, April 8, 2016, https://www.latimes.com/opinion/op-ed/la-oe-0410-orenstein-girls-sex-dutch-20160410-story.html.

19. Diana Hess, *Controversy in the Classroom* (New York: Routledge, 2009); Jonathan Zimmerman and Emily Robertson, *The Case for Contention* (Chicago: University of Chicago Press, 2017).

20. Joyce Martin, Brady Hamilton, Michelle Osterman, Anne Driscoll, and Patrick Drake, "Births: Final Data for 2017," *National Vital Statistics Reports* 67, no. 8 (2018), https://www.cdc.gov/nchs/data/nvsr/nvsr67/nvsr67_08-508.pdf. It is higher for Black and Hispanic girls, lower for whites.

21. United Nations Population Division, "Adolescent Fertility Rate (Births per 1,000 Women Ages 15–19)," https://data.worldbank.org/indicator/SP.ADO.TFRT.

22. See discussion in chapter 6.

23. Rasmussen, *Progressive Sexuality Education.*

24. Svendsen, "Cultural Politics of Sex Education."

25. Svendsen.

26. Lauren Bialystok and Jessica Wright, "'Just Say No': Public Dissent over Sexuality Education and the Canadian National Imaginary," *Discourse: Studies in the Cultural Politics of Education* 40, no. 4 (2019): 343–57.

27. David Finkelhor, Anne Shattuck, Heather Turner, and Sherry Hamby, "The Lifetime Prevalence of Child Sexual Abuse and Sexual Assault Assessed in Late Adolescence," *Journal of Adolescent Health* 55, no. 3 (2014): 329–33.

28. Julia Prodis Sulek, "Los Gatos: Rally to Fight Sexual Assault and Harassment Highlights Slow Change," *San Jose Mercury News*, July 26, 2020, https://www.mercurynews.com/2020/07/26/los-gatos-rally-to-fight-sexual-assault-harassment-highlights-slow-change/.

29. Jackie King and Sonali Muthukrishnan, "Dozens of LGHS Students Come Forward as Survivors of Sexual Assault," *El Gato News* (LGHS student newspaper), July 25, 2020, https://elgatonews.com/2020/07/25/dozens-of-lghs-students-come-forward-as-survivors-of-sexual-assault/.

30. Emily Owens, "Keyword 7: Consent," *Differences: A Journal of Feminist Cultural Studies* 30, no. 1 (2019): 148–56; Laina Bay-Cheng, "Agency Is Everywhere, but Agency Is Not Enough: A Conceptual Analysis of Young Women's Sexual Agency," *Journal of Sex Research* 56, nos. 4–5 (2019): 462–74; Jen Gilbert, "Contesting Consent in Sex Education," *Sex Education* 18, no. 3 (2018): 268–79.

31. Caroline Bologna, "How Sex Educators Talk to Their Sons about Consent," *Huffington Post*, March 6, 2018, https://www.huffingtonpost.ca/entry/consent-sex-education_n_5a9d812be4b089ec353d8e75.

32. Nicole Fava and Laina Bay-Cheng, "Trauma-Informed Sexuality Education: Recognizing the Rights and Resilience of Youth," *Sex Education* 13, no. 4 (2013): 383–94.

33. Jen Gilbert, *Sexuality in School: The Limits of Education* (Minneapolis: University of Minnesota Press, 2014), xi.

INDEX